Node.js 5.0 Reference Manual

A catalogue record for this book is available from the Hong Kong Public Libraries.

Published in Hong Kong by Samurai Media Limited.

Email: info@samuraimedia.org

ISBN 978-988-8381-28-9

Contents

Event: 'error' 169
Class: net.Socket 170
new net.Socket([options]) 170
socket.connect(options[, connectListener]) 170
socket.connect(port[, host][, connectListener]) 170
socket.connect(path[, connectListener]) 170
socket.bufferSize 171
socket.setEncoding([encoding]) 171
socket.write(data[, encoding][, callback]) 171
socket.end([data][, encoding]) 171
socket.destroy() 171
socket.pause() 171
socket.resume() 171
socket.setTimeout(timeout[, callback]) 172
socket.setNoDelay([noDelay]) 172
socket.setKeepAlive([enable][, initialDelay]) 172
socket.address() 172
socket.unref() 172
socket.ref() 172
socket.remoteAddress 172
socket.remoteFamily 173
socket.remotePort 173
socket.localAddress 173
socket.localPort 173
socket.bytesRead 173
socket.bytesWritten 173
Event: 'lookup' 173
Event: 'connect' 173
Event: 'data' 173
Event: 'end' 174
Event: 'timeout' 174
Event: 'drain' 174
Event: 'error' 174
Event: 'close' 174
net.isIP(input) 174
net.isIPv4(input) 174
net.isIPv6(input) 174

OS   **175**
os.tmpdir() 175
os.homedir() 175
os.endianness() 175
os.hostname() 175
os.type() 175
os.platform() 175
os.arch() 175
os.release() 175
os.uptime() 175
os.loadavg() 176
os.totalmem() 176
os.freemem() 176
os.cpus() 176
os.networkInterfaces() 177
os.EOL 178

Path   **179**
path.normalize(p) 179

About this Documentation

The goal of this documentation is to comprehensively explain the Node.js API, both from a reference as well as a conceptual point of view. Each section describes a built-in module or high-level concept.

Where appropriate, property types, method arguments, and the arguments provided to event handlers are detailed in a list underneath the topic heading.

Every `.html` document has a corresponding `.json` document presenting the same information in a structured manner. This feature is experimental, and added for the benefit of IDEs and other utilities that wish to do programmatic things with the documentation.

Every `.html` and `.json` file is generated based on the corresponding `.markdown` file in the `doc/api/` folder in Node.js's source tree. The documentation is generated using the `tools/doc/generate.js` program. The HTML template is located at `doc/template.html`.

Stability Index

Throughout the documentation, you will see indications of a section's stability. The Node.js API is still somewhat changing, and as it matures, certain parts are more reliable than others. Some are so proven, and so relied upon, that they are unlikely to ever change at all. Others are brand new and experimental, or known to be hazardous and in the process of being redesigned.

The stability indices are as follows:

```
Stability: 0 - Deprecated
This feature is known to be problematic, and changes are
planned.  Do not rely on it.  Use of the feature may cause warnings.  Backwards
compatibility should not be expected.
```

```
Stability: 1 - Experimental
This feature is subject to change, and is gated by a command line flag.
It may change or be removed in future versions.
```

```
Stability: 2 - Stable
The API has proven satisfactory. Compatibility with the npm ecosystem
is a high priority, and will not be broken unless absolutely necessary.
```

```
Stability: 3 - Locked
Only fixes related to security, performance, or bug fixes will be accepted.
Please do not suggest API changes in this area; they will be refused.
```

JSON Output

```
Stability: 1 - Experimental
```

Every HTML file in the markdown has a corresponding JSON file with the same data.

This feature was added in node v0.6.12. It is experimental.

Synopsis

An example of a web server written with Node.js which responds with 'Hello World':

```
var http = require('http');

http.createServer(function (request, response) {
  response.writeHead(200, {'Content-Type': 'text/plain'});
  response.end('Hello World\n');
}).listen(8124);

console.log('Server running at http://127.0.0.1:8124/');
```

To run the server, put the code into a file called **example.js** and execute it with the node program

```
> node example.js
Server running at http://127.0.0.1:8124/
```

All of the examples in the documentation can be run similarly.

Assert

`Stability: 3 - Locked`

This module is used so that Node.js can test itself. It can be accessed with `require('assert')`. However, it is recommended that a userland assertion library be used instead.

assert.fail(actual, expected, message, operator)

Throws an exception that displays the values for `actual` and `expected` separated by the provided operator.

assert(value[, message]), assert.ok(value[, message])

Tests if value is truthy. It is equivalent to `assert.equal(!!value, true, message)`.

assert.equal(actual, expected[, message])

Tests shallow, coercive equality with the equal comparison operator (`==`).

assert.notEqual(actual, expected[, message])

Tests shallow, coercive inequality with the not equal comparison operator (`!=`).

assert.deepEqual(actual, expected[, message])

Tests for deep equality. Primitive values are compared with the equal comparison operator (`==`).

This only considers enumerable properties. It does not test object prototypes, attached symbols, or non-enumerable properties. This can lead to some potentially surprising results. For example, this does not throw an `AssertionError` because the properties on the `Error` object are non-enumerable:

```
// WARNING: This does not throw an AssertionError!
assert.deepEqual(Error('a'), Error('b'));
```

assert.notDeepEqual(actual, expected[, message])

Tests for any deep inequality. Opposite of `assert.deepEqual`.

assert.strictEqual(actual, expected[, message])

Tests strict equality as determined by the strict equality operator (`===`).

assert.notStrictEqual(actual, expected[, message])

Tests strict inequality as determined by the strict not equal operator (`!==`).

assert.deepStrictEqual(actual, expected[, message])

Tests for deep equality. Primitive values are compared with the strict equality operator (`===`).

assert.notDeepStrictEqual(actual, expected[, message])

Tests for deep inequality. Opposite of `assert.deepStrictEqual`.

assert.throws(block[, error][, message])

Expects `block` to throw an error. `error` can be a constructor, `RegExp`, or validation function.

Validate instanceof using constructor:

```
assert.throws(
  function() {
    throw new Error("Wrong value");
  },
  Error
);
```

Validate error message using RegExp:

```
assert.throws(
  function() {
    throw new Error("Wrong value");
  },
  /value/
);
```

Custom error validation:

```
assert.throws(
  function() {
    throw new Error("Wrong value");
  },
  function(err) {
    if ( (err instanceof Error) && /value/.test(err) ) {
      return true;
    }
  },
  "unexpected error"
);
```

assert.doesNotThrow(block[, error][, message])

Expects `block` not to throw an error. See assert.throws() for more details.

If `block` throws an error and if it is of a different type from `error`, the thrown error will get propagated back to the caller. The following call will throw the `TypeError`, since we're not matching the error types in the assertion.

```
assert.doesNotThrow(
  function() {
    throw new TypeError("Wrong value");
  },
  SyntaxError
);
```

In case `error` matches with the error thrown by `block`, an `AssertionError` is thrown instead.

```
assert.doesNotThrow(
  function() {
```

```
    throw new TypeError("Wrong value");
  },
  TypeError
);
```

assert.ifError(value)

Throws `value` if `value` is truthy. This is useful when testing the `error` argument in callbacks.

Buffer

`Stability: 2 - Stable`

Pure JavaScript is Unicode friendly but not nice to binary data. When dealing with TCP streams or the file system, it's necessary to handle octet streams. Node.js has several strategies for manipulating, creating, and consuming octet streams.

Raw data is stored in instances of the `Buffer` class. A `Buffer` is similar to an array of integers but corresponds to a raw memory allocation outside the V8 heap. A `Buffer` cannot be resized.

The `Buffer` class is a global, making it very rare that one would need to ever `require('buffer')`.

Converting between Buffers and JavaScript string objects requires an explicit encoding method. Here are the different string encodings.

- `'ascii'` - for 7 bit ASCII data only. This encoding method is very fast, and will strip the high bit if set.

- `'utf8'` - Multibyte encoded Unicode characters. Many web pages and other document formats use UTF-8.

- `'utf16le'` - 2 or 4 bytes, little endian encoded Unicode characters. Surrogate pairs (U+10000 to U+10FFFF) are supported.

- `'ucs2'` - Alias of `'utf16le'`.

- `'base64'` - Base64 string encoding.

- `'binary'` - A way of encoding the buffer into a one-byte (i.e. `latin-1`) encoded string. The string `'latin-1'` is not supported. Instead simply pass `'binary'` to use `'latin-1'` encoding.

- `'hex'` - Encode each byte as two hexadecimal characters.

Creating a typed array from a `Buffer` works with the following caveats:

1. The buffer's memory is copied, not shared.

2. The buffer's memory is interpreted as an array, not a byte array. That is, `new Uint32Array(new Buffer([1,2,3,4]))` creates a 4-element `Uint32Array` with elements `[1,2,3,4]`, not a `Uint32Array` with a single element `[0x1020304]` or `[0x4030201]`.

NOTE: Node.js v0.8 simply retained a reference to the buffer in `array.buffer` instead of cloning it.

While more efficient, it introduces subtle incompatibilities with the typed arrays specification. `ArrayBuffer#slice()` makes a copy of the slice while `Buffer#slice()` creates a view.

Class: Buffer

The Buffer class is a global type for dealing with binary data directly. It can be constructed in a variety of ways.

new Buffer(size)

- `size` Number

Allocates a new buffer of `size` bytes. `size` must be less than 1,073,741,824 bytes (1 GB) on 32 bits architectures or 2,147,483,648 bytes (2 GB) on 64 bits architectures, otherwise a `RangeError` is thrown.

Unlike `ArrayBuffers`, the underlying memory for buffers is not initialized. So the contents of a newly created `Buffer` are unknown and could contain sensitive data. Use `buf.fill(0)` to initialize a buffer to zeroes.

new Buffer(array)

- `array` Array

Allocates a new buffer using an `array` of octets.

new Buffer(buffer)

- `buffer` {Buffer}

Copies the passed `buffer` data onto a new `Buffer` instance.

new Buffer(str[, encoding])

- `str` String - string to encode.
- `encoding` String - encoding to use, Optional.

Allocates a new buffer containing the given `str`. `encoding` defaults to 'utf8'.

Class Method: Buffer.isEncoding(encoding)

- `encoding` {String} The encoding string to test

Returns true if the `encoding` is a valid encoding argument, or false otherwise.

Class Method: Buffer.isBuffer(obj)

- `obj` Object
- Return: Boolean

Tests if `obj` is a `Buffer`.

Class Method: Buffer.byteLength(string[, encoding])

- `string` String
- `encoding` String, Optional, Default: 'utf8'
- Return: Number

Gives the actual byte length of a string. `encoding` defaults to 'utf8'. This is not the same as `String.prototype.length` since that returns the number of *characters* in a string.

Example:

```
str = '\u00bd + \u00bc = \u00be';

console.log(str + ": " + str.length + " characters, " +
  Buffer.byteLength(str, 'utf8') + " bytes");

// ½ + ¼ = ¾: 9 characters, 12 bytes
```

Class Method: Buffer.concat(list[, totalLength])

- `list` {Array} List of Buffer objects to concat
- `totalLength` {Number} Total length of the buffers in the list when concatenated

Returns a buffer which is the result of concatenating all the buffers in the list together.

If the list has no items, or if the totalLength is 0, then it returns a zero-length buffer.

If totalLength is not provided, it is read from the buffers in the list. However, this adds an additional loop to the function, so it is faster to provide the length explicitly.

Example: build a single buffer from a list of three buffers:

```
var buf1 = new Buffer(10);
var buf2 = new Buffer(14);
var buf3 = new Buffer(18);

buf1.fill(0);
buf2.fill(0);
buf3.fill(0);

var buffers = [buf1, buf2, buf3];

var totalLength = 0;
for (var i = 0; i < buffers.length; i++) {
  totalLength += buffers[i].length;
}

console.log(totalLength);
var bufA = Buffer.concat(buffers, totalLength);
console.log(bufA);
console.log(bufA.length);

// 42
// <Buffer 00 00 00 00 ...>
// 42
```

Class Method: Buffer.compare(buf1, buf2)

- buf1 {Buffer}
- buf2 {Buffer}

The same as `buf1.compare(buf2)`. Useful for sorting an Array of Buffers:

```
var arr = [Buffer('1234'), Buffer('0123')];
arr.sort(Buffer.compare);
```

buf.length

- Number

The size of the buffer in bytes. Note that this is not necessarily the size of the contents. `length` refers to the amount of memory allocated for the buffer object. It does not change when the contents of the buffer are changed.

```
buf = new Buffer(1234);

console.log(buf.length);
buf.write("some string", 0, "ascii");
console.log(buf.length);

// 1234
// 1234
```

While the `length` property is not immutable, changing the value of `length` can result in undefined and inconsistent behavior. Applications that wish to modify the length of a buffer should therefore treat `length` as read-only and use `buf.slice` to create a new buffer.

```
buf = new Buffer(10);
buf.write("abcdefghj", 0, "ascii");
console.log(buf.length); // 10
buf = buf.slice(0,5);
console.log(buf.length); // 5
```

buf.write(string[, offset][, length][, encoding])

- `string` String - data to be written to buffer
- `offset` Number, Optional, Default: 0
- `length` Number, Optional, Default: `buffer.length - offset`
- `encoding` String, Optional, Default: 'utf8'

Writes `string` to the buffer at `offset` using the given encoding. `offset` defaults to 0, encoding defaults to 'utf8'. `length` is the number of bytes to write. Returns number of octets written. If `buffer` did not contain enough space to fit the entire string, it will write a partial amount of the string. `length` defaults to `buffer.length - offset`. The method will not write partial characters.

```
buf = new Buffer(256);
len = buf.write('\u00bd + \u00bc = \u00be', 0);
console.log(len + " bytes: " + buf.toString('utf8', 0, len));
```

buf.writeUIntLE(value, offset, byteLength[, noAssert])

buf.writeUIntBE(value, offset, byteLength[, noAssert])

buf.writeIntLE(value, offset, byteLength[, noAssert])

buf.writeIntBE(value, offset, byteLength[, noAssert])

- `value` {Number} Bytes to be written to buffer
- `offset` {Number} 0 <= offset <= buf.length
- `byteLength` {Number} 0 < byteLength <= 6
- `noAssert` {Boolean} Default: false
- Return: {Number}

Writes `value` to the buffer at the specified `offset` and `byteLength`. Supports up to 48 bits of accuracy. For example:

```
var b = new Buffer(6);
b.writeUIntBE(0x1234567890ab, 0, 6);
// <Buffer 12 34 56 78 90 ab>
```

Set `noAssert` to `true` to skip validation of `value` and `offset`. Defaults to `false`.

buf.readUIntLE(offset, byteLength[, noAssert])

buf.readUIntBE(offset, byteLength[, noAssert])

buf.readIntLE(offset, byteLength[, noAssert])

buf.readIntBE(offset, byteLength[, noAssert])

- `offset` {Number} `0 <= offset <= buf.length`
- `byteLength` {Number} `0 < byteLength <= 6`
- `noAssert` {Boolean} Default: false
- Return: {Number}

A generalized version of all numeric read methods. Supports up to 48 bits of accuracy. For example:

```
var b = new Buffer(6);
b.writeUInt16LE(0x90ab, 0);
b.writeUInt32LE(0x12345678, 2);
b.readUIntLE(0, 6).toString(16);   // Specify 6 bytes (48 bits)
// output: '1234567890ab'
```

Set `noAssert` to true to skip validation of `offset`. This means that `offset` may be beyond the end of the buffer. Defaults to `false`.

buf.toString([encoding][, start][, end])

- `encoding` String, Optional, Default: 'utf8'
- `start` Number, Optional, Default: 0
- `end` Number, Optional, Default: `buffer.length`

Decodes and returns a string from buffer data encoded using the specified character set encoding. If `encoding` is undefined or null, then `encoding` defaults to 'utf8'. The `start` and `end` parameters default to 0 and `buffer.length` when undefined.

```
buf = new Buffer(26);
for (var i = 0 ; i < 26 ; i++) {
  buf[i] = i + 97; // 97 is ASCII a
}
buf.toString('ascii'); // outputs: abcdefghijklmnopqrstuvwxyz
buf.toString('ascii',0,5); // outputs: abcde
buf.toString('utf8',0,5); // outputs: abcde
buf.toString(undefined,0,5); // encoding defaults to 'utf8', outputs abcde
```

See `buffer.write()` example, above.

buf.toJSON()

Returns a JSON-representation of the Buffer instance. `JSON.stringify` implicitly calls this function when stringifying a Buffer instance.

Example:

```
var buf = new Buffer('test');
var json = JSON.stringify(buf);

console.log(json);
// '{"type":"Buffer","data":[116,101,115,116]}'
```

```
var copy = JSON.parse(json, function(key, value) {
    return value && value.type === 'Buffer'
      ? new Buffer(value.data)
      : value;
  });

console.log(copy);
// <Buffer 74 65 73 74>
```

buf[index]

Get and set the octet at `index`. The values refer to individual bytes, so the legal range is between 0x00 and 0xFF hex or 0 and 255.

Example: copy an ASCII string into a buffer, one byte at a time:

```
str = "Node.js";
buf = new Buffer(str.length);

for (var i = 0; i < str.length ; i++) {
  buf[i] = str.charCodeAt(i);
}

console.log(buf);

// Node.js
```

buf.equals(otherBuffer)

- otherBuffer {Buffer}

Returns a boolean of whether `this` and `otherBuffer` have the same bytes.

buf.compare(otherBuffer)

- otherBuffer {Buffer}

Returns a number indicating whether `this` comes before or after or is the same as the `otherBuffer` in sort order.

buf.copy(targetBuffer[, targetStart][, sourceStart][, sourceEnd])

- targetBuffer Buffer object - Buffer to copy into
- targetStart Number, Optional, Default: 0
- sourceStart Number, Optional, Default: 0
- sourceEnd Number, Optional, Default: `buffer.length`

Copies data from a region of this buffer to a region in the target buffer even if the target memory region overlaps with the source. If `undefined` the `targetStart` and `sourceStart` parameters default to 0 while `sourceEnd` defaults to `buffer.length`.

Example: build two Buffers, then copy `buf1` from byte 16 through byte 19 into `buf2`, starting at the 8th byte in `buf2`.

```
buf1 = new Buffer(26);
buf2 = new Buffer(26);

for (var i = 0 ; i < 26 ; i++) {
  buf1[i] = i + 97; // 97 is ASCII a
  buf2[i] = 33; // ASCII !
}

buf1.copy(buf2, 8, 16, 20);
console.log(buf2.toString('ascii', 0, 25));
```

```
// !!!!!!!!qrst!!!!!!!!!!!!!!
```

Example: Build a single buffer, then copy data from one region to an overlapping region in the same buffer

```
buf = new Buffer(26);

for (var i = 0 ; i < 26 ; i++) {
  buf[i] = i + 97; // 97 is ASCII a
}

buf.copy(buf, 0, 4, 10);
console.log(buf.toString());
```

```
// efghijghijklmnopqrstuvwxyz
```

buf.slice([start[, end]])

- start Number, Optional, Default: 0
- end Number, Optional, Default: `buffer.length`

Returns a new buffer which references the same memory as the old, but offset and cropped by the `start` (defaults to 0) and `end` (defaults to `buffer.length`) indexes. Negative indexes start from the end of the buffer.

Modifying the new buffer slice will modify memory in the original buffer!

Example: build a Buffer with the ASCII alphabet, take a slice, then modify one byte from the original Buffer.

```
var buf1 = new Buffer(26);

for (var i = 0 ; i < 26 ; i++) {
  buf1[i] = i + 97; // 97 is ASCII a
}

var buf2 = buf1.slice(0, 3);
console.log(buf2.toString('ascii', 0, buf2.length));
buf1[0] = 33;
console.log(buf2.toString('ascii', 0, buf2.length));
```

```
// abc
// !bc
```

buf.indexOf(value[, byteOffset])

- value String, Buffer or Number
- byteOffset Number, Optional, Default: 0
- Return: Number

Operates similar to Array#indexOf(). Accepts a String, Buffer or Number. Strings are interpreted as UTF8. Buffers will use the entire buffer. So in order to compare a partial Buffer use `Buffer#slice()`. Numbers can range from 0 to 255.

buf.readUInt8(offset[, noAssert])

- `offset` Number
- `noAssert` Boolean, Optional, Default: false
- Return: Number

Reads an unsigned 8 bit integer from the buffer at the specified offset.

Set `noAssert` to true to skip validation of `offset`. This means that `offset` may be beyond the end of the buffer. Defaults to `false`.

Example:

```
var buf = new Buffer(4);

buf[0] = 0x3;
buf[1] = 0x4;
buf[2] = 0x23;
buf[3] = 0x42;

for (ii = 0; ii < buf.length; ii++) {
   console.log(buf.readUInt8(ii));
}

// 0x3
// 0x4
// 0x23
// 0x42
```

buf.readUInt16LE(offset[, noAssert])

buf.readUInt16BE(offset[, noAssert])

- `offset` Number
- `noAssert` Boolean, Optional, Default: false
- Return: Number

Reads an unsigned 16 bit integer from the buffer at the specified offset with specified endian format.

Set `noAssert` to true to skip validation of `offset`. This means that `offset` may be beyond the end of the buffer. Defaults to `false`.

Example:

```
var buf = new Buffer(4);

buf[0] = 0x3;
buf[1] = 0x4;
buf[2] = 0x23;
buf[3] = 0x42;

console.log(buf.readUInt16BE(0));
console.log(buf.readUInt16LE(0));
console.log(buf.readUInt16BE(1));
```

```
console.log(buf.readUInt16LE(1));
console.log(buf.readUInt16BE(2));
console.log(buf.readUInt16LE(2));
```

```
// 0x0304
// 0x0403
// 0x0423
// 0x2304
// 0x2342
// 0x4223
```

buf.readUInt32LE(offset[, noAssert])

buf.readUInt32BE(offset[, noAssert])

- offset Number
- noAssert Boolean, Optional, Default: false
- Return: Number

Reads an unsigned 32 bit integer from the buffer at the specified offset with specified endian format.

Set noAssert to true to skip validation of offset. This means that offset may be beyond the end of the buffer. Defaults to false.

Example:

```
var buf = new Buffer(4);
```

```
buf[0] = 0x3;
buf[1] = 0x4;
buf[2] = 0x23;
buf[3] = 0x42;
```

```
console.log(buf.readUInt32BE(0));
console.log(buf.readUInt32LE(0));
```

```
// 0x03042342
// 0x42230403
```

buf.readInt8(offset[, noAssert])

- offset Number
- noAssert Boolean, Optional, Default: false
- Return: Number

Reads a signed 8 bit integer from the buffer at the specified offset.

Set noAssert to true to skip validation of offset. This means that offset may be beyond the end of the buffer. Defaults to false.

Works as buffer.readUInt8, except buffer contents are treated as two's complement signed values.

buf.readInt16LE(offset[, noAssert])

buf.readInt16BE(offset[, noAssert])

- offset Number

- noAssert Boolean, Optional, Default: false
- Return: Number

Reads a signed 16 bit integer from the buffer at the specified offset with specified endian format.

Set noAssert to true to skip validation of offset. This means that offset may be beyond the end of the buffer. Defaults to false.

Works as buffer.readUInt16*, except buffer contents are treated as two's complement signed values.

buf.readInt32LE(offset[, noAssert])

buf.readInt32BE(offset[, noAssert])

- offset Number
- noAssert Boolean, Optional, Default: false
- Return: Number

Reads a signed 32 bit integer from the buffer at the specified offset with specified endian format.

Set noAssert to true to skip validation of offset. This means that offset may be beyond the end of the buffer. Defaults to false.

Works as buffer.readUInt32*, except buffer contents are treated as two's complement signed values.

buf.readFloatLE(offset[, noAssert])

buf.readFloatBE(offset[, noAssert])

- offset Number
- noAssert Boolean, Optional, Default: false
- Return: Number

Reads a 32 bit float from the buffer at the specified offset with specified endian format.

Set noAssert to true to skip validation of offset. This means that offset may be beyond the end of the buffer. Defaults to false.

Example:

```
var buf = new Buffer(4);

buf[0] = 0x00;
buf[1] = 0x00;
buf[2] = 0x80;
buf[3] = 0x3f;

console.log(buf.readFloatLE(0));

// 0x01
```

buf.readDoubleLE(offset[, noAssert])

buf.readDoubleBE(offset[, noAssert])

- offset Number
- noAssert Boolean, Optional, Default: false
- Return: Number

Reads a 64 bit double from the buffer at the specified offset with specified endian format.

Set `noAssert` to true to skip validation of `offset`. This means that `offset` may be beyond the end of the buffer. Defaults to `false`.

Example:

```
var buf = new Buffer(8);

buf[0] = 0x55;
buf[1] = 0x55;
buf[2] = 0x55;
buf[3] = 0x55;
buf[4] = 0x55;
buf[5] = 0x55;
buf[6] = 0xd5;
buf[7] = 0x3f;

console.log(buf.readDoubleLE(0));

// 0.3333333333333333
```

buf.writeUInt8(value, offset[, noAssert])

- value Number
- offset Number
- noAssert Boolean, Optional, Default: false

Writes `value` to the buffer at the specified offset. Note, `value` must be a valid unsigned 8 bit integer.

Set `noAssert` to true to skip validation of `value` and `offset`. This means that `value` may be too large for the specific function and `offset` may be beyond the end of the buffer leading to the values being silently dropped. This should not be used unless you are certain of correctness. Defaults to `false`.

Example:

```
var buf = new Buffer(4);
buf.writeUInt8(0x3, 0);
buf.writeUInt8(0x4, 1);
buf.writeUInt8(0x23, 2);
buf.writeUInt8(0x42, 3);

console.log(buf);

// <Buffer 03 04 23 42>
```

buf.writeUInt16LE(value, offset[, noAssert])

buf.writeUInt16BE(value, offset[, noAssert])

- value Number
- offset Number
- noAssert Boolean, Optional, Default: false

Writes `value` to the buffer at the specified offset with specified endian format. Note, `value` must be a valid unsigned 16 bit integer.

Set `noAssert` to true to skip validation of `value` and `offset`. This means that `value` may be too large for the specific function and `offset` may be beyond the end of the buffer leading to the values being silently dropped. This should not be used unless you are certain of correctness. Defaults to `false`.

Example:

```
var buf = new Buffer(4);
buf.writeUInt16BE(0xdead, 0);
buf.writeUInt16BE(0xbeef, 2);

console.log(buf);

buf.writeUInt16LE(0xdead, 0);
buf.writeUInt16LE(0xbeef, 2);

console.log(buf);

// <Buffer de ad be ef>
// <Buffer ad de ef be>
```

buf.writeUInt32LE(value, offset[, noAssert])

buf.writeUInt32BE(value, offset[, noAssert])

- value Number
- offset Number
- noAssert Boolean, Optional, Default: false

Writes `value` to the buffer at the specified offset with specified endian format. Note, `value` must be a valid unsigned 32 bit integer.

Set `noAssert` to true to skip validation of `value` and `offset`. This means that `value` may be too large for the specific function and `offset` may be beyond the end of the buffer leading to the values being silently dropped. This should not be used unless you are certain of correctness. Defaults to `false`.

Example:

```
var buf = new Buffer(4);
buf.writeUInt32BE(0xfeedface, 0);

console.log(buf);

buf.writeUInt32LE(0xfeedface, 0);

console.log(buf);

// <Buffer fe ed fa ce>
// <Buffer ce fa ed fe>
```

buf.writeInt8(value, offset[, noAssert])

- value Number
- offset Number
- noAssert Boolean, Optional, Default: false

Writes `value` to the buffer at the specified offset. Note, `value` must be a valid signed 8 bit integer.

Set `noAssert` to true to skip validation of `value` and `offset`. This means that `value` may be too large for the specific function and `offset` may be beyond the end of the buffer leading to the values being silently dropped. This should not be used unless you are certain of correctness. Defaults to `false`.

Works as `buffer.writeUInt8`, except value is written out as a two's complement signed integer into `buffer`.

buf.writeInt16LE(value, offset[, noAssert])

buf.writeInt16BE(value, offset[, noAssert])

- `value` Number
- `offset` Number
- `noAssert` Boolean, Optional, Default: false

Writes `value` to the buffer at the specified offset with specified endian format. Note, `value` must be a valid signed 16 bit integer.

Set `noAssert` to true to skip validation of `value` and `offset`. This means that `value` may be too large for the specific function and `offset` may be beyond the end of the buffer leading to the values being silently dropped. This should not be used unless you are certain of correctness. Defaults to `false`.

Works as `buffer.writeUInt16*`, except value is written out as a two's complement signed integer into `buffer`.

buf.writeInt32LE(value, offset[, noAssert])

buf.writeInt32BE(value, offset[, noAssert])

- `value` Number
- `offset` Number
- `noAssert` Boolean, Optional, Default: false

Writes `value` to the buffer at the specified offset with specified endian format. Note, `value` must be a valid signed 32 bit integer.

Set `noAssert` to true to skip validation of `value` and `offset`. This means that `value` may be too large for the specific function and `offset` may be beyond the end of the buffer leading to the values being silently dropped. This should not be used unless you are certain of correctness. Defaults to `false`.

Works as `buffer.writeUInt32*`, except value is written out as a two's complement signed integer into `buffer`.

buf.writeFloatLE(value, offset[, noAssert])

buf.writeFloatBE(value, offset[, noAssert])

- `value` Number
- `offset` Number
- `noAssert` Boolean, Optional, Default: false

Writes `value` to the buffer at the specified offset with specified endian format. Note, behavior is unspecified if `value` is not a 32 bit float.

Set `noAssert` to true to skip validation of `value` and `offset`. This means that `value` may be too large for the specific function and `offset` may be beyond the end of the buffer leading to the values being silently dropped. This should not be used unless you are certain of correctness. Defaults to `false`.

Example:

```
var buf = new Buffer(4);
buf.writeFloatBE(0xcafebabe, 0);

console.log(buf);

buf.writeFloatLE(0xcafebabe, 0);

console.log(buf);
```

```
// <Buffer 4f 4a fe bb>
// <Buffer bb fe 4a 4f>
```

buf.writeDoubleLE(value, offset[, noAssert])

buf.writeDoubleBE(value, offset[, noAssert])

- value Number
- offset Number
- noAssert Boolean, Optional, Default: false

Writes value to the buffer at the specified offset with specified endian format. Note, value must be a valid 64 bit double.

Set noAssert to true to skip validation of value and offset. This means that value may be too large for the specific function and offset may be beyond the end of the buffer leading to the values being silently dropped. This should not be used unless you are certain of correctness. Defaults to false.

Example:

```
var buf = new Buffer(8);
buf.writeDoubleBE(0xdeadbeefcafebabe, 0);

console.log(buf);

buf.writeDoubleLE(0xdeadbeefcafebabe, 0);

console.log(buf);

// <Buffer 43 eb d5 b7 dd f9 5f d7>
// <Buffer d7 5f f9 dd b7 d5 eb 43>
```

buf.fill(value[, offset][, end])

- value
- offset Number, Optional
- end Number, Optional

Fills the buffer with the specified value. If the offset (defaults to 0) and end (defaults to buffer.length) are not given it will fill the entire buffer.

```
var b = new Buffer(50);
b.fill("h");
```

buffer.values()

Creates iterator for buffer values (bytes). This function is called automatically when buffer is used in a for..of statement.

buffer.keys()

Creates iterator for buffer keys (indices).

buffer.entries()

Creates iterator for [index, byte] arrays.

buffer.INSPECT_MAX_BYTES

- Number, Default: 50

How many bytes will be returned when `buffer.inspect()` is called. This can be overridden by user modules.

Note that this is a property on the buffer module returned by `require('buffer')`, not on the Buffer global, or a buffer instance.

ES6 iteration

Buffers can be iterated over using `for..of` syntax:

```
var buf = new Buffer([1, 2, 3]);

for (var b of buf)
  console.log(b)

// 1
// 2
// 3
```

Additionally, `buffer.values()`, `buffer.keys()` and `buffer.entries()` methods can be used to create iterators.

Class: SlowBuffer

Returns an un-pooled `Buffer`.

In order to avoid the garbage collection overhead of creating many individually allocated Buffers, by default allocations under 4KB are sliced from a single larger allocated object. This approach improves both performance and memory usage since v8 does not need to track and cleanup as many `Persistent` objects.

In the case where a developer may need to retain a small chunk of memory from a pool for an indeterminate amount of time it may be appropriate to create an un-pooled Buffer instance using SlowBuffer and copy out the relevant bits.

```
// need to keep around a few small chunks of memory
var store = [];

socket.on('readable', function() {
  var data = socket.read();
  // allocate for retained data
  var sb = new SlowBuffer(10);
  // copy the data into the new allocation
  data.copy(sb, 0, 0, 10);
  store.push(sb);
});
```

Though this should be used sparingly and only be a last resort *after* a developer has actively observed undue memory retention in their applications.

Addons

Addons are dynamically linked shared objects. They can provide glue to C and C++ libraries. The API (at the moment) is rather complex, involving knowledge of several libraries:

- V8 JavaScript, a C++ library. Used for interfacing with JavaScript: creating objects, calling functions, etc. Documented mostly in the **v8.h** header file (**deps/v8/include/v8.h** in the Node.js source tree), which is also available online.

- libuv, C event loop library. Anytime one needs to wait for a file descriptor to become readable, wait for a timer, or wait for a signal to be received one will need to interface with libuv. That is, if you perform any I/O, libuv will need to be used.

- Internal Node.js libraries. Most importantly is the **node::ObjectWrap** class which you will likely want to derive from.

- Others. Look in **deps/** for what else is available.

Node.js statically compiles all its dependencies into the executable. When compiling your module, you don't need to worry about linking to any of these libraries.

All of the following examples are available for download and may be used as a starting-point for your own Addon.

Hello world

To get started let's make a small Addon which is the C++ equivalent of the following JavaScript code:

```
module.exports.hello = function() { return 'world'; };
```

First we create a file **hello.cc**:

```
// hello.cc
#include <node.h>

namespace demo {

using v8::FunctionCallbackInfo;
using v8::Isolate;
using v8::Local;
using v8::Object;
using v8::String;
using v8::Value;

void Method(const FunctionCallbackInfo<Value>& args) {
  Isolate* isolate = args.GetIsolate();
  args.GetReturnValue().Set(String::NewFromUtf8(isolate, "world"));
}

void init(Local<Object> exports) {
  NODE_SET_METHOD(exports, "hello", Method);
}

NODE_MODULE(addon, init)

} // namespace demo
```

Note that all Node.js addons must export an initialization function:

```
void Initialize(Local<Object> exports);
NODE_MODULE(module_name, Initialize)
```

There is no semi-colon after NODE_MODULE as it's not a function (see **node.h**).

The **module_name** needs to match the filename of the final binary (minus the .node suffix).

The source code needs to be built into **addon.node**, the binary Addon. To do this we create a file called **binding.gyp** which describes the configuration to build your module in a JSON-like format. This file gets compiled by node-gyp.

```
{
  "targets": [
    {
      "target_name": "addon",
      "sources": [ "hello.cc" ]
    }
  ]
}
```

The next step is to generate the appropriate project build files for the current platform. Use **node-gyp configure** for that.

Now you will have either a **Makefile** (on Unix platforms) or a **vcxproj** file (on Windows) in the **build/** directory. Next invoke the **node-gyp build** command.

Now you have your compiled **.node** bindings file! The compiled bindings end up in **build/Release/**.

You can now use the binary addon in an Node.js project **hello.js** by pointing **require** to the recently built **hello.node** module:

```
// hello.js
var addon = require('./build/Release/addon');

console.log(addon.hello()); // 'world'
```

Please see patterns below for further information or https://github.com/arturadib/node-qt for an example in production.

Addon patterns

Below are some addon patterns to help you get started. Consult the online v8 reference for help with the various v8 calls, and v8's Embedder's Guide for an explanation of several concepts used such as handles, scopes, function templates, etc.

In order to use these examples you need to compile them using **node-gyp**. Create the following **binding.gyp** file:

```
{
  "targets": [
    {
      "target_name": "addon",
      "sources": [ "addon.cc" ]
    }
  ]
}
```

In cases where there is more than one **.cc** file, simply add the file name to the **sources** array, e.g.:

```
"sources": ["addon.cc", "myexample.cc"]
```

Now that you have your **binding.gyp** ready, you can configure and build the addon:

```
$ node-gyp configure build
```

Function arguments

The following pattern illustrates how to read arguments from JavaScript function calls and return a result.
This is the main and only needed source `addon.cc`:

```cpp
// addon.cc
#include <node.h>

namespace demo {

using v8::Exception;
using v8::FunctionCallbackInfo;
using v8::Isolate;
using v8::Local;
using v8::Number;
using v8::Object;
using v8::String;
using v8::Value;

void Add(const FunctionCallbackInfo<Value>& args) {
  Isolate* isolate = args.GetIsolate();

  if (args.Length() < 2) {
    isolate->ThrowException(Exception::TypeError(
        String::NewFromUtf8(isolate, "Wrong number of arguments")));
    return;
  }

  if (!args[0]->IsNumber() || !args[1]->IsNumber()) {
    isolate->ThrowException(Exception::TypeError(
        String::NewFromUtf8(isolate, "Wrong arguments")));
    return;
  }

  double value = args[0]->NumberValue() + args[1]->NumberValue();
  Local<Number> num = Number::New(isolate, value);

  args.GetReturnValue().Set(num);
}

void Init(Local<Object> exports) {
  NODE_SET_METHOD(exports, "add", Add);
}

NODE_MODULE(addon, Init)

}  // namespace demo
```

You can test it with the following JavaScript snippet:

```js
// test.js
var addon = require('./build/Release/addon');

console.log( 'This should be eight:', addon.add(3,5) );
```

Callbacks

You can pass JavaScript functions to a C++ function and execute them from there. Here's `addon.cc`:

```
// addon.cc
#include <node.h>

namespace demo {

using v8::Function;
using v8::FunctionCallbackInfo;
using v8::Isolate;
using v8::Local;
using v8::Null;
using v8::Object;
using v8::String;
using v8::Value;

void RunCallback(const FunctionCallbackInfo<Value>& args) {
  Isolate* isolate = args.GetIsolate();
  Local<Function> cb = Local<Function>::Cast(args[0]);
  const unsigned argc = 1;
  Local<Value> argv[argc] = { String::NewFromUtf8(isolate, "hello world") };
  cb->Call(Null(isolate), argc, argv);
}

void Init(Local<Object> exports, Local<Object> module) {
  NODE_SET_METHOD(module, "exports", RunCallback);
}

NODE_MODULE(addon, Init)

}  // namespace demo
```

Note that this example uses a two-argument form of `Init()` that receives the full **module** object as the second argument. This allows the addon to completely overwrite **exports** with a single function instead of adding the function as a property of **exports**.

To test it run the following JavaScript snippet:

```
// test.js
var addon = require('./build/Release/addon');

addon(function(msg){
  console.log(msg); // 'hello world'
});
```

Object factory

You can create and return new objects from within a C++ function with this `addon.cc` pattern, which returns an object with property **msg** that echoes the string passed to `createObject()`:

```
// addon.cc
#include <node.h>

namespace demo {

using v8::FunctionCallbackInfo;
```

```
using v8::Isolate;
using v8::Local;
using v8::Object;
using v8::String;
using v8::Value;

void CreateObject(const FunctionCallbackInfo<Value>& args) {
  Isolate* isolate = args.GetIsolate();

  Local<Object> obj = Object::New(isolate);
  obj->Set(String::NewFromUtf8(isolate, "msg"), args[0]->ToString());

  args.GetReturnValue().Set(obj);
}

void Init(Local<Object> exports, Local<Object> module) {
  NODE_SET_METHOD(module, "exports", CreateObject);
}

NODE_MODULE(addon, Init)

}  // namespace demo
```

To test it in JavaScript:

```
// test.js
var addon = require('./build/Release/addon');

var obj1 = addon('hello');
var obj2 = addon('world');
console.log(obj1.msg+' '+obj2.msg); // 'hello world'
```

Function factory

This pattern illustrates how to create and return a JavaScript function that wraps a C++ function:

```
// addon.cc
#include <node.h>

namespace demo {

using v8::Function;
using v8::FunctionCallbackInfo;
using v8::FunctionTemplate;
using v8::Isolate;
using v8::Local;
using v8::Object;
using v8::String;
using v8::Value;

void MyFunction(const FunctionCallbackInfo<Value>& args) {
  Isolate* isolate = args.GetIsolate();
  args.GetReturnValue().Set(String::NewFromUtf8(isolate, "hello world"));
}

void CreateFunction(const FunctionCallbackInfo<Value>& args) {
```

```
  Isolate* isolate = args.GetIsolate();

  Local<FunctionTemplate> tpl = FunctionTemplate::New(isolate, MyFunction);
  Local<Function> fn = tpl->GetFunction();

  // omit this to make it anonymous
  fn->SetName(String::NewFromUtf8(isolate, "theFunction"));

  args.GetReturnValue().Set(fn);
}

void Init(Local<Object> exports, Local<Object> module) {
  NODE_SET_METHOD(module, "exports", CreateFunction);
}

NODE_MODULE(addon, Init)

}  // namespace demo
```

To test:
```
// test.js
var addon = require('./build/Release/addon');

var fn = addon();
console.log(fn()); // 'hello world'
```

Wrapping C++ objects

Here we will create a wrapper for a C++ object/class `MyObject` that can be instantiated in JavaScript through the **new** operator. First prepare the main module `addon.cc`:

```
// addon.cc
#include <node.h>
#include "myobject.h"

namespace demo {

using v8::Local;
using v8::Object;

void InitAll(Local<Object> exports) {
  MyObject::Init(exports);
}

NODE_MODULE(addon, InitAll)

}  // namespace demo
```

Then in `myobject.h` make your wrapper inherit from `node::ObjectWrap`:

```
// myobject.h
#ifndef MYOBJECT_H
#define MYOBJECT_H

#include <node.h>
#include <node_object_wrap.h>
```

```
namespace demo {

class MyObject : public node::ObjectWrap {
 public:
  static void Init(v8::Local<v8::Object> exports);

 private:
  explicit MyObject(double value = 0);
  ~MyObject();

  static void New(const v8::FunctionCallbackInfo<v8::Value>& args);
  static void PlusOne(const v8::FunctionCallbackInfo<v8::Value>& args);
  static v8::Persistent<v8::Function> constructor;
  double value_;
};

}  // namespace demo

#endif
```

And in `myobject.cc` implement the various methods that you want to expose. Here we expose the method `plusOne` by adding it to the constructor's prototype:

```
// myobject.cc
#include "myobject.h"

namespace demo {

using v8::Function;
using v8::FunctionCallbackInfo;
using v8::FunctionTemplate;
using v8::Isolate;
using v8::Local;
using v8::Number;
using v8::Object;
using v8::Persistent;
using v8::String;
using v8::Value;


Persistent<Function> MyObject::constructor;

MyObject::MyObject(double value) : value_(value) {
}

MyObject::~MyObject() {
}

void MyObject::Init(Local<Object> exports) {
  Isolate* isolate = exports->GetIsolate();

  // Prepare constructor template
  Local<FunctionTemplate> tpl = FunctionTemplate::New(isolate, New);
  tpl->SetClassName(String::NewFromUtf8(isolate, "MyObject"));
  tpl->InstanceTemplate()->SetInternalFieldCount(1);

  // Prototype
```

```
    NODE_SET_PROTOTYPE_METHOD(tpl, "plusOne", PlusOne);

    constructor.Reset(isolate, tpl->GetFunction());
    exports->Set(String::NewFromUtf8(isolate, "MyObject"),
                 tpl->GetFunction());
}

void MyObject::New(const FunctionCallbackInfo<Value>& args) {
  Isolate* isolate = args.GetIsolate();

  if (args.IsConstructCall()) {
    // Invoked as constructor: 'new MyObject(...)'
    double value = args[0]->IsUndefined() ? 0 : args[0]->NumberValue();
    MyObject* obj = new MyObject(value);
    obj->Wrap(args.This());
    args.GetReturnValue().Set(args.This());
  } else {
    // Invoked as plain function 'MyObject(...)', turn into construct call.
    const int argc = 1;
    Local<Value> argv[argc] = { args[0] };
    Local<Function> cons = Local<Function>::New(isolate, constructor);
    args.GetReturnValue().Set(cons->NewInstance(argc, argv));
  }
}

void MyObject::PlusOne(const FunctionCallbackInfo<Value>& args) {
  Isolate* isolate = args.GetIsolate();

  MyObject* obj = ObjectWrap::Unwrap<MyObject>(args.Holder());
  obj->value_ += 1;

  args.GetReturnValue().Set(Number::New(isolate, obj->value_));
}

} // namespace demo
```

Test it with:

```
// test.js
var addon = require('./build/Release/addon');

var obj = new addon.MyObject(10);
console.log( obj.plusOne() ); // 11
console.log( obj.plusOne() ); // 12
console.log( obj.plusOne() ); // 13
```

Factory of wrapped objects

This is useful when you want to be able to create native objects without explicitly instantiating them with the new operator in JavaScript, e.g.

```
var obj = addon.createObject();
// instead of:
// var obj = new addon.Object();
```

Let's register our createObject method in addon.cc:

```
// addon.cc
#include <node.h>
#include "myobject.h"

namespace demo {

using v8::FunctionCallbackInfo;
using v8::Isolate;
using v8::Local;
using v8::Object;
using v8::String;
using v8::Value;

void CreateObject(const FunctionCallbackInfo<Value>& args) {
  MyObject::NewInstance(args);
}

void InitAll(Local<Object> exports, Local<Object> module) {
  MyObject::Init(exports->GetIsolate());

  NODE_SET_METHOD(module, "exports", CreateObject);
}

NODE_MODULE(addon, InitAll)

}  // namespace demo
```

In `myobject.h` we now introduce the static method `NewInstance` that takes care of instantiating the object (i.e. it does the job of `new` in JavaScript):

```
// myobject.h
#ifndef MYOBJECT_H
#define MYOBJECT_H

#include <node.h>
#include <node_object_wrap.h>

namespace demo {

class MyObject : public node::ObjectWrap {
 public:
  static void Init(v8::Isolate* isolate);
  static void NewInstance(const v8::FunctionCallbackInfo<v8::Value>& args);

 private:
  explicit MyObject(double value = 0);
  ~MyObject();

  static void New(const v8::FunctionCallbackInfo<v8::Value>& args);
  static void PlusOne(const v8::FunctionCallbackInfo<v8::Value>& args);
  static v8::Persistent<v8::Function> constructor;
  double value_;
};

}  // namespace demo

#endif
```

The implementation is similar to the above in `myobject.cc`:

```
// myobject.cc
#include <node.h>
#include "myobject.h"

namespace demo {

using v8::Function;
using v8::FunctionCallbackInfo;
using v8::FunctionTemplate;
using v8::Isolate;
using v8::Local;
using v8::Number;
using v8::Object;
using v8::Persistent;
using v8::String;
using v8::Value;

Persistent<Function> MyObject::constructor;

MyObject::MyObject(double value) : value_(value) {
}

MyObject::~MyObject() {
}

void MyObject::Init(Isolate* isolate) {
  // Prepare constructor template
  Local<FunctionTemplate> tpl = FunctionTemplate::New(isolate, New);
  tpl->SetClassName(String::NewFromUtf8(isolate, "MyObject"));
  tpl->InstanceTemplate()->SetInternalFieldCount(1);

  // Prototype
  NODE_SET_PROTOTYPE_METHOD(tpl, "plusOne", PlusOne);

  constructor.Reset(isolate, tpl->GetFunction());
}

void MyObject::New(const FunctionCallbackInfo<Value>& args) {
  Isolate* isolate = args.GetIsolate();

  if (args.IsConstructCall()) {
    // Invoked as constructor: 'new MyObject(...)'
    double value = args[0]->IsUndefined() ? 0 : args[0]->NumberValue();
    MyObject* obj = new MyObject(value);
    obj->Wrap(args.This());
    args.GetReturnValue().Set(args.This());
  } else {
    // Invoked as plain function 'MyObject(...)', turn into construct call.
    const int argc = 1;
    Local<Value> argv[argc] = { args[0] };
    Local<Function> cons = Local<Function>::New(isolate, constructor);
    args.GetReturnValue().Set(cons->NewInstance(argc, argv));
  }
}
```

```cpp
void MyObject::NewInstance(const FunctionCallbackInfo<Value>& args) {
  Isolate* isolate = args.GetIsolate();

  const unsigned argc = 1;
  Local<Value> argv[argc] = { args[0] };
  Local<Function> cons = Local<Function>::New(isolate, constructor);
  Local<Object> instance = cons->NewInstance(argc, argv);

  args.GetReturnValue().Set(instance);
}

void MyObject::PlusOne(const FunctionCallbackInfo<Value>& args) {
  Isolate* isolate = args.GetIsolate();

  MyObject* obj = ObjectWrap::Unwrap<MyObject>(args.Holder());
  obj->value_ += 1;

  args.GetReturnValue().Set(Number::New(isolate, obj->value_));
}

} // namespace demo
```

Test it with:

```js
// test.js
var createObject = require('./build/Release/addon');

var obj = createObject(10);
console.log( obj.plusOne() ); // 11
console.log( obj.plusOne() ); // 12
console.log( obj.plusOne() ); // 13

var obj2 = createObject(20);
console.log( obj2.plusOne() ); // 21
console.log( obj2.plusOne() ); // 22
console.log( obj2.plusOne() ); // 23
```

Passing wrapped objects around

In addition to wrapping and returning C++ objects, you can pass them around by unwrapping them with Node.js's `node::ObjectWrap::Unwrap` helper function. In the following `addon.cc` we introduce a function `add()` that can take on two `MyObject` objects:

```cpp
// addon.cc
#include <node.h>
#include <node_object_wrap.h>
#include "myobject.h"

namespace demo {

using v8::FunctionCallbackInfo;
using v8::Isolate;
using v8::Local;
using v8::Number;
using v8::Object;
using v8::String;
```

```
using v8::Value;

void CreateObject(const FunctionCallbackInfo<Value>& args) {
  MyObject::NewInstance(args);
}

void Add(const FunctionCallbackInfo<Value>& args) {
  Isolate* isolate = args.GetIsolate();

  MyObject* obj1 = node::ObjectWrap::Unwrap<MyObject>(
      args[0]->ToObject());
  MyObject* obj2 = node::ObjectWrap::Unwrap<MyObject>(
      args[1]->ToObject());

  double sum = obj1->value() + obj2->value();
  args.GetReturnValue().Set(Number::New(isolate, sum));
}

void InitAll(Local<Object> exports) {
  MyObject::Init(exports->GetIsolate());

  NODE_SET_METHOD(exports, "createObject", CreateObject);
  NODE_SET_METHOD(exports, "add", Add);
}

NODE_MODULE(addon, InitAll)

}  // namespace demo
```

To make things interesting we introduce a public method in `myobject.h` so we can probe private values after unwrapping the object:

```
// myobject.h
#ifndef MYOBJECT_H
#define MYOBJECT_H

#include <node.h>
#include <node_object_wrap.h>

namespace demo {

class MyObject : public node::ObjectWrap {
 public:
  static void Init(v8::Isolate* isolate);
  static void NewInstance(const v8::FunctionCallbackInfo<v8::Value>& args);
  inline double value() const { return value_; }

 private:
  explicit MyObject(double value = 0);
  ~MyObject();

  static void New(const v8::FunctionCallbackInfo<v8::Value>& args);
  static v8::Persistent<v8::Function> constructor;
  double value_;
};

}  // namespace demo
```

```
#endif
```

The implementation of `myobject.cc` is similar as before:

```cpp
// myobject.cc
#include <node.h>
#include "myobject.h"

namespace demo {

using v8::Function;
using v8::FunctionCallbackInfo;
using v8::FunctionTemplate;
using v8::Isolate;
using v8::Local;
using v8::Object;
using v8::Persistent;
using v8::String;
using v8::Value;


Persistent<Function> MyObject::constructor;

MyObject::MyObject(double value) : value_(value) {
}

MyObject::~MyObject() {
}

void MyObject::Init(Isolate* isolate) {
  // Prepare constructor template
  Local<FunctionTemplate> tpl = FunctionTemplate::New(isolate, New);
  tpl->SetClassName(String::NewFromUtf8(isolate, "MyObject"));
  tpl->InstanceTemplate()->SetInternalFieldCount(1);

  constructor.Reset(isolate, tpl->GetFunction());
}

void MyObject::New(const FunctionCallbackInfo<Value>& args) {
  Isolate* isolate = args.GetIsolate();

  if (args.IsConstructCall()) {
    // Invoked as constructor: 'new MyObject(...)'
    double value = args[0]->IsUndefined() ? 0 : args[0]->NumberValue();
    MyObject* obj = new MyObject(value);
    obj->Wrap(args.This());
    args.GetReturnValue().Set(args.This());
  } else {
    // Invoked as plain function 'MyObject(...)', turn into construct call.
    const int argc = 1;
    Local<Value> argv[argc] = { args[0] };
    Local<Function> cons = Local<Function>::New(isolate, constructor);
    args.GetReturnValue().Set(cons->NewInstance(argc, argv));
  }
}

void MyObject::NewInstance(const FunctionCallbackInfo<Value>& args) {
```

```
  Isolate* isolate = args.GetIsolate();

  const unsigned argc = 1;
  Local<Value> argv[argc] = { args[0] };
  Local<Function> cons = Local<Function>::New(isolate, constructor);
  Local<Object> instance = cons->NewInstance(argc, argv);

  args.GetReturnValue().Set(instance);
}

}  // namespace demo
```

Test it with:

```
// test.js
var addon = require('./build/Release/addon');

var obj1 = addon.createObject(10);
var obj2 = addon.createObject(20);
var result = addon.add(obj1, obj2);

console.log(result); // 30
```

AtExit hooks

void AtExit(callback, args)

- callback: void (*)(void*) - A pointer to the function to call at exit.
- args: void* - A pointer to pass to the callback at exit.

Registers exit hooks that run after the event loop has ended, but before the VM is killed.

Callbacks are run in last-in, first-out order. AtExit takes two parameters: a pointer to a callback function to run at exit, and a pointer to untyped context data to be passed to that callback.

The file addon.cc implements AtExit below:

```
// addon.cc
#undef NDEBUG
#include <assert.h>
#include <stdlib.h>
#include <node.h>

namespace demo {

using node::AtExit;
using v8::HandleScope;
using v8::Isolate;
using v8::Local;
using v8::Object;

static char cookie[] = "yum yum";
static int at_exit_cb1_called = 0;
static int at_exit_cb2_called = 0;

static void at_exit_cb1(void* arg) {
  Isolate* isolate = static_cast<Isolate*>(arg);
  HandleScope scope(isolate);
```

```
  Local<Object> obj = Object::New(isolate);
  assert(!obj.IsEmpty()); // assert VM is still alive
  assert(obj->IsObject());
  at_exit_cb1_called++;
}

static void at_exit_cb2(void* arg) {
  assert(arg == static_cast<void*>(cookie));
  at_exit_cb2_called++;
}

static void sanity_check(void*) {
  assert(at_exit_cb1_called == 1);
  assert(at_exit_cb2_called == 2);
}

void init(Local<Object> exports) {
  AtExit(sanity_check);
  AtExit(at_exit_cb2, cookie);
  AtExit(at_exit_cb2, cookie);
  AtExit(at_exit_cb1, exports->GetIsolate());
}

NODE_MODULE(addon, init);

}  // namespace demo
```

Test in JavaScript by running:

```
// test.js
var addon = require('./build/Release/addon');
```

Child Process

`Stability: 2 - Stable`

Node.js provides a tri-directional `popen(3)` facility through the `child_process` module.

It is possible to stream data through a child's `stdin`, `stdout`, and `stderr` in a fully non-blocking way. (Note that some programs use line-buffered I/O internally. That doesn't affect Node.js but it means data you send to the child process may not be immediately consumed.)

To create a child process use `require('child_process').spawn()` or `require('child_process').fork()`. The semantics of each are slightly different, and explained below.

For scripting purposes you may find the synchronous counterparts more convenient.

Class: ChildProcess

`ChildProcess` is an EventEmitter.

Child processes always have three streams associated with them. `child.stdin`, `child.stdout`, and `child.stderr`. These may be shared with the stdio streams of the parent process, or they may be separate stream objects which can be piped to and from.

The ChildProcess class is not intended to be used directly. Use the `spawn()`, `exec()`, `execFile()`, or `fork()` methods to create a Child Process instance.

Event: 'error'

- `err` {Error Object} the error.

Emitted when:

1. The process could not be spawned, or
2. The process could not be killed, or
3. Sending a message to the child process failed for whatever reason.

Note that the `exit`-event may or may not fire after an error has occurred. If you are listening on both events to fire a function, remember to guard against calling your function twice.

See also `ChildProcess#kill()` and `ChildProcess#send()`.

Event: 'exit'

- `code` {Number} the exit code, if it exited normally.
- `signal` {String} the signal passed to kill the child process, if it was killed by the parent.

This event is emitted after the child process ends. If the process terminated normally, `code` is the final exit code of the process, otherwise `null`. If the process terminated due to receipt of a signal, `signal` is the string name of the signal, otherwise `null`.

Note that the child process stdio streams might still be open.

Also, note that Node.js establishes signal handlers for `'SIGINT'` and `'SIGTERM'`, so it will not terminate due to receipt of those signals, it will exit.

See `waitpid(2)`.

Event: 'close'

- `code` {Number} the exit code, if it exited normally.
- `signal` {String} the signal passed to kill the child process, if it was killed by the parent.

This event is emitted when the stdio streams of a child process have all terminated. This is distinct from 'exit', since multiple processes might share the same stdio streams.

Event: 'disconnect'

This event is emitted after calling the `.disconnect()` method in the parent or in the child. After disconnecting it is no longer possible to send messages, and the `.connected` property is false.

Event: 'message'

- `message` {Object} a parsed JSON object or primitive value.
- `sendHandle` {Handle object} a net.Socket or net.Server object, or undefined.

Messages sent by `.send(message, [sendHandle])` are obtained using the `message` event.

child.stdin

- {Stream object}

A `Writable Stream` that represents the child process's `stdin`. If the child is waiting to read all its input, it will not continue until this stream has been closed via `end()`.

If the child was not spawned with `stdio[0]` set to 'pipe', then this will not be set.

`child.stdin` is shorthand for `child.stdio[0]`. Both properties will refer to the same object, or null.

child.stdout

- {Stream object}

A `Readable Stream` that represents the child process's `stdout`.

If the child was not spawned with `stdio[1]` set to 'pipe', then this will not be set.

`child.stdout` is shorthand for `child.stdio[1]`. Both properties will refer to the same object, or null.

child.stderr

- {Stream object}

A `Readable Stream` that represents the child process's `stderr`.

If the child was not spawned with `stdio[2]` set to 'pipe', then this will not be set.

`child.stderr` is shorthand for `child.stdio[2]`. Both properties will refer to the same object, or null.

child.stdio

- {Array}

A sparse array of pipes to the child process, corresponding with positions in the stdio option to spawn that have been set to 'pipe'. Note that streams 0-2 are also available as ChildProcess.stdin, ChildProcess.stdout, and ChildProcess.stderr, respectively.

In the following example, only the child's fd 1 is setup as a pipe, so only the parent's `child.stdio[1]` is a stream, all other values in the array are `null`.

```
var assert = require('assert');
var fs = require('fs');
var child_process = require('child_process');

child = child_process.spawn('ls', {
    stdio: [
      0, // use parents stdin for child
      'pipe', // pipe child's stdout to parent
      fs.openSync('err.out', 'w') // direct child's stderr to a file
    ]
});

assert.equal(child.stdio[0], null);
assert.equal(child.stdio[0], child.stdin);

assert(child.stdout);
assert.equal(child.stdio[1], child.stdout);

assert.equal(child.stdio[2], null);
assert.equal(child.stdio[2], child.stderr);
```

child.pid

- {Integer}

The PID of the child process.

Example:

```
var spawn = require('child_process').spawn,
    grep  = spawn('grep', ['ssh']);

console.log('Spawned child pid: ' + grep.pid);
grep.stdin.end();
```

child.connected

- {Boolean} Set to false after `.disconnect` is called

If `.connected` is false, it is no longer possible to send messages.

child.kill([signal])

- signal {String}

Send a signal to the child process. If no argument is given, the process will be sent `'SIGTERM'`. See `signal(7)` for a list of available signals.

```
var spawn = require('child_process').spawn,
    grep  = spawn('grep', ['ssh']);
```

```
grep.on('close', function (code, signal) {
  console.log('child process terminated due to receipt of signal ' + signal);
});

// send SIGHUP to process
grep.kill('SIGHUP');
```

May emit an **'error'** event when the signal cannot be delivered. Sending a signal to a child process that has already exited is not an error but may have unforeseen consequences: if the PID (the process ID) has been reassigned to another process, the signal will be delivered to that process instead. What happens next is anyone's guess.

Note that while the function is called **kill**, the signal delivered to the child process may not actually kill it. **kill** really just sends a signal to a process.

See **kill(2)**

child.send(message[, sendHandle][, callback])

- **message** {Object}
- **sendHandle** {Handle object}
- **callback** {Function}
- Return: Boolean

When using **child_process.fork()** you can write to the child using **child.send(message[, sendHandle][, callback])** and messages are received by a **'message'** event on the child.

For example:

```
var cp = require('child_process');

var n = cp.fork(__dirname + '/sub.js');

n.on('message', function(m) {
  console.log('PARENT got message:', m);
});

n.send({ hello: 'world' });
```

And then the child script, **'sub.js'** might look like this:

```
process.on('message', function(m) {
  console.log('CHILD got message:', m);
});

process.send({ foo: 'bar' });
```

In the child the **process** object will have a **send()** method, and **process** will emit objects each time it receives a message on its channel.

There is a special case when sending a **{cmd: 'NODE_foo'}** message. All messages containing a **NODE_** prefix in its **cmd** property will not be emitted in the **message** event, since they are internal messages used by Node.js core. Messages containing the prefix are emitted in the **internalMessage** event. Avoid using this feature; it is subject to change without notice.

The **sendHandle** option to **child.send()** is for sending a TCP server or socket object to another process. The child will receive the object as its second argument to the **message** event.

The **callback** option is a function that is invoked after the message is sent but before the target may have received it. It is called with a single argument: **null** on success, or an **Error** object on failure.

`child.send()` emits an `'error'` event if no callback was given and the message cannot be sent, for example because the child process has already exited.

`child.send()` returns `false` if the channel has closed or when the backlog of unsent messages exceeds a threshold that makes it unwise to send more. Otherwise, it returns `true`. Use the callback mechanism to implement flow control.

Example: sending server object   Here is an example of sending a server:

```
var child = require('child_process').fork('child.js');

// Open up the server object and send the handle.
var server = require('net').createServer();
server.on('connection', function (socket) {
  socket.end('handled by parent');
});
server.listen(1337, function() {
  child.send('server', server);
});
```

And the child would then receive the server object as:

```
process.on('message', function(m, server) {
  if (m === 'server') {
    server.on('connection', function (socket) {
      socket.end('handled by child');
    });
  }
});
```

Note that the server is now shared between the parent and child, this means that some connections will be handled by the parent and some by the child.

For `dgram` servers the workflow is exactly the same. Here you listen on a `message` event instead of `connection` and use `server.bind` instead of `server.listen`. (Currently only supported on UNIX platforms.)

Example: sending socket object   Here is an example of sending a socket. It will spawn two children and handle connections with the remote address `74.125.127.100` as VIP by sending the socket to a "special" child process. Other sockets will go to a "normal" process.

```
var normal = require('child_process').fork('child.js', ['normal']);
var special = require('child_process').fork('child.js', ['special']);

// Open up the server and send sockets to child
var server = require('net').createServer();
server.on('connection', function (socket) {

  // if this is a VIP
  if (socket.remoteAddress === '74.125.127.100') {
    special.send('socket', socket);
    return;
  }
  // just the usual...
  normal.send('socket', socket);
});
server.listen(1337);
```

The `child.js` could look like this:

```
process.on('message', function(m, socket) {
  if (m === 'socket') {
    socket.end('You were handled as a ' + process.argv[2] + ' person');
  }
});
```

Note that once a single socket has been sent to a child the parent can no longer keep track of when the socket is destroyed. To indicate this condition the `.connections` property becomes `null`. It is also recommended not to use `.maxConnections` in this condition.

child.disconnect()

Close the IPC channel between parent and child, allowing the child to exit gracefully once there are no other connections keeping it alive. After calling this method the `.connected` flag will be set to `false` in both the parent and child, and it is no longer possible to send messages.

The 'disconnect' event will be emitted when there are no messages in the process of being received, most likely immediately.

Note that you can also call `process.disconnect()` in the child process when the child process has any open IPC channels with the parent (i.e `fork()`).

Asynchronous Process Creation

These methods follow the common async programming patterns (accepting a callback or returning an EventEmitter).

child_process.spawn(command[, args][, options])

- `command` {String} The command to run
- `args` {Array} List of string arguments
- `options` {Object}
- `cwd` {String} Current working directory of the child process
- `env` {Object} Environment key-value pairs
- `stdio` {Array|String} Child's stdio configuration. (See below)
- `detached` {Boolean} Prepare child to run independently of its parent process. Specific behavior depends on the platform, see below)
- `uid` {Number} Sets the user identity of the process. (See setuid(2).)
- `gid` {Number} Sets the group identity of the process. (See setgid(2).)
- return: {ChildProcess object}

Launches a new process with the given `command`, with command line arguments in `args`. If omitted, `args` defaults to an empty Array.

The third argument is used to specify additional options, with these defaults:

```
{ cwd: undefined,
  env: process.env
}
```

Use `cwd` to specify the working directory from which the process is spawned. If not given, the default is to inherit the current working directory.

Use `env` to specify environment variables that will be visible to the new process, the default is `process.env`.

Example of running `ls -lh /usr`, capturing `stdout`, `stderr`, and the exit code:

```
var spawn = require('child_process').spawn,
    ls    = spawn('ls', ['-lh', '/usr']);

ls.stdout.on('data', function (data) {
  console.log('stdout: ' + data);
});

ls.stderr.on('data', function (data) {
  console.log('stderr: ' + data);
});

ls.on('close', function (code) {
  console.log('child process exited with code ' + code);
});
```

Example: A very elaborate way to run 'ps ax | grep ssh'

```
var spawn = require('child_process').spawn,
    ps    = spawn('ps', ['ax']),
    grep  = spawn('grep', ['ssh']);

ps.stdout.on('data', function (data) {
  grep.stdin.write(data);
});

ps.stderr.on('data', function (data) {
  console.log('ps stderr: ' + data);
});

ps.on('close', function (code) {
  if (code !== 0) {
    console.log('ps process exited with code ' + code);
  }
  grep.stdin.end();
});

grep.stdout.on('data', function (data) {
  console.log('' + data);
});

grep.stderr.on('data', function (data) {
  console.log('grep stderr: ' + data);
});

grep.on('close', function (code) {
  if (code !== 0) {
    console.log('grep process exited with code ' + code);
  }
});
```

Example of checking for failed exec:

```
var spawn = require('child_process').spawn,
    child = spawn('bad_command');

child.on('error', function (err) {
  console.log('Failed to start child process.');
```

```
});
```

options.stdio   As a shorthand, the `stdio` argument may be one of the following strings:

- `'pipe'` - `['pipe', 'pipe', 'pipe']`, this is the default value
- `'ignore'` - `['ignore', 'ignore', 'ignore']`
- `'inherit'` - `[process.stdin, process.stdout, process.stderr]` or `[0,1,2]`

Otherwise, the 'stdio' option to `child_process.spawn()` is an array where each index corresponds to a fd in the child. The value is one of the following:

1. `'pipe'` - Create a pipe between the child process and the parent process. The parent end of the pipe is exposed to the parent as a property on the `child_process` object as `ChildProcess.stdio[fd]`. Pipes created for fds 0 - 2 are also available as ChildProcess.stdin, ChildProcess.stdout and ChildProcess.stderr, respectively.

2. `'ipc'` - Create an IPC channel for passing messages/file descriptors between parent and child. A ChildProcess may have at most *one* IPC stdio file descriptor. Setting this option enables the Child-Process.send() method. If the child writes JSON messages to this file descriptor, then this will trigger ChildProcess.on('message'). If the child is an Node.js program, then the presence of an IPC channel will enable process.send() and process.on('message').

3. `'ignore'` - Do not set this file descriptor in the child. Note that Node.js will always open fd 0 - 2 for the processes it spawns. When any of these is ignored Node.js will open `/dev/null` and attach it to the child's fd.

4. `Stream` object - Share a readable or writable stream that refers to a tty, file, socket, or a pipe with the child process. The stream's underlying file descriptor is duplicated in the child process to the fd that corresponds to the index in the `stdio` array. Note that the stream must have an underlying descriptor (file streams do not until the `'open'` event has occurred).

5. Positive integer - The integer value is interpreted as a file descriptor that is is currently open in the parent process. It is shared with the child process, similar to how `Stream` objects can be shared.

6. `null`, `undefined` - Use default value. For stdio fds 0, 1 and 2 (in other words, stdin, stdout, and stderr) a pipe is created. For fd 3 and up, the default is `'ignore'`.

Example:

```
var spawn = require('child_process').spawn;

// Child will use parent's stdios
spawn('prg', [], { stdio: 'inherit' });

// Spawn child sharing only stderr
spawn('prg', [], { stdio: ['pipe', 'pipe', process.stderr] });

// Open an extra fd=4, to interact with programs present a
// startd-style interface.
spawn('prg', [], { stdio: ['pipe', null, null, null, 'pipe'] });
```

options.detached   On Windows, this makes it possible for the child to continue running after the parent exits. The child will have a new console window (this cannot be disabled).

On non-Windows, if the `detached` option is set, the child process will be made the leader of a new process group and session. Note that child processes may continue running after the parent exits whether they are detached or not. See `setsid(2)` for more information.

By default, the parent will wait for the detached child to exit. To prevent the parent from waiting for a given `child`, use the `child.unref()` method, and the parent's event loop will not include the child in its reference count.

Example of detaching a long-running process and redirecting its output to a file:

```
var fs = require('fs'),
    spawn = require('child_process').spawn,
    out = fs.openSync('./out.log', 'a'),
    err = fs.openSync('./out.log', 'a');

var child = spawn('prg', [], {
  detached: true,
  stdio: [ 'ignore', out, err ]
});

child.unref();
```

When using the `detached` option to start a long-running process, the process will not stay running in the background after the parent exits unless it is provided with a `stdio` configuration that is not connected to the parent. If the parent's `stdio` is inherited, the child will remain attached to the controlling terminal.

See also: `child_process.exec()` and `child_process.fork()`

child_process.exec(command[, options], callback)

- `command` {String} The command to run, with space-separated arguments
- `options` {Object}
- `cwd` {String} Current working directory of the child process
- `env` {Object} Environment key-value pairs
- `encoding` {String} (Default: 'utf8')
- `shell` {String} Shell to execute the command with (Default: '/bin/sh' on UNIX, 'cmd.exe' on Windows, The shell should understand the `-c` switch on UNIX or `/s /c` on Windows. On Windows, command line parsing should be compatible with `cmd.exe`.)
- `timeout` {Number} (Default: 0)
- `maxBuffer` {Number} largest amount of data (in bytes) allowed on stdout or stderr - if exceeded child process is killed (Default: 200*1024)
- `killSignal` {String} (Default: 'SIGTERM')
- `uid` {Number} Sets the user identity of the process. (See setuid(2).)
- `gid` {Number} Sets the group identity of the process. (See setgid(2).)
- `callback` {Function} called with the output when process terminates
- `error` {Error}
- `stdout` {Buffer}
- `stderr` {Buffer}
- Return: ChildProcess object

Runs a command in a shell and buffers the output.

```
var exec = require('child_process').exec,
    child;

child = exec('cat *.js bad_file | wc -l',
  function (error, stdout, stderr) {
    console.log('stdout: ' + stdout);
    console.log('stderr: ' + stderr);
    if (error !== null) {
      console.log('exec error: ' + error);
    }
});
```

The callback gets the arguments (`error`, `stdout`, `stderr`). On success, `error` will be `null`. On error, `error` will be an instance of `Error` and `error.code` will be the exit code of the child process, and `error.signal` will be set to the signal that terminated the process.

There is a second optional argument to specify several options. The default options are

```
{ encoding: 'utf8',
  timeout: 0,
  maxBuffer: 200*1024,
  killSignal: 'SIGTERM',
  cwd: null,
  env: null }
```

If `timeout` is greater than 0, then it will kill the child process if it runs longer than `timeout` milliseconds. The child process is killed with `killSignal` (default: 'SIGTERM'). `maxBuffer` specifies the largest amount of data (in bytes) allowed on stdout or stderr - if this value is exceeded then the child process is killed.

Note: Unlike the `exec()` POSIX system call, `child_process.exec()` does not replace the existing process and uses a shell to execute the command.

child_process.execFile(file[, args][, options][, callback])

- `file` {String} The filename of the program to run
- `args` {Array} List of string arguments
- `options` {Object}
- `cwd` {String} Current working directory of the child process
- `env` {Object} Environment key-value pairs
- `encoding` {String} (Default: 'utf8')
- `timeout` {Number} (Default: 0)
- `maxBuffer` {Number} largest amount of data (in bytes) allowed on stdout or stderr - if exceeded child process is killed (Default: 200*1024)
- `killSignal` {String} (Default: 'SIGTERM')
- `uid` {Number} Sets the user identity of the process. (See setuid(2).)
- `gid` {Number} Sets the group identity of the process. (See setgid(2).)
- `callback` {Function} called with the output when process terminates
- `error` {Error}
- `stdout` {Buffer}
- `stderr` {Buffer}
- Return: ChildProcess object

This is similar to `child_process.exec()` except it does not execute a subshell but rather the specified file directly. This makes it slightly leaner than `child_process.exec()`. It has the same options.

child_process.fork(modulePath[, args][, options])

- `modulePath` {String} The module to run in the child
- `args` {Array} List of string arguments
- `options` {Object}
- `cwd` {String} Current working directory of the child process
- `env` {Object} Environment key-value pairs
- `execPath` {String} Executable used to create the child process
- `execArgv` {Array} List of string arguments passed to the executable (Default: `process.execArgv`)
- `silent` {Boolean} If true, stdin, stdout, and stderr of the child will be piped to the parent, otherwise they will be inherited from the parent, see the "pipe" and "inherit" options for `spawn()`'s `stdio` for more details (default is false)
- `uid` {Number} Sets the user identity of the process. (See setuid(2).)
- `gid` {Number} Sets the group identity of the process. (See setgid(2).)
- Return: ChildProcess object

This is a special case of the `child_process.spawn()` functionality for spawning Node.js processes. In addition to having all the methods in a normal ChildProcess instance, the returned object has a communication channel built-in. See `child.send(message, [sendHandle])` for details.

These child Node.js processes are still whole new instances of V8. Assume at least 30ms startup and 10mb memory for each new Node.js. That is, you cannot create many thousands of them.

The `execPath` property in the `options` object allows for a process to be created for the child rather than the current `node` executable. This should be done with care and by default will talk over the fd represented an environmental variable `NODE_CHANNEL_FD` on the child process. The input and output on this fd is expected to be line delimited JSON objects.

Note: Unlike the `fork()` POSIX system call, `child_process.fork()` does not clone the current process.

Synchronous Process Creation

These methods are **synchronous**, meaning they **WILL** block the event loop, pausing execution of your code until the spawned process exits.

Blocking calls like these are mostly useful for simplifying general purpose scripting tasks and for simplifying the loading/processing of application configuration at startup.

child_process.spawnSync(command[, args][, options])

- `command` {String} The command to run
- `args` {Array} List of string arguments
- `options` {Object}
- `cwd` {String} Current working directory of the child process
- `input` {String|Buffer} The value which will be passed as stdin to the spawned process
  – supplying this value will override `stdio[0]`
- `stdio` {Array} Child's stdio configuration.
- `env` {Object} Environment key-value pairs
- `uid` {Number} Sets the user identity of the process. (See setuid(2).)
- `gid` {Number} Sets the group identity of the process. (See setgid(2).)
- `timeout` {Number} In milliseconds the maximum amount of time the process is allowed to run. (Default: undefined)
- `killSignal` {String} The signal value to be used when the spawned process will be killed. (Default: 'SIGTERM')
- `maxBuffer` {Number} largest amount of data (in bytes) allowed on stdout or stderr - if exceeded child process is killed
- `encoding` {String} The encoding used for all stdio inputs and outputs. (Default: 'buffer')
- `return:` {Object}
- `pid` {Number} Pid of the child process
- `output` {Array} Array of results from stdio output
- `stdout` {Buffer|String} The contents of `output[1]`
- `stderr` {Buffer|String} The contents of `output[2]`
- `status` {Number} The exit code of the child process
- `signal` {String} The signal used to kill the child process
- `error` {Error} The error object if the child process failed or timed out

`spawnSync` will not return until the child process has fully closed. When a timeout has been encountered and `killSignal` is sent, the method won't return until the process has completely exited. That is to say, if the process handles the `SIGTERM` signal and doesn't exit, your process will wait until the child process has exited.

child__process.execSync(command[, options])

- `command` {String} The command to run
- `options` {Object}
- `cwd` {String} Current working directory of the child process
- `input` {String|Buffer} The value which will be passed as stdin to the spawned process
  - supplying this value will override `stdio[0]`
- `stdio` {Array} Child's stdio configuration. (Default: 'pipe')
  - `stderr` by default will be output to the parent process' stderr unless `stdio` is specified
- `env` {Object} Environment key-value pairs
- `shell` {String} Shell to execute the command with (Default: '/bin/sh' on UNIX, 'cmd.exe' on Windows, The shell should understand the `-c` switch on UNIX or `/s /c` on Windows. On Windows, command line parsing should be compatible with `cmd.exe`.)
- `uid` {Number} Sets the user identity of the process. (See setuid(2).)
- `gid` {Number} Sets the group identity of the process. (See setgid(2).)
- `timeout` {Number} In milliseconds the maximum amount of time the process is allowed to run. (Default: undefined)
- `killSignal` {String} The signal value to be used when the spawned process will be killed. (Default: 'SIGTERM')
- `maxBuffer` {Number} largest amount of data (in bytes) allowed on stdout or stderr - if exceeded child process is killed
- `encoding` {String} The encoding used for all stdio inputs and outputs. (Default: 'buffer')
- return: {Buffer|String} The stdout from the command

`execSync` will not return until the child process has fully closed. When a timeout has been encountered and `killSignal` is sent, the method won't return until the process has completely exited. That is to say, if the process handles the `SIGTERM` signal and doesn't exit, your process will wait until the child process has exited.

If the process times out, or has a non-zero exit code, this method **will** throw. The `Error` object will contain the entire result from `child_process.spawnSync()`

child__process.execFileSync(file[, args][, options])

- `file` {String} The filename of the program to run
- `args` {Array} List of string arguments
- `options` {Object}
- `cwd` {String} Current working directory of the child process
- `input` {String|Buffer} The value which will be passed as stdin to the spawned process
  - supplying this value will override `stdio[0]`
- `stdio` {Array} Child's stdio configuration. (Default: 'pipe')
  - `stderr` by default will be output to the parent process' stderr unless `stdio` is specified
- `env` {Object} Environment key-value pairs
- `uid` {Number} Sets the user identity of the process. (See setuid(2).)
- `gid` {Number} Sets the group identity of the process. (See setgid(2).)
- `timeout` {Number} In milliseconds the maximum amount of time the process is allowed to run. (Default: undefined)
- `killSignal` {String} The signal value to be used when the spawned process will be killed. (Default: 'SIGTERM')
- `maxBuffer` {Number} largest amount of data (in bytes) allowed on stdout or stderr - if exceeded child process is killed
- `encoding` {String} The encoding used for all stdio inputs and outputs. (Default: 'buffer')
- return: {Buffer|String} The stdout from the command

`execFileSync` will not return until the child process has fully closed. When a timeout has been encountered and `killSignal` is sent, the method won't return until the process has completely exited. That is to say, if the process handles the `SIGTERM` signal and doesn't exit, your process will wait until the child process has exited.

If the process times out, or has a non-zero exit code, this method *will* throw. The `Error` object will contain the entire result from `child_process.spawnSync()`

Cluster

```
Stability: 2 - Stable
```

A single instance of Node.js runs in a single thread. To take advantage of multi-core systems the user will sometimes want to launch a cluster of Node.js processes to handle the load.

The cluster module allows you to easily create child processes that all share server ports.

```
var cluster = require('cluster');
var http = require('http');
var numCPUs = require('os').cpus().length;

if (cluster.isMaster) {
  // Fork workers.
  for (var i = 0; i < numCPUs; i++) {
    cluster.fork();
  }

  cluster.on('exit', function(worker, code, signal) {
    console.log('worker ' + worker.process.pid + ' died');
  });
} else {
  // Workers can share any TCP connection
  // In this case it is an HTTP server
  http.createServer(function(req, res) {
    res.writeHead(200);
    res.end("hello world\n");
  }).listen(8000);
}
```

Running Node.js will now share port 8000 between the workers:

```
% NODE_DEBUG=cluster node server.js
23521,Master Worker 23524 online
23521,Master Worker 23526 online
23521,Master Worker 23523 online
23521,Master Worker 23528 online
```

Please note that, on Windows, it is not yet possible to set up a named pipe server in a worker.

How It Works

The worker processes are spawned using the `child_process.fork` method, so that they can communicate with the parent via IPC and pass server handles back and forth.

The cluster module supports two methods of distributing incoming connections.

The first one (and the default one on all platforms except Windows), is the round-robin approach, where the master process listens on a port, accepts new connections and distributes them across the workers in a round-robin fashion, with some built-in smarts to avoid overloading a worker process.

The second approach is where the master process creates the listen socket and sends it to interested workers. The workers then accept incoming connections directly.

The second approach should, in theory, give the best performance. In practice however, distribution tends to be very unbalanced due to operating system scheduler vagaries. Loads have been observed where over 70% of all connections ended up in just two processes, out of a total of eight.

Because `server.listen()` hands off most of the work to the master process, there are three cases where the behavior between a normal Node.js process and a cluster worker differs:

1. `server.listen({fd:  7})` Because the message is passed to the master, file descriptor 7 **in the parent** will be listened on, and the handle passed to the worker, rather than listening to the worker's idea of what the number 7 file descriptor references.
2. `server.listen(handle)` Listening on handles explicitly will cause the worker to use the supplied handle, rather than talk to the master process. If the worker already has the handle, then it's presumed that you know what you are doing.
3. `server.listen(0)` Normally, this will cause servers to listen on a random port. However, in a cluster, each worker will receive the same "random" port each time they do `listen(0)`. In essence, the port is random the first time, but predictable thereafter. If you want to listen on a unique port, generate a port number based on the cluster worker ID.

There is no routing logic in Node.js, or in your program, and no shared state between the workers. Therefore, it is important to design your program such that it does not rely too heavily on in-memory data objects for things like sessions and login.

Because workers are all separate processes, they can be killed or re-spawned depending on your program's needs, without affecting other workers. As long as there are some workers still alive, the server will continue to accept connections. If no workers are alive, existing connections will be dropped and new connections will be refused. Node.js does not automatically manage the number of workers for you, however. It is your responsibility to manage the worker pool for your application's needs.

cluster.schedulingPolicy

The scheduling policy, either `cluster.SCHED_RR` for round-robin or `cluster.SCHED_NONE` to leave it to the operating system. This is a global setting and effectively frozen once you spawn the first worker or call `cluster.setupMaster()`, whatever comes first.

`SCHED_RR` is the default on all operating systems except Windows. Windows will change to `SCHED_RR` once libuv is able to effectively distribute IOCP handles without incurring a large performance hit.

`cluster.schedulingPolicy` can also be set through the `NODE_CLUSTER_SCHED_POLICY` environment variable. Valid values are `"rr"` and `"none"`.

cluster.settings

- {Object}
- `execArgv` {Array} list of string arguments passed to the Node.js executable. (Default=`process.execArgv`)
- `exec` {String} file path to worker file. (Default=`process.argv[1]`)
- `args` {Array} string arguments passed to worker. (Default=`process.argv.slice(2)`)
- `silent` {Boolean} whether or not to send output to parent's stdio. (Default=`false`)
- `uid` {Number} Sets the user identity of the process. (See setuid(2).)
- `gid` {Number} Sets the group identity of the process. (See setgid(2).)

After calling `.setupMaster()` (or `.fork()`) this settings object will contain the settings, including the default values.

It is effectively frozen after being set, because `.setupMaster()` can only be called once.

This object is not supposed to be changed or set manually, by you.

cluster.isMaster

- {Boolean}

True if the process is a master. This is determined by the `process.env.NODE_UNIQUE_ID`. If `process.env.NODE_UNIQUE_ID` is undefined, then `isMaster` is `true`.

cluster.isWorker

- {Boolean}

True if the process is not a master (it is the negation of `cluster.isMaster`).

Event: 'fork'

- `worker` {Worker object}

When a new worker is forked the cluster module will emit a 'fork' event. This can be used to log worker activity, and create your own timeout.

```
var timeouts = [];
function errorMsg() {
  console.error("Something must be wrong with the connection ...");
}

cluster.on('fork', function(worker) {
  timeouts[worker.id] = setTimeout(errorMsg, 2000);
});
cluster.on('listening', function(worker, address) {
  clearTimeout(timeouts[worker.id]);
});
cluster.on('exit', function(worker, code, signal) {
  clearTimeout(timeouts[worker.id]);
  errorMsg();
});
```

Event: 'online'

- `worker` {Worker object}

After forking a new worker, the worker should respond with an online message. When the master receives an online message it will emit this event. The difference between 'fork' and 'online' is that fork is emitted when the master forks a worker, and 'online' is emitted when the worker is running.

```
cluster.on('online', function(worker) {
  console.log("Yay, the worker responded after it was forked");
});
```

Event: 'listening'

- `worker` {Worker object}
- `address` {Object}

After calling `listen()` from a worker, when the 'listening' event is emitted on the server, a listening event will also be emitted on `cluster` in the master.

The event handler is executed with two arguments, the `worker` contains the worker object and the `address` object contains the following connection properties: `address`, `port` and `addressType`. This is very useful if the worker is listening on more than one address.

```
cluster.on('listening', function(worker, address) {
  console.log("A worker is now connected to " + address.address + ":" + address.port);
});
```

The `addressType` is one of:

- 4 (TCPv4)
- 6 (TCPv6)
- -1 (unix domain socket)
- "udp4" or "udp6" (UDP v4 or v6)

Event: 'disconnect'

- worker {Worker object}

Emitted after the worker IPC channel has disconnected. This can occur when a worker exits gracefully, is killed, or is disconnected manually (such as with worker.disconnect()).

There may be a delay between the **disconnect** and **exit** events. These events can be used to detect if the process is stuck in a cleanup or if there are long-living connections.

```
cluster.on('disconnect', function(worker) {
  console.log('The worker #' + worker.id + ' has disconnected');
});
```

Event: 'exit'

- worker {Worker object}
- code {Number} the exit code, if it exited normally.
- signal {String} the name of the signal (eg. 'SIGHUP') that caused the process to be killed.

When any of the workers die the cluster module will emit the 'exit' event.

This can be used to restart the worker by calling .fork() again.

```
cluster.on('exit', function(worker, code, signal) {
  console.log('worker %d died (%s). restarting...',
    worker.process.pid, signal || code);
  cluster.fork();
});
```

See child_process event: 'exit'.

Event: 'message'

- worker {Worker object}
- message {Object}

Emitted when any worker receives a message.

See child_process event: 'message'.

Event: 'setup'

- settings {Object}

Emitted every time .setupMaster() is called.

The **settings** object is the **cluster.settings** object at the time .setupMaster() was called and is advisory only, since multiple calls to .setupMaster() can be made in a single tick.

If accuracy is important, use **cluster.settings**.

cluster.setupMaster([settings])

- settings {Object}
- exec {String} file path to worker file. (Default=process.argv[1])
- args {Array} string arguments passed to worker. (Default=process.argv.slice(2))
- silent {Boolean} whether or not to send output to parent's stdio. (Default=false)

setupMaster is used to change the default 'fork' behavior. Once called, the settings will be present in cluster.settings.

Note that:

- any settings changes only affect future calls to .fork() and have no effect on workers that are already running
- The *only* attribute of a worker that cannot be set via .setupMaster() is the env passed to .fork()
- the defaults above apply to the first call only, the defaults for later calls is the current value at the time of cluster.setupMaster() is called

Example:

```
var cluster = require('cluster');
cluster.setupMaster({
  exec: 'worker.js',
  args: ['--use', 'https'],
  silent: true
});
cluster.fork(); // https worker
cluster.setupMaster({
  args: ['--use', 'http']
});
cluster.fork(); // http worker
```

This can only be called from the master process.

cluster.fork([env])

- env {Object} Key/value pairs to add to worker process environment.
- return {Worker object}

Spawn a new worker process.

This can only be called from the master process.

cluster.disconnect([callback])

- callback {Function} called when all workers are disconnected and handles are closed

Calls .disconnect() on each worker in cluster.workers.

When they are disconnected all internal handles will be closed, allowing the master process to die gracefully if no other event is waiting.

The method takes an optional callback argument which will be called when finished.

This can only be called from the master process.

cluster.worker

- {Object}

A reference to the current worker object. Not available in the master process.

```
var cluster = require('cluster');

if (cluster.isMaster) {
  console.log('I am master');
  cluster.fork();
  cluster.fork();
} else if (cluster.isWorker) {
  console.log('I am worker #' + cluster.worker.id);
}
```

cluster.workers

- {Object}

A hash that stores the active worker objects, keyed by id field. Makes it easy to loop through all the workers. It is only available in the master process.

A worker is removed from cluster.workers after the worker has disconnected *and* exited. The order between these two events cannot be determined in advance. However, it is guaranteed that the removal from the cluster.workers list happens before last 'disconnect' or 'exit' event is emitted.

```
// Go through all workers
function eachWorker(callback) {
  for (var id in cluster.workers) {
    callback(cluster.workers[id]);
  }
}
eachWorker(function(worker) {
  worker.send('big announcement to all workers');
});
```

Should you wish to reference a worker over a communication channel, using the worker's unique id is the easiest way to find the worker.

```
socket.on('data', function(id) {
  var worker = cluster.workers[id];
});
```

Class: Worker

A Worker object contains all public information and method about a worker. In the master it can be obtained using `cluster.workers`. In a worker it can be obtained using `cluster.worker`.

worker.id

- {Number}

Each new worker is given its own unique id, this id is stored in the id.

While a worker is alive, this is the key that indexes it in cluster.workers

worker.process

- {ChildProcess object}

All workers are created using `child_process.fork()`, the returned object from this function is stored as `.process`. In a worker, the global `process` is stored.

See: Child Process module

Note that workers will call `process.exit(0)` if the `'disconnect'` event occurs on `process` and `.suicide` is not `true`. This protects against accidental disconnection.

worker.suicide

- {Boolean}

Set by calling `.kill()` or `.disconnect()`, until then it is `undefined`.

The boolean `worker.suicide` lets you distinguish between voluntary and accidental exit, the master may choose not to respawn a worker based on this value.

```
cluster.on('exit', function(worker, code, signal) {
  if (worker.suicide === true) {
    console.log('Oh, it was just suicide\' âĂŞ no need to worry').
  }
});

// kill worker
worker.kill();
```

worker.send(message[, sendHandle][, callback])

- `message` {Object}
- `sendHandle` {Handle object}
- `callback` {Function}
- Return: Boolean

Send a message to a worker or master, optionally with a handle.

In the master this sends a message to a specific worker. It is identical to ChildProcess.send().

In a worker this sends a message to the master. It is identical to `process.send()`.

This example will echo back all messages from the master:

```
if (cluster.isMaster) {
  var worker = cluster.fork();
  worker.send('hi there');

} else if (cluster.isWorker) {
  process.on('message', function(msg) {
    process.send(msg);
  });
}
```

worker.kill([signal='SIGTERM'])

- `signal` {String} Name of the kill signal to send to the worker process.

This function will kill the worker. In the master, it does this by disconnecting the `worker.process`, and once disconnected, killing with `signal`. In the worker, it does it by disconnecting the channel, and then exiting with code 0.

Causes `.suicide` to be set.

This method is aliased as `worker.destroy()` for backwards compatibility.

Note that in a worker, `process.kill()` exists, but it is not this function, it is kill.

worker.disconnect()

In a worker, this function will close all servers, wait for the 'close' event on those servers, and then disconnect the IPC channel.

In the master, an internal message is sent to the worker causing it to call `.disconnect()` on itself.

Causes `.suicide` to be set.

Note that after a server is closed, it will no longer accept new connections, but connections may be accepted by any other listening worker. Existing connections will be allowed to close as usual. When no more connections exist, see server.close(), the IPC channel to the worker will close allowing it to die gracefully.

The above applies *only* to server connections, client connections are not automatically closed by workers, and disconnect does not wait for them to close before exiting.

Note that in a worker, `process.disconnect` exists, but it is not this function, it is disconnect.

Because long living server connections may block workers from disconnecting, it may be useful to send a message, so application specific actions may be taken to close them. It also may be useful to implement a timeout, killing a worker if the `disconnect` event has not been emitted after some time.

```
if (cluster.isMaster) {
  var worker = cluster.fork();
  var timeout;

  worker.on('listening', function(address) {
    worker.send('shutdown');
    worker.disconnect();
    timeout = setTimeout(function() {
      worker.kill();
    }, 2000);
  });

  worker.on('disconnect', function() {
    clearTimeout(timeout);
  });

} else if (cluster.isWorker) {
  var net = require('net');
  var server = net.createServer(function(socket) {
    // connections never end
  });

  server.listen(8000);

  process.on('message', function(msg) {
    if(msg === 'shutdown') {
      // initiate graceful close of any connections to server
    }
  });
}
```

worker.isDead()

This function returns `true` if the worker's process has terminated (either because of exiting or being signaled). Otherwise, it returns `false`.

worker.isConnected()

This function returns `true` if the worker is connected to its master via its IPC channel, `false` otherwise. A worker is connected to its master after it's been created. It is disconnected after the `disconnect` event is emitted.

Event: 'message'

- message {Object}

Similar to the `cluster.on('message')` event, but specific to this worker.

This event is the same as the one provided by `child_process.fork()`.

In a worker you can also use `process.on('message')`.

As an example, here is a cluster that keeps count of the number of requests in the master process using the message system:

```
var cluster = require('cluster');
var http = require('http');

if (cluster.isMaster) {

  // Keep track of http requests
  var numReqs = 0;
  setInterval(function() {
    console.log("numReqs =", numReqs);
  }, 1000);

  // Count requests
  function messageHandler(msg) {
    if (msg.cmd && msg.cmd == 'notifyRequest') {
      numReqs += 1;
    }
  }

  // Start workers and listen for messages containing notifyRequest
  var numCPUs = require('os').cpus().length;
  for (var i = 0; i < numCPUs; i++) {
    cluster.fork();
  }

  Object.keys(cluster.workers).forEach(function(id) {
    cluster.workers[id].on('message', messageHandler);
  });

} else {

  // Worker processes have a http server.
  http.Server(function(req, res) {
    res.writeHead(200);
    res.end("hello world\n");
```

```
    // notify master about the request
    process.send({ cmd: 'notifyRequest' });
  }).listen(8000);
}
```

Event: 'online'

Similar to the `cluster.on('online')` event, but specific to this worker.

```
cluster.fork().on('online', function() {
  // Worker is online
});
```

It is not emitted in the worker.

Event: 'listening'

- `address` {Object}

Similar to the `cluster.on('listening')` event, but specific to this worker.

```
cluster.fork().on('listening', function(address) {
  // Worker is listening
});
```

It is not emitted in the worker.

Event: 'disconnect'

Similar to the `cluster.on('disconnect')` event, but specific to this worker.

```
cluster.fork().on('disconnect', function() {
  // Worker has disconnected
});
```

Event: 'exit'

- `code` {Number} the exit code, if it exited normally.
- `signal` {String} the name of the signal (eg. `'SIGHUP'`) that caused the process to be killed.

Similar to the `cluster.on('exit')` event, but specific to this worker.

```
var worker = cluster.fork();
worker.on('exit', function(code, signal) {
  if( signal ) {
    console.log("worker was killed by signal: "+signal);
  } else if( code !== 0 ) {
    console.log("worker exited with error code: "+code);
  } else {
    console.log("worker success!");
  }
});
```

Event: 'error'

This event is the same as the one provided by `child_process.fork()`.

In a worker you can also use `process.on('error')`.

Console

```
Stability: 2 - Stable
```

The module defines a **Console** class and exports a **console** object.

The **console** object is a special instance of **Console** whose output is sent to stdout or stderr.

For ease of use, **console** is defined as a global object and can be used directly without **require**.

console

- {Object}

For printing to stdout and stderr. Similar to the console object functions provided by most web browsers, here the output is sent to stdout or stderr.

The console functions are synchronous when the destination is a terminal or a file (to avoid lost messages in case of premature exit) and asynchronous when it's a pipe (to avoid blocking for long periods of time).

That is, in the following example, stdout is non-blocking while stderr is blocking:

```
$ node script.js 2> error.log | tee info.log
```

In daily use, the blocking/non-blocking dichotomy is not something you should worry about unless you log huge amounts of data.

console.log([data][, ...])

Prints to stdout with newline. This function can take multiple arguments in a **printf()**-like way. Example:

```
var count = 5;
console.log('count: %d', count);
// prints 'count: 5'
```

If formatting elements are not found in the first string then **util.inspect** is used on each argument. See util.format() for more information.

console.info([data][, ...])

Same as **console.log**.

console.error([data][, ...])

Same as **console.log** but prints to stderr.

console.warn([data][, ...])

Same as **console.error**.

console.dir(obj[, options])

Uses **util.inspect** on **obj** and prints resulting string to stdout. This function bypasses any custom **inspect()** function on **obj**. An optional *options* object may be passed that alters certain aspects of the formatted string:

- **showHidden** - if **true** then the object's non-enumerable and symbol properties will be shown too. Defaults to **false**.

- `depth` - tells `inspect` how many times to recurse while formatting the object. This is useful for inspecting large complicated objects. Defaults to 2. To make it recurse indefinitely pass `null`.

- `colors` - if `true`, then the output will be styled with ANSI color codes. Defaults to `false`. Colors are customizable, see below.

console.time(timerName)

Starts a timer that can be used to compute the duration of an operation. Timers are identified by a unique name. Use the same name when you call `console.timeEnd()` to stop the timer and output the elapsed time in milliseconds. Timer durations are accurate to the sub-millisecond.

console.timeEnd(timerName)

Stops a timer that was previously started by calling `console.time()` and prints the result to the console.

Example:

```
console.time('100-elements');
for (var i = 0; i < 100; i++) {
  ;
}
console.timeEnd('100-elements');
// prints 100-elements: 225.438ms
```

console.trace(message[, ...])

Print to stderr `'Trace :'`, followed by the formatted message and stack trace to the current position.

console.assert(value[, message][, ...])

Similar to assert.ok(), but the error message is formatted as `util.format(message...)`.

Class: Console

Use `require('console').Console` or `console.Console` to access this class.

```
var Console = require('console').Console;
var Console = console.Console;
```

You can use `Console` class to custom simple logger like `console`, but with different output streams.

new Console(stdout[, stderr])

Create a new `Console` by passing one or two writable stream instances. `stdout` is a writable stream to print log or info output. `stderr` is used for warning or error output. If `stderr` isn't passed, the warning and error output will be sent to the `stdout`.

```
var output = fs.createWriteStream('./stdout.log');
var errorOutput = fs.createWriteStream('./stderr.log');
// custom simple logger
var logger = new Console(output, errorOutput);
// use it like console
var count = 5;
logger.log('count: %d', count);
// in stdout.log: count 5
```

The global `console` is a special `Console` whose output is sent to `process.stdout` and `process.stderr`:

```
new Console(process.stdout, process.stderr);
```

Crypto

Stability: 2 - Stable

Use `require('crypto')` to access this module.

The crypto module offers a way of encapsulating secure credentials to be used as part of a secure HTTPS net or http connection.

It also offers a set of wrappers for OpenSSL's hash, hmac, cipher, decipher, sign and verify methods.

crypto.setEngine(engine[, flags])

Load and set engine for some/all OpenSSL functions (selected by flags).

`engine` could be either an id or a path to the engine's shared library.

`flags` is optional and has `ENGINE_METHOD_ALL` value by default. It could take one of or mix of following flags (defined in `constants` module):

- `ENGINE_METHOD_RSA`
- `ENGINE_METHOD_DSA`
- `ENGINE_METHOD_DH`
- `ENGINE_METHOD_RAND`
- `ENGINE_METHOD_ECDH`
- `ENGINE_METHOD_ECDSA`
- `ENGINE_METHOD_CIPHERS`
- `ENGINE_METHOD_DIGESTS`
- `ENGINE_METHOD_STORE`
- `ENGINE_METHOD_PKEY_METH`
- `ENGINE_METHOD_PKEY_ASN1_METH`
- `ENGINE_METHOD_ALL`
- `ENGINE_METHOD_NONE`

crypto.getCiphers()

Returns an array with the names of the supported ciphers.

Example:

```
var ciphers = crypto.getCiphers();
console.log(ciphers); // ['aes-128-cbc', 'aes-128-ccm', ...]
```

crypto.getHashes()

Returns an array with the names of the supported hash algorithms.

Example:

```
var hashes = crypto.getHashes();
console.log(hashes); // ['sha', 'sha1', 'sha1WithRSAEncryption', ...]
```

crypto.getCurves()

Returns an array with the names of the supported elliptic curves.

Example:

```
var curves = crypto.getCurves();
console.log(curves); // ['secp256k1', 'secp384r1', ...]
```

crypto.createCredentials(details)

Stability: 0 - Deprecated: Use [tls.createSecureContext][] instead.

Creates a credentials object, with the optional details being a dictionary with keys:

- pfx : A string or buffer holding the PFX or PKCS12 encoded private key, certificate and CA certificates
- key : A string holding the PEM encoded private key
- passphrase : A string of passphrase for the private key or pfx
- cert : A string holding the PEM encoded certificate
- ca : Either a string or list of strings of PEM encoded CA certificates to trust.
- crl : Either a string or list of strings of PEM encoded CRLs (Certificate Revocation List)
- ciphers: A string describing the ciphers to use or exclude. Consult http://www.openssl.org/docs/apps/ciphers.html#CIPHER_LIST_FORMAT for details on the format.

If no 'ca' details are given, then Node.js will use the default publicly trusted list of CAs as given in http://mxr.mozilla.org/mozilla/source/security/nss/lib/ckfw/builtins/certdata.txt.

crypto.createHash(algorithm)

Creates and returns a hash object, a cryptographic hash with the given algorithm which can be used to generate hash digests.

algorithm is dependent on the available algorithms supported by the version of OpenSSL on the platform. Examples are 'sha256', 'sha512', etc. On recent releases, openssl list-message-digest-algorithms will display the available digest algorithms.

Example: this program that takes the sha256 sum of a file

```
var filename = process.argv[2];
var crypto = require('crypto');
var fs = require('fs');

var shasum = crypto.createHash('sha256');

var s = fs.ReadStream(filename);
s.on('data', function(d) {
  shasum.update(d);
});

s.on('end', function() {
  var d = shasum.digest('hex');
  console.log(d + '  ' + filename);
});
```

Class: Hash

The class for creating hash digests of data.

It is a stream that is both readable and writable. The written data is used to compute the hash. Once the writable side of the stream is ended, use the read() method to get the computed hash digest. The legacy update and digest methods are also supported.

Returned by crypto.createHash.

hash.update(data[, input_encoding])

Updates the hash content with the given `data`, the encoding of which is given in `input_encoding` and can be `'utf8'`, `'ascii'` or `'binary'`. If no encoding is provided, and the input is a string, an encoding of `'binary'` is enforced. If `data` is a Buffer then `input_encoding` is ignored.

This can be called many times with new data as it is streamed.

hash.digest([encoding])

Calculates the digest of all of the passed data to be hashed. The `encoding` can be `'hex'`, `'binary'` or `'base64'`. If no encoding is provided, then a buffer is returned.

Note: `hash` object can not be used after `digest()` method has been called.

crypto.createHmac(algorithm, key)

Creates and returns a hmac object, a cryptographic hmac with the given algorithm and key.

It is a stream that is both readable and writable. The written data is used to compute the hmac. Once the writable side of the stream is ended, use the `read()` method to get the computed digest. The legacy `update` and `digest` methods are also supported.

`algorithm` is dependent on the available algorithms supported by OpenSSL - see createHash above. `key` is the hmac key to be used.

Class: Hmac

Class for creating cryptographic hmac content.

Returned by `crypto.createHmac`.

hmac.update(data)

Update the hmac content with the given `data`. This can be called many times with new data as it is streamed.

hmac.digest([encoding])

Calculates the digest of all of the passed data to the hmac. The `encoding` can be `'hex'`, `'binary'` or `'base64'`. If no encoding is provided, then a buffer is returned.

Note: `hmac` object can not be used after `digest()` method has been called.

crypto.createCipher(algorithm, password)

Creates and returns a cipher object, with the given algorithm and password.

`algorithm` is dependent on OpenSSL, examples are `'aes192'`, etc. On recent releases, `openssl list-cipher-algorithms` will display the available cipher algorithms. `password` is used to derive key and IV, which must be a `'binary'` encoded string or a buffer.

It is a stream that is both readable and writable. The written data is used to compute the hash. Once the writable side of the stream is ended, use the `read()` method to get the enciphered contents. The legacy `update` and `final` methods are also supported.

Note: `createCipher` derives keys with the OpenSSL function EVP_BytesToKey with the digest algorithm set to MD5, one iteration, and no salt. The lack of salt allows dictionary attacks as the same password always creates the same key. The low iteration count and non-cryptographically secure hash algorithm allow passwords to be tested very rapidly.

In line with OpenSSL's recommendation to use pbkdf2 instead of EVP_BytesToKey it is recommended you derive a key and iv yourself with crypto.pbkdf2 and to then use createCipheriv() to create the cipher stream.

crypto.createCipheriv(algorithm, key, iv)

Creates and returns a cipher object, with the given algorithm, key and iv.

`algorithm` is the same as the argument to `createCipher()`. `key` is the raw key used by the algorithm. `iv` is an initialization vector.

`key` and `iv` must be 'binary' encoded strings or buffers.

Class: Cipher

Class for encrypting data.

Returned by `crypto.createCipher` and `crypto.createCipheriv`.

Cipher objects are streams that are both readable and writable. The written plain text data is used to produce the encrypted data on the readable side. The legacy `update` and `final` methods are also supported.

cipher.update(data[, input_encoding][, output_encoding])

Updates the cipher with `data`, the encoding of which is given in `input_encoding` and can be 'utf8', 'ascii' or 'binary'. If no encoding is provided, then a buffer is expected. If `data` is a `Buffer` then `input_encoding` is ignored.

The `output_encoding` specifies the output format of the enciphered data, and can be 'binary', 'base64' or 'hex'. If no encoding is provided, then a buffer is returned.

Returns the enciphered contents, and can be called many times with new data as it is streamed.

cipher.final([output_encoding])

Returns any remaining enciphered contents, with `output_encoding` being one of: 'binary', 'base64' or 'hex'. If no encoding is provided, then a buffer is returned.

Note: `cipher` object can not be used after `final()` method has been called.

cipher.setAutoPadding(auto_padding=true)

You can disable automatic padding of the input data to block size. If `auto_padding` is false, the length of the entire input data must be a multiple of the cipher's block size or `final` will fail. Useful for non-standard padding, e.g. using 0x0 instead of PKCS padding. You must call this before `cipher.final`.

cipher.getAuthTag()

For authenticated encryption modes (currently supported: GCM), this method returns a `Buffer` that represents the *authentication tag* that has been computed from the given data. Should be called after encryption has been completed using the `final` method!

cipher.setAAD(buffer)

For authenticated encryption modes (currently supported: GCM), this method sets the value used for the additional authenticated data (AAD) input parameter.

crypto.createDecipher(algorithm, password)

Creates and returns a decipher object, with the given algorithm and key. This is the mirror of the createCipher() above.

crypto.createDecipheriv(algorithm, key, iv)

Creates and returns a decipher object, with the given algorithm, key and iv. This is the mirror of the createCipheriv() above.

Class: Decipher

Class for decrypting data.

Returned by `crypto.createDecipher` and `crypto.createDecipheriv`.

Decipher objects are streams that are both readable and writable. The written enciphered data is used to produce the plain-text data on the the readable side. The legacy `update` and `final` methods are also supported.

decipher.update(data[, input_encoding][, output_encoding])

Updates the decipher with `data`, which is encoded in 'binary', 'base64' or 'hex'. If no encoding is provided, then a buffer is expected. If `data` is a `Buffer` then `input_encoding` is ignored.

The `output_decoding` specifies in what format to return the deciphered plaintext: 'binary', 'ascii' or 'utf8'. If no encoding is provided, then a buffer is returned.

decipher.final([output_encoding])

Returns any remaining plaintext which is deciphered, with `output_encoding` being one of: 'binary', 'ascii' or 'utf8'. If no encoding is provided, then a buffer is returned.

Note: `decipher` object can not be used after `final()` method has been called.

decipher.setAutoPadding(auto_padding=true)

You can disable auto padding if the data has been encrypted without standard block padding to prevent `decipher.final` from checking and removing it. This will only work if the input data's length is a multiple of the ciphers block size. You must call this before streaming data to `decipher.update`.

decipher.setAuthTag(buffer)

For authenticated encryption modes (currently supported: GCM), this method must be used to pass in the received *authentication tag*. If no tag is provided or if the ciphertext has been tampered with, `final` will throw, thus indicating that the ciphertext should be discarded due to failed authentication.

decipher.setAAD(buffer)

For authenticated encryption modes (currently supported: GCM), this method sets the value used for the additional authenticated data (AAD) input parameter.

crypto.createSign(algorithm)

Creates and returns a signing object, with the given algorithm. On recent OpenSSL releases, `openssl list-public-key-algorithms` will display the available signing algorithms. Examples are `'RSA-SHA256'`.

Class: Sign

Class for generating signatures.

Returned by `crypto.createSign`.

Sign objects are writable streams. The written data is used to generate the signature. Once all of the data has been written, the `sign` method will return the signature. The legacy `update` method is also supported.

sign.update(data)

Updates the sign object with data. This can be called many times with new data as it is streamed.

sign.sign(private_key[, output_format])

Calculates the signature on all the updated data passed through the sign.

`private_key` can be an object or a string. If `private_key` is a string, it is treated as the key with no passphrase.

`private_key`:

- `key` : A string holding the PEM encoded private key
- `passphrase` : A string of passphrase for the private key

Returns the signature in `output_format` which can be `'binary'`, `'hex'` or `'base64'`. If no encoding is provided, then a buffer is returned.

Note: `sign` object can not be used after `sign()` method has been called.

crypto.createVerify(algorithm)

Creates and returns a verification object, with the given algorithm. This is the mirror of the signing object above.

Class: Verify

Class for verifying signatures.

Returned by `crypto.createVerify`.

Verify objects are writable streams. The written data is used to validate against the supplied signature. Once all of the data has been written, the `verify` method will return true if the supplied signature is valid. The legacy `update` method is also supported.

verifier.update(data)

Updates the verifier object with data. This can be called many times with new data as it is streamed.

verifier.verify(object, signature[, signature_format])

Verifies the signed data by using the `object` and `signature`. `object` is a string containing a PEM encoded object, which can be one of RSA public key, DSA public key, or X.509 certificate. `signature` is the previously calculated signature for the data, in the `signature_format` which can be 'binary', 'hex' or 'base64'. If no encoding is specified, then a buffer is expected.

Returns true or false depending on the validity of the signature for the data and public key.

Note: `verifier` object can not be used after `verify()` method has been called.

crypto.createDiffieHellman(prime_length[, generator])

Creates a Diffie-Hellman key exchange object and generates a prime of `prime_length` bits and using an optional specific numeric `generator`. If no `generator` is specified, then 2 is used.

crypto.createDiffieHellman(prime[, prime_encoding][, generator][, generator_encoding])

Creates a Diffie-Hellman key exchange object using the supplied `prime` and an optional specific `generator`. `generator` can be a number, string, or Buffer. If no `generator` is specified, then 2 is used. `prime_encoding` and `generator_encoding` can be 'binary', 'hex', or 'base64'. If no `prime_encoding` is specified, then a Buffer is expected for `prime`. If no `generator_encoding` is specified, then a Buffer is expected for `generator`.

Class: DiffieHellman

The class for creating Diffie-Hellman key exchanges.

Returned by `crypto.createDiffieHellman`.

diffieHellman.verifyError

A bit field containing any warnings and/or errors as a result of a check performed during initialization. The following values are valid for this property (defined in `constants` module):

- DH_CHECK_P_NOT_SAFE_PRIME
- DH_CHECK_P_NOT_PRIME
- DH_UNABLE_TO_CHECK_GENERATOR
- DH_NOT_SUITABLE_GENERATOR

diffieHellman.generateKeys([encoding])

Generates private and public Diffie-Hellman key values, and returns the public key in the specified encoding. This key should be transferred to the other party. Encoding can be 'binary', 'hex', or 'base64'. If no encoding is provided, then a buffer is returned.

diffieHellman.computeSecret(other_public_key[, input_encoding][, output_encoding])

Computes the shared secret using `other_public_key` as the other party's public key and returns the computed shared secret. Supplied key is interpreted using specified `input_encoding`, and secret is encoded using specified `output_encoding`. Encodings can be `'binary'`, `'hex'`, or `'base64'`. If the input encoding is not provided, then a buffer is expected.

If no output encoding is given, then a buffer is returned.

diffieHellman.getPrime([encoding])

Returns the Diffie-Hellman prime in the specified encoding, which can be `'binary'`, `'hex'`, or `'base64'`. If no encoding is provided, then a buffer is returned.

diffieHellman.getGenerator([encoding])

Returns the Diffie-Hellman generator in the specified encoding, which can be `'binary'`, `'hex'`, or `'base64'`. If no encoding is provided, then a buffer is returned.

diffieHellman.getPublicKey([encoding])

Returns the Diffie-Hellman public key in the specified encoding, which can be `'binary'`, `'hex'`, or `'base64'`. If no encoding is provided, then a buffer is returned.

diffieHellman.getPrivateKey([encoding])

Returns the Diffie-Hellman private key in the specified encoding, which can be `'binary'`, `'hex'`, or `'base64'`. If no encoding is provided, then a buffer is returned.

diffieHellman.setPublicKey(public_key[, encoding])

Sets the Diffie-Hellman public key. Key encoding can be `'binary'`, `'hex'` or `'base64'`. If no encoding is provided, then a buffer is expected.

diffieHellman.setPrivateKey(private_key[, encoding])

Sets the Diffie-Hellman private key. Key encoding can be `'binary'`, `'hex'` or `'base64'`. If no encoding is provided, then a buffer is expected.

crypto.getDiffieHellman(group_name)

Creates a predefined Diffie-Hellman key exchange object. The supported groups are: `'modp1'`, `'modp2'`, `'modp5'` (defined in RFC 2412, but see Caveats) and `'modp14'`, `'modp15'`, `'modp16'`, `'modp17'`, `'modp18'` (defined in RFC 3526). The returned object mimics the interface of objects created by crypto.createDiffieHellman() above, but will not allow changing the keys (with diffieHellman.setPublicKey() for example). The advantage of using this routine is that the parties do not have to generate nor exchange group modulus beforehand, saving both processor and communication time.

Example (obtaining a shared secret):

```
var crypto = require('crypto');
var alice = crypto.getDiffieHellman('modp14');
var bob = crypto.getDiffieHellman('modp14');

alice.generateKeys();
bob.generateKeys();

var alice_secret = alice.computeSecret(bob.getPublicKey(), null, 'hex');
var bob_secret = bob.computeSecret(alice.getPublicKey(), null, 'hex');

/* alice_secret and bob_secret should be the same */
console.log(alice_secret == bob_secret);
```

crypto.createECDH(curve_name)

Creates an Elliptic Curve (EC) Diffie-Hellman key exchange object using a predefined curve specified by the `curve_name` string. Use getCurves() to obtain a list of available curve names. On recent releases, `openssl ecparam -list_curves` will also display the name and description of each available elliptic curve.

Class: ECDH

The class for creating EC Diffie-Hellman key exchanges.

Returned by `crypto.createECDH`.

ECDH.generateKeys([encoding[, format]])

Generates private and public EC Diffie-Hellman key values, and returns the public key in the specified format and encoding. This key should be transferred to the other party.

Format specifies point encoding and can be 'compressed', 'uncompressed', or 'hybrid'. If no format is provided - the point will be returned in 'uncompressed' format.

Encoding can be 'binary', 'hex', or 'base64'. If no encoding is provided, then a buffer is returned.

ECDH.computeSecret(other_public_key[, input_encoding][, output_encoding])

Computes the shared secret using `other_public_key` as the other party's public key and returns the computed shared secret. Supplied key is interpreted using specified `input_encoding`, and secret is encoded using specified `output_encoding`. Encodings can be 'binary', 'hex', or 'base64'. If the input encoding is not provided, then a buffer is expected.

If no output encoding is given, then a buffer is returned.

ECDH.getPublicKey([encoding[, format]])

Returns the EC Diffie-Hellman public key in the specified encoding and format.

Format specifies point encoding and can be 'compressed', 'uncompressed', or 'hybrid'. If no format is provided - the point will be returned in 'uncompressed' format.

Encoding can be 'binary', 'hex', or 'base64'. If no encoding is provided, then a buffer is returned.

ECDH.getPrivateKey([encoding])

Returns the EC Diffie-Hellman private key in the specified encoding, which can be 'binary', 'hex', or 'base64'. If no encoding is provided, then a buffer is returned.

ECDH.setPublicKey(public_key[, encoding])

Sets the EC Diffie-Hellman public key. Key encoding can be 'binary', 'hex' or 'base64'. If no encoding is provided, then a buffer is expected.

ECDH.setPrivateKey(private_key[, encoding])

Sets the EC Diffie-Hellman private key. Key encoding can be 'binary', 'hex' or 'base64'. If no encoding is provided, then a buffer is expected.

Example (obtaining a shared secret):

```
var crypto = require('crypto');
var alice = crypto.createECDH('secp256k1');
var bob = crypto.createECDH('secp256k1');

alice.generateKeys();
bob.generateKeys();

var alice_secret = alice.computeSecret(bob.getPublicKey(), null, 'hex');
var bob_secret = bob.computeSecret(alice.getPublicKey(), null, 'hex');

/* alice_secret and bob_secret should be the same */
console.log(alice_secret == bob_secret);
```

crypto.pbkdf2(password, salt, iterations, keylen[, digest], callback)

Asynchronous PBKDF2 function. Applies the selected HMAC digest function (default: SHA1) to derive a key of the requested byte length from the password, salt and number of iterations. The callback gets two arguments: (err, derivedKey).

Example:

```
crypto.pbkdf2('secret', 'salt', 4096, 64, 'sha256', function(err, key) {
  if (err)
    throw err;
  console.log(key.toString('hex'));  // 'c5e478d...1469e50'
});
```

You can get a list of supported digest functions with crypto.getHashes().

crypto.pbkdf2Sync(password, salt, iterations, keylen[, digest])

Synchronous PBKDF2 function. Returns derivedKey or throws error.

crypto.randomBytes(size[, callback])

Generates cryptographically strong pseudo-random data. Usage:

```
// async
crypto.randomBytes(256, function(ex, buf) {
  if (ex) throw ex;
  console.log('Have %d bytes of random data: %s', buf.length, buf);
});

// sync
const buf = crypto.randomBytes(256);
console.log('Have %d bytes of random data: %s', buf.length, buf);
```

NOTE: This will block if there is insufficient entropy, although it should normally never take longer than a few milliseconds. The only time when this may conceivably block is right after boot, when the whole system is still low on entropy.

Class: Certificate

The class used for working with signed public key & challenges. The most common usage for this series of functions is when dealing with the <keygen> element. http://www.openssl.org/docs/apps/spkac.html

Returned by crypto.Certificate.

Certificate.verifySpkac(spkac)

Returns true of false based on the validity of the SPKAC.

Certificate.exportChallenge(spkac)

Exports the encoded challenge associated with the SPKAC.

Certificate.exportPublicKey(spkac)

Exports the encoded public key from the supplied SPKAC.

crypto.publicEncrypt(public_key, buffer)

Encrypts buffer with public_key. Only RSA is currently supported.

public_key can be an object or a string. If public_key is a string, it is treated as the key with no passphrase and will use RSA_PKCS1_OAEP_PADDING. Since RSA public keys may be derived from private keys you may pass a private key to this method.

public_key:

- key : A string holding the PEM encoded private key
- passphrase : An optional string of passphrase for the private key
- padding : An optional padding value, one of the following:
- constants.RSA_NO_PADDING
- constants.RSA_PKCS1_PADDING
- constants.RSA_PKCS1_OAEP_PADDING

NOTE: All paddings are defined in constants module.

crypto.publicDecrypt(public_key, buffer)

See above for details. Has the same API as crypto.publicEncrypt. Default padding is RSA_PKCS1_PADDING.

crypto.privateDecrypt(private_key, buffer)

Decrypts `buffer` with `private_key`.

`private_key` can be an object or a string. If `private_key` is a string, it is treated as the key with no passphrase and will use `RSA_PKCS1_OAEP_PADDING`.

`private_key`:

- `key` : A string holding the PEM encoded private key
- `passphrase` : An optional string of passphrase for the private key
- `padding` : An optional padding value, one of the following:
- `constants.RSA_NO_PADDING`
- `constants.RSA_PKCS1_PADDING`
- `constants.RSA_PKCS1_OAEP_PADDING`

NOTE: All paddings are defined in `constants` module.

crypto.privateEncrypt(private_key, buffer)

See above for details. Has the same API as `crypto.privateDecrypt`. Default padding is `RSA_PKCS1_PADDING`.

crypto.DEFAULT_ENCODING

The default encoding to use for functions that can take either strings or buffers. The default value is `'buffer'`, which makes it default to using Buffer objects. This is here to make the crypto module more easily compatible with legacy programs that expected `'binary'` to be the default encoding.

Note that new programs will probably expect buffers, so only use this as a temporary measure.

Recent API Changes

The Crypto module was added to Node.js before there was the concept of a unified Stream API, and before there were Buffer objects for handling binary data.

As such, the streaming classes don't have the typical methods found on other Node.js classes, and many methods accepted and returned Binary-encoded strings by default rather than Buffers. This was changed to use Buffers by default instead.

This is a breaking change for some use cases, but not all.

For example, if you currently use the default arguments to the Sign class, and then pass the results to the Verify class, without ever inspecting the data, then it will continue to work as before. Where you once got a binary string and then presented the binary string to the Verify object, you'll now get a Buffer, and present the Buffer to the Verify object.

However, if you were doing things with the string data that will not work properly on Buffers (such as, concatenating them, storing in databases, etc.), or you are passing binary strings to the crypto functions without an encoding argument, then you will need to start providing encoding arguments to specify which encoding you'd like to use. To switch to the previous style of using binary strings by default, set the `crypto.DEFAULT_ENCODING` field to 'binary'. Note that new programs will probably expect buffers, so only use this as a temporary measure.

Caveats

The crypto module still supports some algorithms which are already compromised. And the API also allows the use of ciphers and hashes with a small key size that are considered to be too weak for safe use.

Users should take full responsibility for selecting the crypto algorithm and key size according to their security requirements.

Based on the recommendations of NIST SP 800-131A:

- MD5 and SHA-1 are no longer acceptable where collision resistance is required such as digital signatures.
- The key used with RSA, DSA and DH algorithms is recommended to have at least 2048 bits and that of the curve of ECDSA and ECDH at least 224 bits, to be safe to use for several years.
- The DH groups of `modp1`, `modp2` and `modp5` have a key size smaller than 2048 bits and are not recommended.

See the reference for other recommendations and details.

Debugger

Stability: 2 - Stable

V8 comes with an extensive debugger which is accessible out-of-process via a simple TCP protocol. Node.js has a built-in client for this debugger. To use this, start Node.js with the **debug** argument; a prompt will appear:

```
% node debug myscript.js
< debugger listening on port 5858
connecting... ok
break in /home/indutny/Code/git/indutny/myscript.js:1
  1 x = 5;
  2 setTimeout(function () {
  3   debugger;
debug>
```

Node.js's debugger client doesn't support the full range of commands, but simple step and inspection is possible. By putting the statement **debugger;** into the source code of your script, you will enable a breakpoint.

For example, suppose **myscript.js** looked like this:

```
// myscript.js
x = 5;
setTimeout(function () {
  debugger;
  console.log("world");
}, 1000);
console.log("hello");
```

Then once the debugger is run, it will break on line 4.

```
% node debug myscript.js
< debugger listening on port 5858
connecting... ok
break in /home/indutny/Code/git/indutny/myscript.js:1
  1 x = 5;
  2 setTimeout(function () {
  3   debugger;
debug> cont
< hello
break in /home/indutny/Code/git/indutny/myscript.js:3
  1 x = 5;
  2 setTimeout(function () {
  3   debugger;
  4   console.log("world");
  5 }, 1000);
debug> next
break in /home/indutny/Code/git/indutny/myscript.js:4
  2 setTimeout(function () {
  3   debugger;
  4   console.log("world");
  5 }, 1000);
  6 console.log("hello");
debug> repl
Press Ctrl + C to leave debug repl
> x
5
> 2+2
```

```
4
debug> next
< world
break in /home/indutny/Code/git/indutny/myscript.js:5
  3   debugger;
  4   console.log("world");
  5 }, 1000);
  6 console.log("hello");
  7
debug> quit
%
```

The `repl` command allows you to evaluate code remotely. The `next` command steps over to the next line. There are a few other commands available and more to come. Type `help` to see others.

Watchers

You can watch expression and variable values while debugging your code. On every breakpoint each expression from the watchers list will be evaluated in the current context and displayed just before the breakpoint's source code listing.

To start watching an expression, type `watch("my_expression")`. `watchers` prints the active watchers. To remove a watcher, type `unwatch("my_expression")`.

Commands reference

Stepping

- `cont`, `c` - Continue execution
- `next`, `n` - Step next
- `step`, `s` - Step in
- `out`, `o` - Step out
- `pause` - Pause running code (like pause button in Developer Tools)

Breakpoints

- `setBreakpoint()`, `sb()` - Set breakpoint on current line
- `setBreakpoint(line)`, `sb(line)` - Set breakpoint on specific line
- `setBreakpoint('fn()')`, `sb(...)` - Set breakpoint on a first statement in functions body
- `setBreakpoint('script.js', 1)`, `sb(...)` - Set breakpoint on first line of script.js
- `clearBreakpoint('script.js', 1)`, `cb(...)` - Clear breakpoint in script.js on line 1

It is also possible to set a breakpoint in a file (module) that isn't loaded yet:

```
% ./node debug test/fixtures/break-in-module/main.js
< debugger listening on port 5858
connecting to port 5858... ok
break in test/fixtures/break-in-module/main.js:1
  1 var mod = require('./mod.js');
  2 mod.hello();
  3 mod.hello();
debug> setBreakpoint('mod.js', 23)
Warning: script 'mod.js' was not loaded yet.
  1 var mod = require('./mod.js');
  2 mod.hello();
```

```
 3 mod.hello();
debug> c
break in test/fixtures/break-in-module/mod.js:23
 21
 22 exports.hello = function() {
 23   return 'hello from module';
 24 };
 25
debug>
```

Info

- `backtrace, bt` - Print backtrace of current execution frame
- `list(5)` - List scripts source code with 5 line context (5 lines before and after)
- `watch(expr)` - Add expression to watch list
- `unwatch(expr)` - Remove expression from watch list
- `watchers` - List all watchers and their values (automatically listed on each breakpoint)
- `repl` - Open debugger's repl for evaluation in debugging script's context

Execution control

- `run` - Run script (automatically runs on debugger's start)
- `restart` - Restart script
- `kill` - Kill script

Various

- `scripts` - List all loaded scripts
- `version` - Display v8's version

Advanced Usage

The V8 debugger can be enabled and accessed either by starting Node.js with the `--debug` command-line flag or by signaling an existing Node.js process with `SIGUSR1`.

Once a process has been set in debug mode with this it can be connected to with the Node.js debugger. Either connect to the `pid` or the URI to the debugger. The syntax is:

- `node debug -p <pid>` - Connects to the process via the `pid`
- `node debug <URI>` - Connects to the process via the URI such as localhost:5858

DNS

```
Stability: 2 - Stable
```

Use `require('dns')` to access this module.

This module contains functions that belong to two different categories:

1) Functions that use the underlying operating system facilities to perform name resolution, and that do not necessarily do any network communication. This category contains only one function: `dns.lookup()`. **Developers looking to perform name resolution in the same way that other applications on the same operating system behave should use `dns.lookup()`.**

Here is an example that does a lookup of `www.google.com`.

```
var dns = require('dns');

dns.lookup('www.google.com', function onLookup(err, addresses, family) {
  console.log('addresses:', addresses);
});
```

2) Functions that connect to an actual DNS server to perform name resolution, and that *always* use the network to perform DNS queries. This category contains all functions in the `dns` module but `dns.lookup()`. These functions do not use the same set of configuration files than what `dns.lookup()` uses. For instance, *they do not use the configuration from /etc/hosts*. These functions should be used by developers who do not want to use the underlying operating system's facilities for name resolution, and instead want to *always* perform DNS queries.

Here is an example which resolves `'www.google.com'` then reverse resolves the IP addresses which are returned.

```
var dns = require('dns');

dns.resolve4('www.google.com', function (err, addresses) {
  if (err) throw err;

  console.log('addresses: ' + JSON.stringify(addresses));

  addresses.forEach(function (a) {
    dns.reverse(a, function (err, hostnames) {
      if (err) {
        throw err;
      }

      console.log('reverse for ' + a + ': ' + JSON.stringify(hostnames));
    });
  });
});
```

There are subtle consequences in choosing one or another, please consult the Implementation considerations section for more information.

dns.lookup(hostname[, options], callback)

Resolves a hostname (e.g. `'google.com'`) into the first found A (IPv4) or AAAA (IPv6) record. `options` can be an object or integer. If `options` is not provided, then IP v4 and v6 addresses are both valid. If `options` is an integer, then it must be **4** or **6**.

Alternatively, `options` can be an object containing these properties:

- `family` {Number} - The record family. If present, must be the integer 4 or 6. If not provided, both IP v4 and v6 addresses are accepted.
- `hints`: {Number} - If present, it should be one or more of the supported `getaddrinfo` flags. If `hints` is not provided, then no flags are passed to `getaddrinfo`. Multiple flags can be passed through `hints` by logically `OR`ing their values. See supported `getaddrinfo` flags below for more information on supported flags.
- `all`: {Boolean} - When `true`, the callback returns all resolved addresses in an array, otherwise returns a single address. Defaults to `false`.

All properties are optional. An example usage of options is shown below.

```
{
  family: 4,
  hints: dns.ADDRCONFIG | dns.V4MAPPED,
  all: false
}
```

The callback has arguments `(err, address, family)`. `address` is a string representation of an IP v4 or v6 address. `family` is either the integer 4 or 6 and denotes the family of `address` (not necessarily the value initially passed to `lookup`).

With the `all` option set, the arguments change to `(err, addresses)`, with `addresses` being an array of objects with the properties `address` and `family`.

On error, `err` is an `Error` object, where `err.code` is the error code. Keep in mind that `err.code` will be set to `'ENOENT'` not only when the hostname does not exist but also when the lookup fails in other ways such as no available file descriptors.

`dns.lookup()` doesn't necessarily have anything to do with the DNS protocol. It's only an operating system facility that can associate name with addresses, and vice versa.

Its implementation can have subtle but important consequences on the behavior of any Node.js program. Please take some time to consult the Implementation considerations section before using it.

dns.lookupService(address, port, callback)

Resolves the given address and port into a hostname and service using `getnameinfo`.

The callback has arguments `(err, hostname, service)`. The `hostname` and `service` arguments are strings (e.g. `'localhost'` and `'http'` respectively).

On error, `err` is an `Error` object, where `err.code` is the error code.

dns.resolve(hostname[, rrtype], callback)

Resolves a hostname (e.g. `'google.com'`) into an array of the record types specified by rrtype.

Valid rrtypes are:

- `'A'` (IPV4 addresses, default)
- `'AAAA'` (IPV6 addresses)
- `'MX'` (mail exchange records)
- `'TXT'` (text records)
- `'SRV'` (SRV records)
- `'PTR'` (used for reverse IP lookups)
- `'NS'` (name server records)
- `'CNAME'` (canonical name records)
- `'SOA'` (start of authority record)

The callback has arguments (`err, addresses`). The type of each item in `addresses` is determined by the record type, and described in the documentation for the corresponding lookup methods below.

On error, `err` is an `Error` object, where `err.code` is one of the error codes listed below.

dns.resolve4(hostname, callback)

The same as `dns.resolve()`, but only for IPv4 queries (`A` records). `addresses` is an array of IPv4 addresses (e.g. [`'74.125.79.104'`, `'74.125.79.105'`, `'74.125.79.106'`]).

dns.resolve6(hostname, callback)

The same as `dns.resolve4()` except for IPv6 queries (an `AAAA` query).

dns.resolveMx(hostname, callback)

The same as `dns.resolve()`, but only for mail exchange queries (`MX` records).

`addresses` is an array of MX records, each with a priority and an exchange attribute (e.g. [{`'priority'`: 10, `'exchange'`: `'mx.example.com'`},...]).

dns.resolveTxt(hostname, callback)

The same as `dns.resolve()`, but only for text queries (`TXT` records). `addresses` is a 2-d array of the text records available for `hostname` (e.g., [[`'v=spf1 ip4:0.0.0.0 '`, `'~all'`]]). Each sub-array contains TXT chunks of one record. Depending on the use case, the could be either joined together or treated separately.

dns.resolveSrv(hostname, callback)

The same as `dns.resolve()`, but only for service records (`SRV` records). `addresses` is an array of the SRV records available for `hostname`. Properties of SRV records are priority, weight, port, and name (e.g., [{`'priority'`: 10, `'weight'`: 5, `'port'`: 21223, `'name'`: `'service.example.com'`}, ...]).

dns.resolveSoa(hostname, callback)

The same as `dns.resolve()`, but only for start of authority record queries (`SOA` record).

`addresses` is an object with the following structure:

```
{
  nsname: 'ns.example.com',
  hostmaster: 'root.example.com',
  serial: 2013101809,
  refresh: 10000,
  retry: 2400,
  expire: 604800,
  minttl: 3600
}
```

dns.resolveNs(hostname, callback)

The same as `dns.resolve()`, but only for name server records (`NS` records). `addresses` is an array of the name server records available for `hostname` (e.g., [`'ns1.example.com'`, `'ns2.example.com'`]).

dns.resolveCname(hostname, callback)

The same as `dns.resolve()`, but only for canonical name records (`CNAME` records). `addresses` is an array of the canonical name records available for `hostname` (e.g., `['bar.example.com']`).

dns.reverse(ip, callback)

Reverse resolves an ip address to an array of hostnames.

The callback has arguments `(err, hostnames)`.

On error, `err` is an `Error` object, where `err.code` is one of the error codes listed below.

dns.getServers()

Returns an array of IP addresses as strings that are currently being used for resolution

dns.setServers(servers)

Given an array of IP addresses as strings, set them as the servers to use for resolving

If you specify a port with the address it will be stripped, as the underlying library doesn't support that.

This will throw if you pass invalid input.

Error codes

Each DNS query can return one of the following error codes:

- `dns.NODATA`: DNS server returned answer with no data.
- `dns.FORMERR`: DNS server claims query was misformatted.
- `dns.SERVFAIL`: DNS server returned general failure.
- `dns.NOTFOUND`: Domain name not found.
- `dns.NOTIMP`: DNS server does not implement requested operation.
- `dns.REFUSED`: DNS server refused query.
- `dns.BADQUERY`: Misformatted DNS query.
- `dns.BADNAME`: Misformatted hostname.
- `dns.BADFAMILY`: Unsupported address family.
- `dns.BADRESP`: Misformatted DNS reply.
- `dns.CONNREFUSED`: Could not contact DNS servers.
- `dns.TIMEOUT`: Timeout while contacting DNS servers.
- `dns.EOF`: End of file.
- `dns.FILE`: Error reading file.
- `dns.NOMEM`: Out of memory.
- `dns.DESTRUCTION`: Channel is being destroyed.
- `dns.BADSTR`: Misformatted string.
- `dns.BADFLAGS`: Illegal flags specified.
- `dns.NONAME`: Given hostname is not numeric.
- `dns.BADHINTS`: Illegal hints flags specified.
- `dns.NOTINITIALIZED`: c-ares library initialization not yet performed.
- `dns.LOADIPHLPAPI`: Error loading iphlpapi.dll.
- `dns.ADDRGETNETWORKPARAMS`: Could not find GetNetworkParams function.
- `dns.CANCELLED`: DNS query cancelled.

Supported getaddrinfo flags

The following flags can be passed as hints to `dns.lookup()`.

- `dns.ADDRCONFIG`: Returned address types are determined by the types of addresses supported by the current system. For example, IPv4 addresses are only returned if the current system has at least one IPv4 address configured. Loopback addresses are not considered.
- `dns.V4MAPPED`: If the IPv6 family was specified, but no IPv6 addresses were found, then return IPv4 mapped IPv6 addresses. Note that it is not supported on some operating systems (e.g FreeBSD 10.1).

Implementation considerations

Although `dns.lookup()` and `dns.resolve*()`/`dns.reverse()` functions have the same goal of associating a network name with a network address (or vice versa), their behavior is quite different. These differences can have subtle but significant consequences on the behavior of Node.js programs.

dns.lookup

Under the hood, `dns.lookup()` uses the same operating system facilities as most other programs. For instance, `dns.lookup()` will almost always resolve a given name the same way as the `ping` command. On most POSIX-like operating systems, the behavior of the `dns.lookup()` function can be tweaked by changing settings in `nsswitch.conf(5)` and/or `resolv.conf(5)`, but be careful that changing these files will change the behavior of all other programs running on the same operating system.

Though the call will be asynchronous from JavaScript's perspective, it is implemented as a synchronous call to `getaddrinfo(3)` that runs on libuv's threadpool. Because libuv's threadpool has a fixed size, it means that if for whatever reason the call to `getaddrinfo(3)` takes a long time, other operations that could run on libuv's threadpool (such as filesystem operations) will experience degraded performance. In order to mitigate this issue, one potential solution is to increase the size of libuv's threadpool by setting the 'UV_THREADPOOL_SIZE' environment variable to a value greater than 4 (its current default value). For more information on libuv's threadpool, see the official libuv documentation.

dns.resolve, functions starting with dns.resolve and dns.reverse

These functions are implemented quite differently than `dns.lookup()`. They do not use `getaddrinfo(3)` and they *always* perform a DNS query on the network. This network communication is always done asynchronously, and does not use libuv's threadpool.

As a result, these functions cannot have the same negative impact on other processing that happens on libuv's threadpool that `dns.lookup()` can have.

They do not use the same set of configuration files than what `dns.lookup()` uses. For instance, *they do not use the configuration from /etc/hosts.*

Domain

```
Stability: 0 - Deprecated
```

This module is pending deprecation. Once a replacement API has been finalized, this module will be fully deprecated. Most end users should **not** have cause to use this module. Users who absolutely must have the functionality that domains provide may rely on it for the time being but should expect to have to migrate to a different solution in the future.

Domains provide a way to handle multiple different IO operations as a single group. If any of the event emitters or callbacks registered to a domain emit an **error** event, or throw an error, then the domain object will be notified, rather than losing the context of the error in the `process.on('uncaughtException')` handler, or causing the program to exit immediately with an error code.

Warning: Don't Ignore Errors!

Domain error handlers are not a substitute for closing down your process when an error occurs.

By the very nature of how **throw** works in JavaScript, there is almost never any way to safely "pick up where you left off", without leaking references, or creating some other sort of undefined brittle state.

The safest way to respond to a thrown error is to shut down the process. Of course, in a normal web server, you might have many connections open, and it is not reasonable to abruptly shut those down because an error was triggered by someone else.

The better approach is to send an error response to the request that triggered the error, while letting the others finish in their normal time, and stop listening for new requests in that worker.

In this way, **domain** usage goes hand-in-hand with the cluster module, since the master process can fork a new worker when a worker encounters an error. For Node.js programs that scale to multiple machines, the terminating proxy or service registry can take note of the failure, and react accordingly.

For example, this is not a good idea:

```
// XXX WARNING!  BAD IDEA!

var d = require('domain').create();
d.on('error', function(er) {
  // The error won't crash the process, but what it does is worse!
  // Though we've prevented abrupt process restarting, we are leaking
  // resources like crazy if this ever happens.
  // This is no better than process.on('uncaughtException')!
  console.log('error, but oh well', er.message);
});
d.run(function() {
  require('http').createServer(function(req, res) {
    handleRequest(req, res);
  }).listen(PORT);
});
```

By using the context of a domain, and the resilience of separating our program into multiple worker processes, we can react more appropriately, and handle errors with much greater safety.

```
// Much better!

var cluster = require('cluster');
var PORT = +process.env.PORT || 1337;

if (cluster.isMaster) {
```

```
    // In real life, you'd probably use more than just 2 workers,
    // and perhaps not put the master and worker in the same file.
    //
    // You can also of course get a bit fancier about logging, and
    // implement whatever custom logic you need to prevent DoS
    // attacks and other bad behavior.
    //
    // See the options in the cluster documentation.
    //
    // The important thing is that the master does very little,
    // increasing our resilience to unexpected errors.

    cluster.fork();
    cluster.fork();

    cluster.on('disconnect', function(worker) {
      console.error('disconnect!');
      cluster.fork();
    });

} else {
    // the worker
    //
    // This is where we put our bugs!

    var domain = require('domain');

    // See the cluster documentation for more details about using
    // worker processes to serve requests.  How it works, caveats, etc.

    var server = require('http').createServer(function(req, res) {
      var d = domain.create();
      d.on('error', function(er) {
        console.error('error', er.stack);

        // Note: we're in dangerous territory!
        // By definition, something unexpected occurred,
        // which we probably didn't want.
        // Anything can happen now!  Be very careful!

        try {
          // make sure we close down within 30 seconds
          var killtimer = setTimeout(function() {
            process.exit(1);
          }, 30000);
          // But don't keep the process open just for that!
          killtimer.unref();

          // stop taking new requests.
          server.close();

          // Let the master know we're dead.  This will trigger a
          // 'disconnect' in the cluster master, and then it will fork
          // a new worker.
          cluster.worker.disconnect();
```

```
        // try to send an error to the request that triggered the problem
        res.statusCode = 500;
        res.setHeader('content-type', 'text/plain');
        res.end('Oops, there was a problem!\n');
      } catch (er2) {
        // oh well, not much we can do at this point.
        console.error('Error sending 500!', er2.stack);
      }
    });

    // Because req and res were created before this domain existed,
    // we need to explicitly add them.
    // See the explanation of implicit vs explicit binding below.
    d.add(req);
    d.add(res);

    // Now run the handler function in the domain.
    d.run(function() {
      handleRequest(req, res);
    });
  });
  server.listen(PORT);
}

// This part isn't important.  Just an example routing thing.
// You'd put your fancy application logic here.
function handleRequest(req, res) {
  switch(req.url) {
    case '/error':
      // We do some async stuff, and then...
      setTimeout(function() {
        // Whoops!
        flerb.bark();
      });
      break;
    default:
      res.end('ok');
  }
}
```

Additions to Error objects

Any time an Error object is routed through a domain, a few extra fields are added to it.

- `error.domain` The domain that first handled the error.
- `error.domainEmitter` The event emitter that emitted an 'error' event with the error object.
- `error.domainBound` The callback function which was bound to the domain, and passed an error as its first argument.
- `error.domainThrown` A boolean indicating whether the error was thrown, emitted, or passed to a bound callback function.

Implicit Binding

If domains are in use, then all **new** EventEmitter objects (including Stream objects, requests, responses, etc.) will be implicitly bound to the active domain at the time of their creation.

Additionally, callbacks passed to lowlevel event loop requests (such as to fs.open, or other callback-taking methods) will automatically be bound to the active domain. If they throw, then the domain will catch the error.

In order to prevent excessive memory usage, Domain objects themselves are not implicitly added as children of the active domain. If they were, then it would be too easy to prevent request and response objects from being properly garbage collected.

If you *want* to nest Domain objects as children of a parent Domain, then you must explicitly add them.

Implicit binding routes thrown errors and 'error' events to the Domain's error event, but does not register the EventEmitter on the Domain, so domain.dispose() will not shut down the EventEmitter. Implicit binding only takes care of thrown errors and 'error' events.

Explicit Binding

Sometimes, the domain in use is not the one that ought to be used for a specific event emitter. Or, the event emitter could have been created in the context of one domain, but ought to instead be bound to some other domain.

For example, there could be one domain in use for an HTTP server, but perhaps we would like to have a separate domain to use for each request.

That is possible via explicit binding.

For example:

```
// create a top-level domain for the server
var serverDomain = domain.create();

serverDomain.run(function() {
  // server is created in the scope of serverDomain
  http.createServer(function(req, res) {
    // req and res are also created in the scope of serverDomain
    // however, we'd prefer to have a separate domain for each request.
    // create it first thing, and add req and res to it.
    var reqd = domain.create();
    reqd.add(req);
    reqd.add(res);
    reqd.on('error', function(er) {
      console.error('Error', er, req.url);
      try {
        res.writeHead(500);
        res.end('Error occurred, sorry.');
      } catch (er) {
        console.error('Error sending 500', er, req.url);
      }
    });
  }).listen(1337);
});
```

domain.create()

- return: {Domain}

Returns a new Domain object.

Class: Domain

The Domain class encapsulates the functionality of routing errors and uncaught exceptions to the active Domain object.

Domain is a child class of EventEmitter. To handle the errors that it catches, listen to its **error** event.

domain.run(fn[, arg][, ...])

- fn {Function}

Run the supplied function in the context of the domain, implicitly binding all event emitters, timers, and lowlevel requests that are created in that context. Optionally, arguments can be passed to the function.

This is the most basic way to use a domain.

Example:

```
var d = domain.create();
d.on('error', function(er) {
  console.error('Caught error!', er);
});
d.run(function() {
  process.nextTick(function() {
    setTimeout(function() { // simulating some various async stuff
      fs.open('non-existent file', 'r', function(er, fd) {
        if (er) throw er;
        // proceed...
      });
    }, 100);
  });
});
```

In this example, the **d.on('error')** handler will be triggered, rather than crashing the program.

domain.members

- {Array}

An array of timers and event emitters that have been explicitly added to the domain.

domain.add(emitter)

- emitter {EventEmitter | Timer} emitter or timer to be added to the domain

Explicitly adds an emitter to the domain. If any event handlers called by the emitter throw an error, or if the emitter emits an **error** event, it will be routed to the domain's **error** event, just like with implicit binding.

This also works with timers that are returned from **setInterval** and **setTimeout**. If their callback function throws, it will be caught by the domain 'error' handler.

If the Timer or EventEmitter was already bound to a domain, it is removed from that one, and bound to this one instead.

domain.remove(emitter)

- emitter {EventEmitter | Timer} emitter or timer to be removed from the domain

The opposite of **domain.add(emitter)**. Removes domain handling from the specified emitter.

domain.bind(callback)

- callback {Function} The callback function
- return: {Function} The bound function

The returned function will be a wrapper around the supplied callback function. When the returned function is called, any errors that are thrown will be routed to the domain's **error** event.

```
var d = domain.create();

function readSomeFile(filename, cb) {
  fs.readFile(filename, 'utf8', d.bind(function(er, data) {
    // if this throws, it will also be passed to the domain
    return cb(er, data ? JSON.parse(data) : null);
  }));
}

d.on('error', function(er) {
  // an error occurred somewhere.
  // if we throw it now, it will crash the program
  // with the normal line number and stack message.
});
```

Example

domain.intercept(callback)

- callback {Function} The callback function
- return: {Function} The intercepted function

This method is almost identical to **domain.bind(callback)**. However, in addition to catching thrown errors, it will also intercept **Error** objects sent as the first argument to the function.

In this way, the common **if (er) return callback(er);** pattern can be replaced with a single error handler in a single place.

```
var d = domain.create();

function readSomeFile(filename, cb) {
  fs.readFile(filename, 'utf8', d.intercept(function(data) {
    // note, the first argument is never passed to the
    // callback since it is assumed to be the 'Error' argument
    // and thus intercepted by the domain.

    // if this throws, it will also be passed to the domain
    // so the error-handling logic can be moved to the 'error'
    // event on the domain instead of being repeated throughout
    // the program.
    return cb(null, JSON.parse(data));
  }));
}

d.on('error', function(er) {
  // an error occurred somewhere.
```

```
    // if we throw it now, it will crash the program
    // with the normal line number and stack message.
});
```

Example

domain.enter()

The `enter` method is plumbing used by the **run**, **bind**, and **intercept** methods to set the active domain. It sets `domain.active` and `process.domain` to the domain, and implicitly pushes the domain onto the domain stack managed by the domain module (see `domain.exit()` for details on the domain stack). The call to `enter` delimits the beginning of a chain of asynchronous calls and I/O operations bound to a domain.

Calling `enter` changes only the active domain, and does not alter the domain itself. Enter and `exit` can be called an arbitrary number of times on a single domain.

If the domain on which `enter` is called has been disposed, `enter` will return without setting the domain.

domain.exit()

The `exit` method exits the current domain, popping it off the domain stack. Any time execution is going to switch to the context of a different chain of asynchronous calls, it's important to ensure that the current domain is exited. The call to `exit` delimits either the end of or an interruption to the chain of asynchronous calls and I/O operations bound to a domain.

If there are multiple, nested domains bound to the current execution context, `exit` will exit any domains nested within this domain.

Calling `exit` changes only the active domain, and does not alter the domain itself. Enter and `exit` can be called an arbitrary number of times on a single domain.

If the domain on which `exit` is called has been disposed, `exit` will return without exiting the domain.

domain.dispose()

```
Stability: 0 - Deprecated.  Please recover from failed IO actions
explicitly via error event handlers set on the domain.
```

Once `dispose` has been called, the domain will no longer be used by callbacks bound into the domain via **run**, **bind**, or **intercept**, and a **dispose** event is emitted.

Events

Stability: 2 - Stable

Many objects in Node.js emit events: a `net.Server` emits an event each time a peer connects to it, a `fs.readStream` emits an event when the file is opened. All objects which emit events are instances of `events.EventEmitter`. You can access this module by doing: `require("events");`

Typically, event names are represented by a camel-cased string, however, there aren't any strict restrictions on that, as any string will be accepted.

Functions can then be attached to objects, to be executed when an event is emitted. These functions are called *listeners*. Inside a listener function, `this` refers to the `EventEmitter` that the listener was attached to.

Class: events.EventEmitter

Use `require('events')` to access the EventEmitter class.

`var EventEmitter = require('events');`

When an `EventEmitter` instance experiences an error, the typical action is to emit an `'error'` event. Error events are treated as a special case in Node.js. If there is no listener for it, then the default action is to print a stack trace and exit the program.

All EventEmitters emit the event `'newListener'` when new listeners are added and `'removeListener'` when a listener is removed.

emitter.addListener(event, listener)

emitter.on(event, listener)

Adds a listener to the end of the listeners array for the specified `event`. No checks are made to see if the `listener` has already been added. Multiple calls passing the same combination of `event` and `listener` will result in the `listener` being added multiple times.

```
server.on('connection', function (stream) {
  console.log('someone connected!');
});
```

Returns emitter, so calls can be chained.

emitter.once(event, listener)

Adds a **one time** listener for the event. This listener is invoked only the next time the event is fired, after which it is removed.

```
server.once('connection', function (stream) {
  console.log('Ah, we have our first user!');
});
```

Returns emitter, so calls can be chained.

emitter.removeListener(event, listener)

Removes a listener from the listener array for the specified event. **Caution**: changes array indices in the listener array behind the listener.

```
var callback = function(stream) {
  console.log('someone connected!');
};
server.on('connection', callback);
// ...
server.removeListener('connection', callback);
```

removeListener will remove, at most, one instance of a listener from the listener array. If any single listener has been added multiple times to the listener array for the specified event, then removeListener must be called multiple times to remove each instance.

Returns emitter, so calls can be chained.

emitter.removeAllListeners([event])

Removes all listeners, or those of the specified event. It's not a good idea to remove listeners that were added elsewhere in the code, especially when it's on an emitter that you didn't create (e.g. sockets or file streams).

Returns emitter, so calls can be chained.

emitter.setMaxListeners(n)

By default EventEmitters will print a warning if more than 10 listeners are added for a particular event. This is a useful default which helps finding memory leaks. Obviously not all Emitters should be limited to 10. This function allows that to be increased. Set to Infinity (or 0) for unlimited.

Returns emitter, so calls can be chained.

emitter.getMaxListeners()

Returns the current max listener value for the emitter which is either set by emitter.setMaxListeners(n) or defaults to EventEmitter.defaultMaxListeners.

This can be useful to increment/decrement max listeners to avoid the warning while not being irresponsible and setting a too big number.

```
emitter.setMaxListeners(emitter.getMaxListeners() + 1);
emitter.once('event', function () {
  // do stuff
  emitter.setMaxListeners(Math.max(emitter.getMaxListeners() - 1, 0));
});
```

EventEmitter.defaultMaxListeners

emitter.setMaxListeners(n) sets the maximum on a per-instance basis. This class property lets you set it for *all* EventEmitter instances, current and future, effective immediately. Use with care.

Note that emitter.setMaxListeners(n) still has precedence over EventEmitter.defaultMaxListeners.

emitter.listeners(event)

Returns a copy of the array of listeners for the specified event.

```
server.on('connection', function (stream) {
  console.log('someone connected!');
});
console.log(util.inspect(server.listeners('connection'))); // [ [Function] ]
```

emitter.emit(event[, arg1][, arg2][, . . .])

Calls each of the listeners in order with the supplied arguments.

Returns `true` if event had listeners, `false` otherwise.

emitter.listenerCount(type)

- `type` {Value} The type of event

Returns the number of listeners listening to the `type` of event.

Class Method: EventEmitter.listenerCount(emitter, event)

Stability: `0 - Deprecated: Use [emitter.listenerCount][]` instead.

Returns the number of listeners for a given event.

Event: 'newListener'

- `event` {String} The event name
- `listener` {Function} The event handler function

This event is emitted *before* a listener is added. When this event is triggered, the listener has not been added to the array of listeners for the `event`. Any listeners added to the event `name` in the newListener event callback will be added *before* the listener that is in the process of being added.

Event: 'removeListener'

- `event` {String} The event name
- `listener` {Function} The event handler function

This event is emitted *after* a listener is removed. When this event is triggered, the listener has been removed from the array of listeners for the `event`.

Inheriting from 'EventEmitter'

Inheriting from `EventEmitter` is no different from inheriting from any other constructor function. For example:

```
'use strict';
const util = require('util');
const EventEmitter = require('events');

function MyEventEmitter() {
  // Initialize necessary properties from 'EventEmitter' in this instance
  EventEmitter.call(this);
}

// Inherit functions from 'EventEmitter''s prototype
util.inherits(MyEventEmitter, EventEmitter);
```

Errors

Errors generated by Node.js fall into two categories: JavaScript errors and system errors. All errors inherit from or are instances of JavaScript's Error class and are guaranteed to provide *at least* the attributes available on that class.

When an operation is not permitted due to language-syntax or language-runtime-level reasons, a **JavaScript error** is generated and thrown as an **exception**. If an operation is not allowed due to system-level restrictions, a **system error** is generated. Client code is then given the opportunity to **intercept** this error based on how the API **propagates** it.

The style of API called determines how generated errors are handed back, or **propagated**, to client code, which in turn informs how the client may **intercept** the error. Exceptions can be intercepted using the `try /` `catch` construct; other propagation strategies are covered below.

JavaScript Errors

JavaScript errors typically denote that an API is being used incorrectly, or that there is a problem with the program as written.

Class: Error

A general error object. Unlike other error objects, `Error` instances do not denote any specific circumstance of why the error occurred. Errors capture a "stack trace" detailing the point in the program at which they were instantiated, and may provide a description of the error.

Note: Node.js will generate this class of error to encapsulate system errors as well as plain JavaScript errors.

new Error(message)   Instantiates a new Error object and sets its `.message` property to the provided message. Its `.stack` will represent the point in the program at which `new Error` was called. Stack traces are subject to V8's stack trace API. Stack traces only extend to the beginning of synchronous code execution, *or a* number of frames given by `Error.stackTraceLimit`, whichever is smaller.

error.message   A string of the value passed to `Error()` upon instantiation. The message will also appear in the first line of the stack trace of the error. Changing this property *may not* change the first line of the stack trace.

error.stack   A property that, when **accessed**, returns a string representing the point in the program at which this error was instantiated. An example stacktrace follows:

```
Error: Things keep happening!
   at /home/gbusey/file.js:525:2
   at Frobnicator.refrobulate (/home/gbusey/business-logic.js:424:21)
   at Actor.<anonymous> (/home/gbusey/actors.js:400:8)
   at increaseSynergy (/home/gbusey/actors.js:701:6)
```

The first line is formatted as `<error class name>:   <error message>`, and it is followed by a series of stack frames (each line beginning with "at"). Each frame describes a call site in the program that lead to the error being generated. V8 attempts to display a name for each function (by variable name, function name, or object method name), but occasionally it will not be able to find a suitable name. If V8 cannot determine a name for the function, only location information will be displayed for that frame. Otherwise, the determined function name will be displayed with location information appended in parentheses.

Frames are **only** generated for JavaScript functions. If, for example, execution synchronously passes through a C++ addon function called `cheetahify`, which itself calls a JavaScript function, the frame representing the `cheetahify` call will **not** be present in stacktraces:

```
var cheetahify = require('./native-binding.node');

function makeFaster() {
  // cheetahify *synchronously* calls speedy.
  cheetahify(function speedy() {
    throw new Error('oh no!');
  });
}

makeFaster(); // will throw:
// /home/gbusey/file.js:6
//     throw new Error('oh no!');
//           ^
// Error: oh no!
//     at speedy (/home/gbusey/file.js:6:11)
//     at makeFaster (/home/gbusey/file.js:5:3)
//     at Object.<anonymous> (/home/gbusey/file.js:10:1)
//     at Module._compile (module.js:456:26)
//     at Object.Module._extensions..js (module.js:474:10)
//     at Module.load (module.js:356:32)
//     at Function.Module._load (module.js:312:12)
//     at Function.Module.runMain (module.js:497:10)
//     at startup (node.js:119:16)
//     at node.js:906:3
```

The location information will be one of:

- `native`, if the frame represents a call internal to V8 (as in `[].forEach`).
- `plain-filename.js:line:column`, if the frame represents a call internal to Node.js.
- `/absolute/path/to/file.js:line:column`, if the frame represents a call in a user program, or its dependencies.

It is important to note that the string representing the stacktrace is only generated on **access**: it is lazily generated.

The number of frames captured by the stack trace is bounded by the smaller of `Error.stackTraceLimit` or the number of available frames on the current event loop tick.

System-level errors are generated as augmented Error instances, which are detailed below.

Error.captureStackTrace(targetObject[, constructorOpt]) Creates a `.stack` property on `targetObject`, which when accessed returns a string representing the location in the program at which `Error.captureStackTrace` was called.

```
var myObject = {};

Error.captureStackTrace(myObject);

myObject.stack  // similar to 'new Error().stack'
```

The first line of the trace, instead of being prefixed with `ErrorType:  message`, will be the result of `targetObject.toString()`.

`constructorOpt` optionally accepts a function. If given, all frames above `constructorOpt`, including `constructorOpt`, will be omitted from the generated stack trace.

This is useful for hiding implementation details of error generation from the end user. A common way of using this parameter is to pass the current Error constructor to it:

```
function MyError() {
  Error.captureStackTrace(this, MyError);
}

// without passing MyError to captureStackTrace, the MyError
// frame would should up in the .stack property. by passing
// the constructor, we omit that frame and all frames above it.
new MyError().stack
```

Error.stackTraceLimit   Property that determines the number of stack frames collected by a stack trace (whether generated by `new Error().stack` or `Error.captureStackTrace(obj)`).

The initial value is `10`. It may be set to any valid JavaScript number, which will affect any stack trace captured *after* the value has been changed. If set to a non-number value, stack traces will not capture any frames and will report `undefined` on access.

Class: RangeError

A subclass of Error that indicates that a provided argument was not within the set or range of acceptable values for a function; whether that be a numeric range, or outside the set of options for a given function parameter. An example:

```
require('net').connect(-1);   // throws RangeError, port should be > 0 && < 65536
```

Node.js will generate and throw RangeError instances *immediately* – they are a form of argument validation.

Class: TypeError

A subclass of Error that indicates that a provided argument is not an allowable type. For example, passing a function to a parameter which expects a string would be considered a TypeError.

```
require('url').parse(function() { }); // throws TypeError, since it expected a string
```

Node.js will generate and throw TypeError instances *immediately* – they are a form of argument validation.

Class: ReferenceError

A subclass of Error that indicates that an attempt is being made to access a variable that is not defined. Most commonly it indicates a typo, or an otherwise broken program. While client code may generate and propagate these errors, in practice only V8 will do so.

```
doesNotExist; // throws ReferenceError, doesNotExist is not a variable in this program.
```

ReferenceError instances will have an `.arguments` member that is an array containing one element – a string representing the variable that was not defined.

```
try {
  doesNotExist;
} catch(err) {
  err.arguments[0] === 'doesNotExist';
}
```

Unless the userland program is dynamically generating and running code, ReferenceErrors should always be considered a bug in the program, or its dependencies.

Class: SyntaxError

A subclass of Error that indicates that a program is not valid JavaScript. These errors may only be generated and propagated as a result of code evaluation. Code evaluation may happen as a result of eval, Function, require, or vm. These errors are almost always indicative of a broken program.

```
try {
  require("vm").runInThisContext("binary ! isNotOk");
} catch(err) {
  // err will be a SyntaxError
}
```

SyntaxErrors are unrecoverable from the context that created them – they may only be caught by other contexts.

Exceptions vs. Errors

A JavaScript "exception" is a value that is thrown as a result of an invalid operation or as the target of a throw statement. While it is not required that these values inherit from Error, all exceptions thrown by Node.js or the JavaScript runtime *will* be instances of Error.

Some exceptions are *unrecoverable* at the JavaScript layer. These exceptions will always bring down the process. These are usually failed assert() checks or abort() calls in the C++ layer.

System Errors

System errors are generated in response to a program's runtime environment. Ideally, they represent operational errors that the program needs to be able to react to. They are generated at the syscall level: an exhaustive list of error codes and their meanings is available by running man 2 intro or man 3 errno on most Unices; or online.

In Node.js, system errors are represented as augmented Error objects – not full subclasses, but instead an error instance with added members.

Class: System Error

error.syscall A string representing the syscall that failed.

error.errno

error.code A string representing the error code, which is always E followed by capital letters, and may be referenced in man 2 intro.

Common System Errors

This list is **not exhaustive**, but enumerates many of the common system errors when writing a Node.js program. An exhaustive list may be found here.

EPERM: Operation not permitted An attempt was made to perform an operation that requires appropriate privileges.

ENOENT: No such file or directory Commonly raised by fs operations; a component of the specified pathname does not exist – no entity (file or directory) could be found by the given path.

EACCES: Permission denied An attempt was made to access a file in a way forbidden by its file access permissions.

EEXIST: File exists An existing file was the target of an operation that required that the target not exist.

ENOTDIR: Not a directory A component of the given pathname existed, but was not a directory as expected. Commonly raised by fs.readdir.

EISDIR: Is a directory An operation expected a file, but the given pathname was a directory.

EMFILE: Too many open files in system Maximum number of file descriptors allowable on the system has been reached, and requests for another descriptor cannot be fulfilled until at least one has been closed.

Commonly encountered when opening many files at once in parallel, especially on systems (in particular, OS X) where there is a low file descriptor limit for processes. To remedy a low limit, run `ulimit -n 2048` in the same shell that will run the Node.js process.

EPIPE: Broken pipe A write on a pipe, socket, or FIFO for which there is no process to read the data. Commonly encountered at the net and http layers, indicative that the remote side of the stream being written to has been closed.

EADDRINUSE: Address already in use An attempt to bind a server (net, http, or https) to a local address failed due to another server on the local system already occupying that address.

ECONNRESET: Connection reset by peer A connection was forcibly closed by a peer. This normally results from a loss of the connection on the remote socket due to a timeout or reboot. Commonly encountered via the http and net modules.

ECONNREFUSED: Connection refused No connection could be made because the target machine actively refused it. This usually results from trying to connect to a service that is inactive on the foreign host.

ENOTEMPTY: Directory not empty A directory with entries was the target of an operation that requires an empty directory – usually fs.unlink.

ETIMEDOUT: Operation timed out A connect or send request failed because the connected party did not properly respond after a period of time. Usually encountered by http or net – often a sign that a connected socket was not `.end()`'d appropriately.

Error Propagation and Interception

All Node.js APIs will treat invalid arguments as exceptional – that is, if passed invalid arguments, they will *immediately* generate and throw the error as an exception, even if they are an otherwise asynchronous API.

Synchronous APIs (like fs.readFileSync) will throw the error. The act of *throwing* a value (in this case, the error) turns the value into an **exception**. Exceptions may be caught using the `try { } catch(err) { }` construct.

Asynchronous APIs have **two** mechanisms for error propagation; one mechanism for APIs that represent a single operation, and one for APIs that represent multiple operations over time.

Node style callbacks

Single operation APIs take "node style callbacks" – a function provided to the API as an argument. The node style callback takes at least **one** argument – `error` – that will either be `null` (if no error was encountered) or an `Error` instance. For instance:

```
var fs = require('fs');

fs.readFile('/some/file/that/does-not-exist', function nodeStyleCallback(err, data) {
  console.log(err)   // Error: ENOENT
  console.log(data)  // undefined / null
});

fs.readFile('/some/file/that/does-exist', function(err, data) {
  console.log(err)   // null
  console.log(data)  // <Buffer: ba dd ca fe>
})
```

Note that `try { } catch(err) { }` **cannot** intercept errors generated by asynchronous APIs. A common mistake for beginners is to try to use `throw` inside their node style callback:

```
// THIS WILL NOT WORK:
var fs = require('fs');

try {
  fs.readFile('/some/file/that/does-not-exist', function(err, data) {
    // mistaken assumption: throwing here...
    if (err) {
      throw err;
    }
  });
} catch(err) {
  // ... will be caught here -- this is incorrect!
  console.log(err); // Error: ENOENT
}
```

This will not work! By the time the node style callback has been called, the surrounding code (including the `try { } catch(err) { }` will have already exited. Throwing an error inside a node style callback **will crash the process** in most cases. If domains are enabled, they may intercept the thrown error; similarly, if a handler has been added to `process.on('uncaughtException')`, it will intercept the error.

Error events

The other mechanism for providing errors is the "error" event. This is typically used by stream-based and event emitter-based APIs, which themselves represent a series of asynchronous operations over time (versus a single operation that may pass or fail). If no "error" event handler is attached to the source of the error, the error will be thrown. At this point, it will crash the process as an unhandled exception unless domains are employed appropriately or process.on('uncaughtException') has a handler.

```
var net = require('net');

var connection = net.connect('localhost');

// adding an "error" event handler to a stream:
connection.on('error', function(err) {
  // if the connection is reset by the server, or if it can't
  // connect at all, or on any sort of error encountered by
  // the connection, the error will be sent here.
```

```
  console.error(err);
});
```

```
connection.pipe(process.stdout);
```

The "throw when no error handlers are attached behavior" is not limited to APIs provided by Node.js – even user created event emitters and streams will throw errors when no error handlers are attached. An example:

```
var EventEmitter = require('events');
```

```
var ee = new EventEmitter();
```

```
setImmediate(function() {
  // this will crash the process because no "error" event
  // handler has been added.
  ee.emit('error', new Error('This will crash'));
});
```

As with node style callbacks, errors generated this way *cannot* be intercepted by `try { } catch(err) { }` – they happen *after* the calling code has already exited.

File System

`Stability: 2 - Stable`

File I/O is provided by simple wrappers around standard POSIX functions. To use this module do `require('fs')`. All the methods have asynchronous and synchronous forms.

The asynchronous form always takes a completion callback as its last argument. The arguments passed to the completion callback depend on the method, but the first argument is always reserved for an exception. If the operation was completed successfully, then the first argument will be `null` or `undefined`.

When using the synchronous form any exceptions are immediately thrown. You can use try/catch to handle exceptions or allow them to bubble up.

Here is an example of the asynchronous version:

```
var fs = require('fs');

fs.unlink('/tmp/hello', function (err) {
  if (err) throw err;
  console.log('successfully deleted /tmp/hello');
});
```

Here is the synchronous version:

```
var fs = require('fs');

fs.unlinkSync('/tmp/hello');
console.log('successfully deleted /tmp/hello');
```

With the asynchronous methods there is no guaranteed ordering. So the following is prone to error:

```
fs.rename('/tmp/hello', '/tmp/world', function (err) {
  if (err) throw err;
  console.log('renamed complete');
});
fs.stat('/tmp/world', function (err, stats) {
  if (err) throw err;
  console.log('stats: ' + JSON.stringify(stats));
});
```

It could be that `fs.stat` is executed before `fs.rename`. The correct way to do this is to chain the callbacks.

```
fs.rename('/tmp/hello', '/tmp/world', function (err) {
  if (err) throw err;
  fs.stat('/tmp/world', function (err, stats) {
    if (err) throw err;
    console.log('stats: ' + JSON.stringify(stats));
  });
});
```

In busy processes, the programmer is *strongly encouraged* to use the asynchronous versions of these calls. The synchronous versions will block the entire process until they complete–halting all connections.

The relative path to a filename can be used. Remember, however, that this path will be relative to `process.cwd()`.

Most fs functions let you omit the callback argument. If you do, a default callback is used that rethrows errors. To get a trace to the original call site, set the NODE_DEBUG environment variable:

```
$ cat script.js
function bad() {
```

```
    require('fs').readFile('/');
}
bad();

$ env NODE_DEBUG=fs node script.js
fs.js:66
        throw err;
              ^
Error: EISDIR, read
    at rethrow (fs.js:61:21)
    at maybeCallback (fs.js:79:42)
    at Object.fs.readFile (fs.js:153:18)
    at bad (/path/to/script.js:2:17)
    at Object.<anonymous> (/path/to/script.js:5:1)
    <etc.>
```

fs.rename(oldPath, newPath, callback)

Asynchronous rename(2). No arguments other than a possible exception are given to the completion callback.

fs.renameSync(oldPath, newPath)

Synchronous rename(2). Returns `undefined`.

fs.ftruncate(fd, len, callback)

Asynchronous ftruncate(2). No arguments other than a possible exception are given to the completion callback.

fs.ftruncateSync(fd, len)

Synchronous ftruncate(2). Returns `undefined`.

fs.truncate(path, len, callback)

Asynchronous truncate(2). No arguments other than a possible exception are given to the completion callback. A file descriptor can also be passed as the first argument. In this case, `fs.ftruncate()` is called.

fs.truncateSync(path, len)

Synchronous truncate(2). Returns `undefined`.

fs.chown(path, uid, gid, callback)

Asynchronous chown(2). No arguments other than a possible exception are given to the completion callback.

fs.chownSync(path, uid, gid)

Synchronous chown(2). Returns `undefined`.

fs.fchown(fd, uid, gid, callback)

Asynchronous fchown(2). No arguments other than a possible exception are given to the completion callback.

fs.fchownSync(fd, uid, gid)

Synchronous fchown(2). Returns `undefined`.

fs.lchown(path, uid, gid, callback)

Asynchronous lchown(2). No arguments other than a possible exception are given to the completion callback.

fs.lchownSync(path, uid, gid)

Synchronous lchown(2). Returns `undefined`.

fs.chmod(path, mode, callback)

Asynchronous chmod(2). No arguments other than a possible exception are given to the completion callback.

fs.chmodSync(path, mode)

Synchronous chmod(2). Returns `undefined`.

fs.fchmod(fd, mode, callback)

Asynchronous fchmod(2). No arguments other than a possible exception are given to the completion callback.

fs.fchmodSync(fd, mode)

Synchronous fchmod(2). Returns `undefined`.

fs.lchmod(path, mode, callback)

Asynchronous lchmod(2). No arguments other than a possible exception are given to the completion callback. Only available on Mac OS X.

fs.lchmodSync(path, mode)

Synchronous lchmod(2). Returns `undefined`.

fs.stat(path, callback)

Asynchronous stat(2). The callback gets two arguments (`err, stats`) where `stats` is a fs.Stats object. See the fs.Stats section below for more information.

fs.lstat(path, callback)

Asynchronous lstat(2). The callback gets two arguments (`err, stats`) where stats is a `fs.Stats` object. `lstat()` is identical to `stat()`, except that if `path` is a symbolic link, then the link itself is stat-ed, not the file that it refers to.

fs.fstat(fd, callback)

Asynchronous fstat(2). The callback gets two arguments (`err, stats`) where stats is a `fs.Stats` object. `fstat()` is identical to `stat()`, except that the file to be stat-ed is specified by the file descriptor `fd`.

fs.statSync(path)

Synchronous stat(2). Returns an instance of `fs.Stats`.

fs.lstatSync(path)

Synchronous lstat(2). Returns an instance of `fs.Stats`.

fs.fstatSync(fd)

Synchronous fstat(2). Returns an instance of `fs.Stats`.

fs.link(srcpath, dstpath, callback)

Asynchronous link(2). No arguments other than a possible exception are given to the completion callback.

fs.linkSync(srcpath, dstpath)

Synchronous link(2). Returns `undefined`.

fs.symlink(destination, path[, type], callback)

Asynchronous symlink(2). No arguments other than a possible exception are given to the completion callback. The `type` argument can be set to `'dir'`, `'file'`, or `'junction'` (default is `'file'`) and is only available on Windows (ignored on other platforms). Note that Windows junction points require the destination path to be absolute. When using `'junction'`, the `destination` argument will automatically be normalized to absolute path.

fs.symlinkSync(destination, path[, type])

Synchronous symlink(2). Returns `undefined`.

fs.readlink(path, callback)

Asynchronous readlink(2). The callback gets two arguments (`err, linkString`).

fs.readlinkSync(path)

Synchronous readlink(2). Returns the symbolic link's string value.

fs.realpath(path[, cache], callback)

Asynchronous realpath(2). The `callback` gets two arguments (`err, resolvedPath`). May use `process.cwd` to resolve relative paths. `cache` is an object literal of mapped paths that can be used to force a specific path resolution or avoid additional `fs.stat` calls for known real paths.

Example:

```
var cache = {'/etc':'/private/etc'};
fs.realpath('/etc/passwd', cache, function (err, resolvedPath) {
  if (err) throw err;
  console.log(resolvedPath);
});
```

fs.realpathSync(path[, cache])

Synchronous realpath(2). Returns the resolved path.

fs.unlink(path, callback)

Asynchronous unlink(2). No arguments other than a possible exception are given to the completion callback.

fs.unlinkSync(path)

Synchronous unlink(2). Returns `undefined`.

fs.rmdir(path, callback)

Asynchronous rmdir(2). No arguments other than a possible exception are given to the completion callback.

fs.rmdirSync(path)

Synchronous rmdir(2). Returns `undefined`.

fs.mkdir(path[, mode], callback)

Asynchronous mkdir(2). No arguments other than a possible exception are given to the completion callback. `mode` defaults to 0o777.

fs.mkdirSync(path[, mode])

Synchronous mkdir(2). Returns `undefined`.

fs.readdir(path, callback)

Asynchronous readdir(3). Reads the contents of a directory. The callback gets two arguments (`err, files`) where `files` is an array of the names of the files in the directory excluding '.' and '..'.

fs.readdirSync(path)

Synchronous readdir(3). Returns an array of filenames excluding '.' and '..'.

fs.close(fd, callback)

Asynchronous close(2). No arguments other than a possible exception are given to the completion callback.

fs.closeSync(fd)

Synchronous close(2). Returns `undefined`.

fs.open(path, flags[, mode], callback)

Asynchronous file open. See open(2). `flags` can be:

- `'r'` - Open file for reading. An exception occurs if the file does not exist.
- `'r+'` - Open file for reading and writing. An exception occurs if the file does not exist.
- `'rs'` - Open file for reading in synchronous mode. Instructs the operating system to bypass the local file system cache.

This is primarily useful for opening files on NFS mounts as it allows you to skip the potentially stale local cache. It has a very real impact on I/O performance so don't use this flag unless you need it.

Note that this doesn't turn `fs.open()` into a synchronous blocking call. If that's what you want then you should be using `fs.openSync()`

- `'rs+'` - Open file for reading and writing, telling the OS to open it synchronously. See notes for `'rs'` about using this with caution.
- `'w'` - Open file for writing. The file is created (if it does not exist) or truncated (if it exists).
- `'wx'` - Like `'w'` but fails if `path` exists.
- `'w+'` - Open file for reading and writing. The file is created (if it does not exist) or truncated (if it exists).
- `'wx+'` - Like `'w+'` but fails if `path` exists.
- `'a'` - Open file for appending. The file is created if it does not exist.
- `'ax'` - Like `'a'` but fails if `path` exists.
- `'a+'` - Open file for reading and appending. The file is created if it does not exist.
- `'ax+'` - Like `'a+'` but fails if `path` exists.

`mode` sets the file mode (permission and sticky bits), but only if the file was created. It defaults to `0666`, readable and writeable.

The callback gets two arguments (`err, fd`).

The exclusive flag `'x'` (`O_EXCL` flag in open(2)) ensures that `path` is newly created. On POSIX systems, `path` is considered to exist even if it is a symlink to a non-existent file. The exclusive flag may or may not work with network file systems.

On Linux, positional writes don't work when the file is opened in append mode. The kernel ignores the position argument and always appends the data to the end of the file.

fs.openSync(path, flags[, mode])

Synchronous version of `fs.open()`. Returns an integer representing the file descriptor.

fs.utimes(path, atime, mtime, callback)

Change file timestamps of the file referenced by the supplied path.

Note: the arguments `atime` and `mtime` of the following related functions does follow the below rules:

- If the value is a numberable string like "123456789", the value would get converted to corresponding number.
- If the value is `NaN` or `Infinity`, the value would get converted to `Date.now()`.

fs.utimesSync(path, atime, mtime)

Synchronous version of `fs.utimes()`. Returns `undefined`.

fs.futimes(fd, atime, mtime, callback)

Change the file timestamps of a file referenced by the supplied file descriptor.

fs.futimesSync(fd, atime, mtime)

Synchronous version of `fs.futimes()`. Returns `undefined`.

fs.fsync(fd, callback)

Asynchronous fsync(2). No arguments other than a possible exception are given to the completion callback.

fs.fsyncSync(fd)

Synchronous fsync(2). Returns `undefined`.

fs.write(fd, buffer, offset, length[, position], callback)

Write `buffer` to the file specified by `fd`.

`offset` and `length` determine the part of the buffer to be written.

`position` refers to the offset from the beginning of the file where this data should be written. If `typeof position !== 'number'`, the data will be written at the current position. See pwrite(2).

The callback will be given three arguments (`err, written, buffer`) where `written` specifies how many *bytes* were written from `buffer`.

Note that it is unsafe to use `fs.write` multiple times on the same file without waiting for the callback. For this scenario, `fs.createWriteStream` is strongly recommended.

On Linux, positional writes don't work when the file is opened in append mode. The kernel ignores the position argument and always appends the data to the end of the file.

fs.write(fd, data[, position[, encoding]], callback)

Write `data` to the file specified by `fd`. If `data` is not a Buffer instance then the value will be coerced to a string.

`position` refers to the offset from the beginning of the file where this data should be written. If `typeof position !== 'number'` the data will be written at the current position. See pwrite(2).

`encoding` is the expected string encoding.

The callback will receive the arguments `(err, written, string)` where `written` specifies how many *bytes* the passed string required to be written. Note that bytes written is not the same as string characters. See Buffer.byteLength.

Unlike when writing `buffer`, the entire string must be written. No substring may be specified. This is because the byte offset of the resulting data may not be the same as the string offset.

Note that it is unsafe to use `fs.write` multiple times on the same file without waiting for the callback. For this scenario, `fs.createWriteStream` is strongly recommended.

On Linux, positional writes don't work when the file is opened in append mode. The kernel ignores the position argument and always appends the data to the end of the file.

fs.writeSync(fd, buffer, offset, length[, position])

fs.writeSync(fd, data[, position[, encoding]])

Synchronous versions of `fs.write()`. Returns the number of bytes written.

fs.read(fd, buffer, offset, length, position, callback)

Read data from the file specified by `fd`.

`buffer` is the buffer that the data will be written to.

`offset` is the offset in the buffer to start writing at.

`length` is an integer specifying the number of bytes to read.

`position` is an integer specifying where to begin reading from in the file. If `position` is `null`, data will be read from the current file position.

The callback is given the three arguments, `(err, bytesRead, buffer)`.

fs.readSync(fd, buffer, offset, length, position)

Synchronous version of `fs.read`. Returns the number of `bytesRead`.

fs.readFile(file[, options], callback)

- `file` {String | Integer} filename or file descriptor
- `options` {Object | String}
- `encoding` {String | Null} default = `null`
- `flag` {String} default = `'r'`
- `callback` {Function}

Asynchronously reads the entire contents of a file. Example:

```
fs.readFile('/etc/passwd', function (err, data) {
  if (err) throw err;
  console.log(data);
});
```

The callback is passed two arguments (`err, data`), where `data` is the contents of the file.

If no encoding is specified, then the raw buffer is returned.

If `options` is a string, then it specifies the encoding. Example:

```
fs.readFile('/etc/passwd', 'utf8', callback);
```

Any specified file descriptor has to support reading.

Note: Specified file descriptors will not be closed automatically.

fs.readFileSync(file[, options])

Synchronous version of `fs.readFile`. Returns the contents of the `file`.

If the `encoding` option is specified then this function returns a string. Otherwise it returns a buffer.

fs.writeFile(file, data[, options], callback)

- `file` {String | Integer} filename or file descriptor
- `data` {String | Buffer}
- `options` {Object | String}
- `encoding` {String | Null} default = 'utf8'
- `mode` {Number} default = 0o666
- `flag` {String} default = 'w'
- `callback` {Function}

Asynchronously writes data to a file, replacing the file if it already exists. `data` can be a string or a buffer.

The `encoding` option is ignored if `data` is a buffer. It defaults to 'utf8'.

Example:

```
fs.writeFile('message.txt', 'Hello Node.js', function (err) {
  if (err) throw err;
  console.log('It\'s saved!');
});
```

If `options` is a string, then it specifies the encoding. Example:

```
fs.writeFile('message.txt', 'Hello Node.js', 'utf8', callback);
```

Any specified file descriptor has to support writing.

Note that it is unsafe to use `fs.writeFile` multiple times on the same file without waiting for the callback. For this scenario, `fs.createWriteStream` is strongly recommended.

Note: Specified file descriptors will not be closed automatically.

fs.writeFileSync(file, data[, options])

The synchronous version of `fs.writeFile`. Returns `undefined`.

fs.appendFile(file, data[, options], callback)

- `file` {String | Integer} filename or file descriptor
- `data` {String | Buffer}
- `options` {Object | String}
- `encoding` {String | Null} default = 'utf8'
- `mode` {Number} default = 0o666
- `flag` {String} default = 'a'
- `callback` {Function}

Asynchronously append data to a file, creating the file if it does not yet exist. `data` can be a string or a buffer.

Example:

```
fs.appendFile('message.txt', 'data to append', function (err) {
  if (err) throw err;
  console.log('The "data to append" was appended to file!');
});
```

If `options` is a string, then it specifies the encoding. Example:

```
fs.appendFile('message.txt', 'data to append', 'utf8', callback);
```

Any specified file descriptor has to have been opened for appending.

Note: Specified file descriptors will not be closed automatically.

fs.appendFileSync(file, data[, options])

The synchronous version of `fs.appendFile`. Returns `undefined`.

fs.watchFile(filename[, options], listener)

Watch for changes on `filename`. The callback `listener` will be called each time the file is accessed.

The `options` argument may be omitted. If provided, it should be an object. The `options` object may contain a boolean named `persistent` that indicates whether the process should continue to run as long as files are being watched. The `options` object may specify an `interval` property indicating how often the target should be polled in milliseconds. The default is `{ persistent: true, interval: 5007 }`.

The `listener` gets two arguments the current stat object and the previous stat object:

```
fs.watchFile('message.text', function (curr, prev) {
  console.log('the current mtime is: ' + curr.mtime);
  console.log('the previous mtime was: ' + prev.mtime);
});
```

These stat objects are instances of `fs.Stat`.

If you want to be notified when the file was modified, not just accessed, you need to compare `curr.mtime` and `prev.mtime`.

Note: when an `fs.watchFile` operation results in an ENOENT error, it will invoke the listener once, with all the fields zeroed (or, for dates, the Unix Epoch). In Windows, `blksize` and `blocks` fields will be undefined, instead of zero. If the file is created later on, the listener will be called again, with the latest stat objects. This is a change in functionality since v0.10.

Note: `fs.watch` is more efficient than `fs.watchFile` and `fs.unwatchFile`. `fs.watch` should be used instead of `fs.watchFile` and `fs.unwatchFile` when possible.

fs.unwatchFile(filename[, listener])

Stop watching for changes on `filename`. If `listener` is specified, only that particular listener is removed. Otherwise, *all* listeners are removed and you have effectively stopped watching `filename`.

Calling `fs.unwatchFile()` with a filename that is not being watched is a no-op, not an error.

Note: `fs.watch` is more efficient than `fs.watchFile` and `fs.unwatchFile`. `fs.watch` should be used instead of `fs.watchFile` and `fs.unwatchFile` when possible.

fs.watch(filename[, options][, listener])

Watch for changes on `filename`, where `filename` is either a file or a directory. The returned object is a fs.FSWatcher.

The second argument is optional. The `options` if provided should be an object. The supported boolean members are `persistent` and `recursive`. `persistent` indicates whether the process should continue to run as long as files are being watched. `recursive` indicates whether all subdirectories should be watched, or only the current directory. This applies when a directory is specified, and only on supported platforms (See Caveats below).

The default is { `persistent: true, recursive: false` }.

The listener callback gets two arguments (`event, filename`). `event` is either 'rename' or 'change', and `filename` is the name of the file which triggered the event.

Caveats

The `fs.watch` API is not 100% consistent across platforms, and is unavailable in some situations.

The recursive option is only supported on OS X and Windows.

Availability　　This feature depends on the underlying operating system providing a way to be notified of filesystem changes.

- On Linux systems, this uses `inotify`.
- On BSD systems, this uses `kqueue`.
- On OS X, this uses `kqueue` for files and 'FSEvents' for directories.
- On SunOS systems (including Solaris and SmartOS), this uses `event ports`.
- On Windows systems, this feature depends on `ReadDirectoryChangesW`.

If the underlying functionality is not available for some reason, then `fs.watch` will not be able to function. For example, watching files or directories on network file systems (NFS, SMB, etc.) often doesn't work reliably or at all.

You can still use `fs.watchFile`, which uses stat polling, but it is slower and less reliable.

Filename Argument　　Providing `filename` argument in the callback is only supported on Linux and Windows. Even on supported platforms, `filename` is not always guaranteed to be provided. Therefore, don't assume that `filename` argument is always provided in the callback, and have some fallback logic if it is null.

```
fs.watch('somedir', function (event, filename) {
  console.log('event is: ' + event);
  if (filename) {
    console.log('filename provided: ' + filename);
  } else {
    console.log('filename not provided');
  }
});
```

fs.exists(path, callback)

Stability: 0 - Deprecated: Use [fs.stat][] or [fs.access][] instead.

Test whether or not the given path exists by checking with the file system. Then call the `callback` argument with either true or false. Example:

```
fs.exists('/etc/passwd', function (exists) {
  console.log(exists ? "it's there" : 'no passwd!');
});
```

`fs.exists()` should not be used to check if a file exists before calling `fs.open()`. Doing so introduces a race condition since other processes may change the file's state between the two calls. Instead, user code should call `fs.open()` directly and handle the error raised if the file is non-existent.

fs.existsSync(path)

Synchronous version of `fs.exists`. Returns `true` if the file exists, `false` otherwise.

Stability: 0 - Deprecated: Use [fs.statSync][] or [fs.accessSync][] instead.

fs.access(path[, mode], callback)

Tests a user's permissions for the file specified by `path`. `mode` is an optional integer that specifies the accessibility checks to be performed. The following constants define the possible values of `mode`. It is possible to create a mask consisting of the bitwise OR of two or more values.

- `fs.F_OK` - File is visible to the calling process. This is useful for determining if a file exists, but says nothing about `rwx` permissions. Default if no `mode` is specified.
- `fs.R_OK` - File can be read by the calling process.
- `fs.W_OK` - File can be written by the calling process.
- `fs.X_OK` - File can be executed by the calling process. This has no effect on Windows (will behave like `fs.F_OK`).

The final argument, `callback`, is a callback function that is invoked with a possible error argument. If any of the accessibility checks fail, the error argument will be populated. The following example checks if the file /etc/passwd can be read and written by the current process.

```
fs.access('/etc/passwd', fs.R_OK | fs.W_OK, function (err) {
  console.log(err ? 'no access!' : 'can read/write');
});
```

fs.accessSync(path[, mode])

Synchronous version of `fs.access`. This throws if any accessibility checks fail, and does nothing otherwise.

Class: fs.Stats

Objects returned from `fs.stat()`, `fs.lstat()` and `fs.fstat()` and their synchronous counterparts are of this type.

- `stats.isFile()`
- `stats.isDirectory()`
- `stats.isBlockDevice()`
- `stats.isCharacterDevice()`

- `stats.isSymbolicLink()` (only valid with `fs.lstat()`)
- `stats.isFIFO()`
- `stats.isSocket()`

For a regular file `util.inspect(stats)` would return a string very similar to this:

```
{ dev: 2114,
  ino: 48064969,
  mode: 33188,
  nlink: 1,
  uid: 85,
  gid: 100,
  rdev: 0,
  size: 527,
  blksize: 4096,
  blocks: 8,
  atime: Mon, 10 Oct 2011 23:24:11 GMT,
  mtime: Mon, 10 Oct 2011 23:24:11 GMT,
  ctime: Mon, 10 Oct 2011 23:24:11 GMT,
  birthtime: Mon, 10 Oct 2011 23:24:11 GMT }
```

Please note that `atime`, `mtime`, `birthtime`, and `ctime` are instances of Date object and to compare the values of these objects you should use appropriate methods. For most general uses getTime() will return the number of milliseconds elapsed since *1 January 1970 00:00:00 UTC* and this integer should be sufficient for any comparison, however there are additional methods which can be used for displaying fuzzy information. More details can be found in the MDN JavaScript Reference page.

Stat Time Values

The times in the stat object have the following semantics:

- `atime` "Access Time" - Time when file data last accessed. Changed by the `mknod(2)`, `utimes(2)`, and `read(2)` system calls.
- `mtime` "Modified Time" - Time when file data last modified. Changed by the `mknod(2)`, `utimes(2)`, and `write(2)` system calls.
- `ctime` "Change Time" - Time when file status was last changed (inode data modification). Changed by the `chmod(2)`, `chown(2)`, `link(2)`, `mknod(2)`, `rename(2)`, `unlink(2)`, `utimes(2)`, `read(2)`, and `write(2)` system calls.
- `birthtime` "Birth Time" - Time of file creation. Set once when the file is created. On filesystems where birthtime is not available, this field may instead hold either the `ctime` or `1970-01-01T00:00Z` (ie, unix epoch timestamp 0). On Darwin and other FreeBSD variants, also set if the `atime` is explicitly set to an earlier value than the current `birthtime` using the `utimes(2)` system call.

Prior to Node v0.12, the `ctime` held the `birthtime` on Windows systems. Note that as of v0.12, `ctime` is not "creation time", and on Unix systems, it never was.

fs.createReadStream(path[, options])

Returns a new ReadStream object (See `Readable Stream`).

Be aware that, unlike the default value set for `highWaterMark` on a readable stream (16 kb), the stream returned by this method has a default value of 64 kb for the same parameter.

`options` is an object or string with the following defaults:

```
{ flags: 'r',
  encoding: null,
  fd: null,
```

```
    mode: 0o666,
    autoClose: true
}
```

options can include **start** and **end** values to read a range of bytes from the file instead of the entire file. Both **start** and **end** are inclusive and start at 0. The **encoding** can be any one of those accepted by Buffer.

If **fd** is specified, **ReadStream** will ignore the **path** argument and will use the specified file descriptor. This means that no **open** event will be emitted.

If **autoClose** is false, then the file descriptor won't be closed, even if there's an error. It is your responsibility to close it and make sure there's no file descriptor leak. If **autoClose** is set to true (default behavior), on **error** or **end** the file descriptor will be closed automatically.

mode sets the file mode (permission and sticky bits), but only if the file was created.

An example to read the last 10 bytes of a file which is 100 bytes long:

```
fs.createReadStream('sample.txt', {start: 90, end: 99});
```

If **options** is a string, then it specifies the encoding.

Class: fs.ReadStream

ReadStream is a Readable Stream.

Event: 'open'

  • **fd** {Integer} file descriptor used by the ReadStream.

Emitted when the ReadStream's file is opened.

fs.createWriteStream(path[, options])

Returns a new WriteStream object (See **Writable Stream**).

options is an object or string with the following defaults:

```
{ flags: 'w',
  defaultEncoding: 'utf8',
  fd: null,
  mode: 0o666 }
```

options may also include a **start** option to allow writing data at some position past the beginning of the file. Modifying a file rather than replacing it may require a **flags** mode of **r+** rather than the default mode **w**. The **defaultEncoding** can be any one of those accepted by Buffer.

Like **ReadStream** above, if **fd** is specified, **WriteStream** will ignore the **path** argument and will use the specified file descriptor. This means that no **open** event will be emitted.

If **options** is a string, then it specifies the encoding.

Class: fs.WriteStream

WriteStream is a Writable Stream.

Event: 'open'

- `fd` {Integer} file descriptor used by the WriteStream.

Emitted when the WriteStream's file is opened.

file.bytesWritten

The number of bytes written so far. Does not include data that is still queued for writing.

Class: fs.FSWatcher

Objects returned from `fs.watch()` are of this type.

watcher.close()

Stop watching for changes on the given `fs.FSWatcher`.

Event: 'change'

- `event` {String} The type of fs change
- `filename` {String} The filename that changed (if relevant/available)

Emitted when something changes in a watched directory or file. See more details in fs.watch.

Event: 'error'

- `error` {Error object}

Emitted when an error occurs.

Global Objects

These objects are available in all modules. Some of these objects aren't actually in the global scope but in the module scope - this will be noted.

global

- {Object} The global namespace object.

In browsers, the top-level scope is the global scope. That means that in browsers if you're in the global scope `var something` will define a global variable. In Node.js this is different. The top-level scope is not the global scope; `var something` inside an Node.js module will be local to that module.

process

- {Object}

The process object. See the process object section.

console

- {Object}

Used to print to stdout and stderr. See the console section.

Class: Buffer

- {Function}

Used to handle binary data. See the buffer section

require()

- {Function}

To require modules. See the Modules section. `require` isn't actually a global but rather local to each module.

require.resolve()

Use the internal `require()` machinery to look up the location of a module, but rather than loading the module, just return the resolved filename.

require.cache

- {Object}

Modules are cached in this object when they are required. By deleting a key value from this object, the next `require` will reload the module.

---

require.extensions

```
Stability: 0 - Deprecated
```

- {Object}

Instruct **require** on how to handle certain file extensions.

Process files with the extension **.sjs** as **.js**:

```
require.extensions['.sjs'] = require.extensions['.js'];
```

Deprecated In the past, this list has been used to load non-JavaScript modules into Node.js by compiling them on-demand. However, in practice, there are much better ways to do this, such as loading modules via some other Node.js program, or compiling them to JavaScript ahead of time.

Since the Module system is locked, this feature will probably never go away. However, it may have subtle bugs and complexities that are best left untouched.

___filename

- {String}

The filename of the code being executed. This is the resolved absolute path of this code file. For a main program this is not necessarily the same filename used in the command line. The value inside a module is the path to that module file.

Example: running **node example.js** from **/Users/mjr**

```
console.log(__filename);
// /Users/mjr/example.js
```

__filename isn't actually a global but rather local to each module.

___dirname

- {String}

The name of the directory that the currently executing script resides in.

Example: running **node example.js** from **/Users/mjr**

```
console.log(__dirname);
// /Users/mjr
```

__dirname isn't actually a global but rather local to each module.

module

- {Object}

A reference to the current module. In particular **module.exports** is used for defining what a module exports and makes available through **require()**.

module isn't actually a global but rather local to each module.

See the module system documentation for more information.

exports

A reference to the `module.exports` that is shorter to type. See module system documentation for details on when to use `exports` and when to use `module.exports`.

`exports` isn't actually a global but rather local to each module.

See the module system documentation for more information.

setTimeout(cb, ms)

Run callback `cb` after *at least* `ms` milliseconds. The actual delay depends on external factors like OS timer granularity and system load.

The timeout must be in the range of 1-2,147,483,647 inclusive. If the value is outside that range, it's changed to 1 millisecond. Broadly speaking, a timer cannot span more than 24.8 days.

Returns an opaque value that represents the timer.

clearTimeout(t)

Stop a timer that was previously created with `setTimeout()`. The callback will not execute.

setInterval(cb, ms)

Run callback `cb` repeatedly every `ms` milliseconds. Note that the actual interval may vary, depending on external factors like OS timer granularity and system load. It's never less than `ms` but it may be longer.

The interval must be in the range of 1-2,147,483,647 inclusive. If the value is outside that range, it's changed to 1 millisecond. Broadly speaking, a timer cannot span more than 24.8 days.

Returns an opaque value that represents the timer.

clearInterval(t)

Stop a timer that was previously created with `setInterval()`. The callback will not execute.

The timer functions are global variables. See the timers section.

HTTP

`Stability: 2 - Stable`

To use the HTTP server and client one must `require('http')`.

The HTTP interfaces in Node.js are designed to support many features of the protocol which have been traditionally difficult to use. In particular, large, possibly chunk-encoded, messages. The interface is careful to never buffer entire requests or responses–the user is able to stream data.

HTTP message headers are represented by an object like this:

```
{ 'content-length': '123',
  'content-type': 'text/plain',
  'connection': 'keep-alive',
  'host': 'mysite.com',
  'accept': '*/*' }
```

Keys are lowercased. Values are not modified.

In order to support the full spectrum of possible HTTP applications, Node.js's HTTP API is very low-level. It deals with stream handling and message parsing only. It parses a message into headers and body but it does not parse the actual headers or the body.

Defined headers that allow multiple values are concatenated with a , character, except for the `set-cookie` and `cookie` headers which are represented as an array of values. Headers such as `content-length` which can only have a single value are parsed accordingly, and only a single value is represented on the parsed object.

The raw headers as they were received are retained in the `rawHeaders` property, which is an array of `[key, value, key2, value2, ...]`. For example, the previous message header object might have a `rawHeaders` list like the following:

```
[ 'ConTent-Length', '123456',
  'content-LENGTH', '123',
  'content-type', 'text/plain',
  'CONNECTION', 'keep-alive',
  'Host', 'mysite.com',
  'accepT', '*/*' ]
```

http.METHODS

- {Array}

A list of the HTTP methods that are supported by the parser.

http.STATUS_CODES

- {Object}

A collection of all the standard HTTP response status codes, and the short description of each. For example, `http.STATUS_CODES[404] === 'Not Found'`.

http.createServer([requestListener])

Returns a new instance of http.Server.

The `requestListener` is a function which is automatically added to the `'request'` event.

http.createClient([port][, host])

Stability: 0 - Deprecated: Use [http.request][] instead.

Constructs a new HTTP client. port and host refer to the server to be connected to.

Class: http.Server

This is an EventEmitter with the following events:

Event: 'request'

function (request, response) { }

Emitted each time there is a request. Note that there may be multiple requests per connection (in the case of keep-alive connections). request is an instance of http.IncomingMessage and response is an instance of http.ServerResponse.

Event: 'connection'

function (socket) { }

When a new TCP stream is established. socket is an object of type net.Socket. Usually users will not want to access this event. In particular, the socket will not emit readable events because of how the protocol parser attaches to the socket. The socket can also be accessed at request.connection.

Event: 'close'

function () { }

Emitted when the server closes.

Event: 'checkContinue'

function (request, response) { }

Emitted each time a request with an http Expect: 100-continue is received. If this event isn't listened for, the server will automatically respond with a 100 Continue as appropriate.

Handling this event involves calling response.writeContinue() if the client should continue to send the request body, or generating an appropriate HTTP response (e.g., 400 Bad Request) if the client should not continue to send the request body.

Note that when this event is emitted and handled, the request event will not be emitted.

Event: 'connect'

function (request, socket, head) { }

Emitted each time a client requests a http CONNECT method. If this event isn't listened for, then clients requesting a CONNECT method will have their connections closed.

- request is the arguments for the http request, as it is in the request event.
- socket is the network socket between the server and client.
- head is an instance of Buffer, the first packet of the tunneling stream, this may be empty.

After this event is emitted, the request's socket will not have a data event listener, meaning you will need to bind to it in order to handle data sent to the server on that socket.

Event: 'upgrade'

```
function (request, socket, head) { }
```

Emitted each time a client requests a http upgrade. If this event isn't listened for, then clients requesting an upgrade will have their connections closed.

- **request** is the arguments for the http request, as it is in the request event.
- **socket** is the network socket between the server and client.
- **head** is an instance of Buffer, the first packet of the upgraded stream, this may be empty.

After this event is emitted, the request's socket will not have a **data** event listener, meaning you will need to bind to it in order to handle data sent to the server on that socket.

Event: 'clientError'

```
function (exception, socket) { }
```

If a client connection emits an 'error' event, it will be forwarded here.

socket is the **net.Socket** object that the error originated from.

server.listen(port[, hostname][, backlog][, callback])

Begin accepting connections on the specified **port** and **hostname**. If the **hostname** is omitted, the server will accept connections on any IPv6 address (::) when IPv6 is available, or any IPv4 address (0.0.0.0) otherwise. A port value of zero will assign a random port.

To listen to a unix socket, supply a filename instead of port and hostname.

Backlog is the maximum length of the queue of pending connections. The actual length will be determined by your OS through sysctl settings such as **tcp_max_syn_backlog** and **somaxconn** on linux. The default value of this parameter is 511 (not 512).

This function is asynchronous. The last parameter **callback** will be added as a listener for the 'listening' event. See also net.Server.listen(port).

server.listen(path[, callback])

Start a UNIX socket server listening for connections on the given **path**.

This function is asynchronous. The last parameter **callback** will be added as a listener for the 'listening' event. See also net.Server.listen(path).

server.listen(handle[, callback])

- **handle** {Object}
- **callback** {Function}

The **handle** object can be set to either a server or socket (anything with an underlying **_handle** member), or a **{fd: <n>}** object.

This will cause the server to accept connections on the specified handle, but it is presumed that the file descriptor or handle has already been bound to a port or domain socket.

Listening on a file descriptor is not supported on Windows.

This function is asynchronous. The last parameter **callback** will be added as a listener for the 'listening' event. See also net.Server.listen().

server.close([callback])

Stops the server from accepting new connections. See net.Server.close().

server.maxHeadersCount

Limits maximum incoming headers count, equal to 1000 by default. If set to 0 - no limit will be applied.

server.setTimeout(msecs, callback)

- msecs {Number}
- callback {Function}

Sets the timeout value for sockets, and emits a 'timeout' event on the Server object, passing the socket as an argument, if a timeout occurs.

If there is a 'timeout' event listener on the Server object, then it will be called with the timed-out socket as an argument.

By default, the Server's timeout value is 2 minutes, and sockets are destroyed automatically if they time out. However, if you assign a callback to the Server's 'timeout' event, then you are responsible for handling socket timeouts.

Returns server.

server.timeout

- {Number} Default = 120000 (2 minutes)

The number of milliseconds of inactivity before a socket is presumed to have timed out.

Note that the socket timeout logic is set up on connection, so changing this value only affects *new* connections to the server, not any existing connections.

Set to 0 to disable any kind of automatic timeout behavior on incoming connections.

Class: http.ServerResponse

This object is created internally by a HTTP server–not by the user. It is passed as the second parameter to the 'request' event.

The response implements the Writable Stream interface. This is an EventEmitter with the following events:

Event: 'close'

```
function () { }
```

Indicates that the underlying connection was terminated before response.end() was called or able to flush.

Event: 'finish'

```
function () { }
```

Emitted when the response has been sent. More specifically, this event is emitted when the last segment of the response headers and body have been handed off to the operating system for transmission over the network. It does not imply that the client has received anything yet.

After this event, no more events will be emitted on the response object.

response.writeContinue()

Sends a HTTP/1.1 100 Continue message to the client, indicating that the request body should be sent. See the 'checkContinue' event on `Server`.

response.writeHead(statusCode[, statusMessage][, headers])

Sends a response header to the request. The status code is a 3-digit HTTP status code, like 404. The last argument, `headers`, are the response headers. Optionally one can give a human-readable `statusMessage` as the second argument.

Example:

```
var body = 'hello world';
response.writeHead(200, {
  'Content-Length': body.length,
  'Content-Type': 'text/plain' });
```

This method must only be called once on a message and it must be called before response.end() is called.

If you call response.write() or response.end() before calling this, the implicit/mutable headers will be calculated and call this function for you.

Note that Content-Length is given in bytes not characters. The above example works because the string `'hello world'` contains only single byte characters. If the body contains higher coded characters then `Buffer.byteLength()` should be used to determine the number of bytes in a given encoding. And Node.js does not check whether Content-Length and the length of the body which has been transmitted are equal or not.

response.setTimeout(msecs, callback)

- `msecs` {Number}
- `callback` {Function}

Sets the Socket's timeout value to `msecs`. If a callback is provided, then it is added as a listener on the `'timeout'` event on the response object.

If no `'timeout'` listener is added to the request, the response, or the server, then sockets are destroyed when they time out. If you assign a handler on the request, the response, or the server's `'timeout'` events, then it is your responsibility to handle timed out sockets.

Returns `response`.

response.statusCode

When using implicit headers (not calling response.writeHead() explicitly), this property controls the status code that will be sent to the client when the headers get flushed.

Example:

```
response.statusCode = 404;
```

After response header was sent to the client, this property indicates the status code which was sent out.

response.statusMessage

When using implicit headers (not calling `response.writeHead()` explicitly), this property controls the status message that will be sent to the client when the headers get flushed. If this is left as `undefined` then the standard message for the status code will be used.

Example:

```
response.statusMessage = 'Not found';
```

After response header was sent to the client, this property indicates the status message which was sent out.

response.setHeader(name, value)

Sets a single header value for implicit headers. If this header already exists in the to-be-sent headers, its value will be replaced. Use an array of strings here if you need to send multiple headers with the same name.

Example:

```
response.setHeader("Content-Type", "text/html");
```

or

```
response.setHeader("Set-Cookie", ["type=ninja", "language=javascript"]);
```

Attempting to set a header field name that contains invalid characters will result in a **TypeError** being thrown.

response.headersSent

Boolean (read-only). True if headers were sent, false otherwise.

response.sendDate

When true, the Date header will be automatically generated and sent in the response if it is not already present in the headers. Defaults to true.

This should only be disabled for testing; HTTP requires the Date header in responses.

response.getHeader(name)

Reads out a header that's already been queued but not sent to the client. Note that the name is case insensitive. This can only be called before headers get implicitly flushed.

Example:

```
var contentType = response.getHeader('content-type');
```

response.removeHeader(name)

Removes a header that's queued for implicit sending.

Example:

```
response.removeHeader("Content-Encoding");
```

response.write(chunk[, encoding][, callback])

If this method is called and response.writeHead() has not been called, it will switch to implicit header mode and flush the implicit headers.

This sends a chunk of the response body. This method may be called multiple times to provide successive parts of the body.

chunk can be a string or a buffer. If `chunk` is a string, the second parameter specifies how to encode it into a byte stream. By default the `encoding` is `'utf8'`. The last parameter `callback` will be called when this chunk of data is flushed.

Note: This is the raw HTTP body and has nothing to do with higher-level multi-part body encodings that may be used.

The first time `response.write()` is called, it will send the buffered header information and the first body to the client. The second time `response.write()` is called, Node.js assumes you're going to be streaming data, and sends that separately. That is, the response is buffered up to the first chunk of body.

Returns `true` if the entire data was flushed successfully to the kernel buffer. Returns `false` if all or part of the data was queued in user memory. `'drain'` will be emitted when the buffer is free again.

response.addTrailers(headers)

This method adds HTTP trailing headers (a header but at the end of the message) to the response.

Trailers will **only** be emitted if chunked encoding is used for the response; if it is not (e.g., if the request was HTTP/1.0), they will be silently discarded.

Note that HTTP requires the `Trailer` header to be sent if you intend to emit trailers, with a list of the header fields in its value. E.g.,

```
response.writeHead(200, { 'Content-Type': 'text/plain',
                          'Trailer': 'Content-MD5' });
response.write(fileData);
response.addTrailers({'Content-MD5': "7895bf4b8828b55ceaf47747b4bca667"});
response.end();
```

Attempting to set a trailer field name that contains invalid characters will result in a `TypeError` being thrown.

response.end([data][, encoding][, callback])

This method signals to the server that all of the response headers and body have been sent; that server should consider this message complete. The method, `response.end()`, MUST be called on each response.

If `data` is specified, it is equivalent to calling `response.write(data, encoding)` followed by `response.end(callback)`.

If `callback` is specified, it will be called when the response stream is finished.

response.finished

Boolean value that indicates whether the response has completed. Starts as `false`. After `response.end()` executes, the value will be `true`.

http.request(options[, callback])

Node.js maintains several connections per server to make HTTP requests. This function allows one to transparently issue requests.

`options` can be an object or a string. If `options` is a string, it is automatically parsed with url.parse().

Options:

- `protocol`: Protocol to use. Defaults to `'http'`.
- `host`: A domain name or IP address of the server to issue the request to. Defaults to `'localhost'`.
- `hostname`: Alias for `host`. To support `url.parse()` `hostname` is preferred over `host`.

- family: IP address family to use when resolving host and hostname. Valid values are 4 or 6. When unspecified, both IP v4 and v6 will be used.
- port: Port of remote server. Defaults to 80.
- localAddress: Local interface to bind for network connections.
- socketPath: Unix Domain Socket (use one of host:port or socketPath).
- method: A string specifying the HTTP request method. Defaults to 'GET'.
- path: Request path. Defaults to '/'. Should include query string if any. E.G. '/index.html?page=12'. An exception is thrown when the request path contains illegal characters. Currently, only spaces are rejected but that may change in the future.
- headers: An object containing request headers.
- auth: Basic authentication i.e. 'user:password' to compute an Authorization header.
- agent: Controls Agent behavior. When an Agent is used request will default to Connection: keep-alive. Possible values:
- undefined (default): use globalAgent for this host and port.
- Agent object: explicitly use the passed in Agent.
- false: opts out of connection pooling with an Agent, defaults request to Connection: close.

The optional callback parameter will be added as a one time listener for the 'response' event.

http.request() returns an instance of the http.ClientRequest class. The ClientRequest instance is a writable stream. If one needs to upload a file with a POST request, then write to the ClientRequest object.

Example:

```
var postData = querystring.stringify({
  'msg' : 'Hello World!'
});

var options = {
  hostname: 'www.google.com',
  port: 80,
  path: '/upload',
  method: 'POST',
  headers: {
    'Content-Type': 'application/x-www-form-urlencoded',
    'Content-Length': postData.length
  }
};

var req = http.request(options, function(res) {
  console.log('STATUS: ' + res.statusCode);
  console.log('HEADERS: ' + JSON.stringify(res.headers));
  res.setEncoding('utf8');
  res.on('data', function (chunk) {
    console.log('BODY: ' + chunk);
  });
  res.on('end', function() {
    console.log('No more data in response.')
  })
});

req.on('error', function(e) {
  console.log('problem with request: ' + e.message);
});

// write data to request body
req.write(postData);
req.end();
```

Note that in the example `req.end()` was called. With `http.request()` one must always call `req.end()` to signify that you're done with the request - even if there is no data being written to the request body.

If any error is encountered during the request (be that with DNS resolution, TCP level errors, or actual HTTP parse errors) an `'error'` event is emitted on the returned request object.

There are a few special headers that should be noted.

- Sending a 'Connection: keep-alive' will notify Node.js that the connection to the server should be persisted until the next request.

- Sending a 'Content-length' header will disable the default chunked encoding.

- Sending an 'Expect' header will immediately send the request headers. Usually, when sending 'Expect: 100-continue', you should both set a timeout and listen for the `continue` event. See RFC2616 Section 8.2.3 for more information.

- Sending an Authorization header will override using the `auth` option to compute basic authentication.

http.get(options[, callback])

Since most requests are GET requests without bodies, Node.js provides this convenience method. The only difference between this method and `http.request()` is that it sets the method to GET and calls `req.end()` automatically.

Example:

```
http.get("http://www.google.com/index.html", function(res) {
  console.log("Got response: " + res.statusCode);
}).on('error', function(e) {
  console.log("Got error: " + e.message);
});
```

Class: http.Agent

The HTTP Agent is used for pooling sockets used in HTTP client requests.

The HTTP Agent also defaults client requests to using Connection:keep-alive. If no pending HTTP requests are waiting on a socket to become free the socket is closed. This means that Node.js's pool has the benefit of keep-alive when under load but still does not require developers to manually close the HTTP clients using KeepAlive.

If you opt into using HTTP KeepAlive, you can create an Agent object with that flag set to `true`. (See the constructor options below.) Then, the Agent will keep unused sockets in a pool for later use. They will be explicitly marked so as to not keep the Node.js process running. However, it is still a good idea to explicitly `destroy()` KeepAlive agents when they are no longer in use, so that the Sockets will be shut down.

Sockets are removed from the agent's pool when the socket emits either a "close" event or a special "agentRemove" event. This means that if you intend to keep one HTTP request open for a long time and don't want it to stay in the pool you can do something along the lines of:

```
http.get(options, function(res) {
  // Do stuff
}).on("socket", function (socket) {
  socket.emit("agentRemove");
});
```

Alternatively, you could just opt out of pooling entirely using `agent:false`:

```
http.get({
  hostname: 'localhost',
  port: 80,
  path: '/',
  agent: false  // create a new agent just for this one request
}, function (res) {
  // Do stuff with response
})
```

new Agent([options])

- `options` {Object} Set of configurable options to set on the agent. Can have the following fields:
- `keepAlive` {Boolean} Keep sockets around in a pool to be used by other requests in the future. Default = `false`
- `keepAliveMsecs` {Integer} When using HTTP KeepAlive, how often to send TCP KeepAlive packets over sockets being kept alive. Default = 1000. Only relevant if `keepAlive` is set to `true`.
- `maxSockets` {Number} Maximum number of sockets to allow per host. Default = `Infinity`.
- `maxFreeSockets` {Number} Maximum number of sockets to leave open in a free state. Only relevant if `keepAlive` is set to `true`. Default = 256.

The default `http.globalAgent` that is used by `http.request` has all of these values set to their respective defaults.

To configure any of them, you must create your own `Agent` object.

```
var http = require('http');
var keepAliveAgent = new http.Agent({ keepAlive: true });
options.agent = keepAliveAgent;
http.request(options, onResponseCallback);
```

agent.maxSockets

By default set to Infinity. Determines how many concurrent sockets the agent can have open per origin. Origin is either a 'host:port' or 'host:port:localAddress' combination.

agent.maxFreeSockets

By default set to 256. For Agents supporting HTTP KeepAlive, this sets the maximum number of sockets that will be left open in the free state.

agent.sockets

An object which contains arrays of sockets currently in use by the Agent. Do not modify.

agent.freeSockets

An object which contains arrays of sockets currently awaiting use by the Agent when HTTP KeepAlive is used. Do not modify.

agent.requests

An object which contains queues of requests that have not yet been assigned to sockets. Do not modify.

agent.destroy()

Destroy any sockets that are currently in use by the agent.

It is usually not necessary to do this. However, if you are using an agent with KeepAlive enabled, then it is best to explicitly shut down the agent when you know that it will no longer be used. Otherwise, sockets may hang open for quite a long time before the server terminates them.

agent.getName(options)

Get a unique name for a set of request options, to determine whether a connection can be reused. In the http agent, this returns `host:port:localAddress`. In the https agent, the name includes the CA, cert, ciphers, and other HTTPS/TLS-specific options that determine socket reusability.

http.globalAgent

Global instance of Agent which is used as the default for all http client requests.

Class: http.ClientRequest

This object is created internally and returned from `http.request()`. It represents an *in-progress* request whose header has already been queued. The header is still mutable using the `setHeader(name, value)`, `getHeader(name)`, `removeHeader(name)` API. The actual header will be sent along with the first data chunk or when closing the connection.

To get the response, add a listener for `'response'` to the request object. `'response'` will be emitted from the request object when the response headers have been received. The `'response'` event is executed with one argument which is an instance of http.IncomingMessage.

During the `'response'` event, one can add listeners to the response object; particularly to listen for the `'data'` event.

If no `'response'` handler is added, then the response will be entirely discarded. However, if you add a `'response'` event handler, then you **must** consume the data from the response object, either by calling `response.read()` whenever there is a `'readable'` event, or by adding a `'data'` handler, or by calling the `.resume()` method. Until the data is consumed, the `'end'` event will not fire. Also, until the data is read it will consume memory that can eventually lead to a 'process out of memory' error.

Note: Node.js does not check whether Content-Length and the length of the body which has been transmitted are equal or not.

The request implements the Writable Stream interface. This is an EventEmitter with the following events:

Event: 'response'

```
function (response) { }
```

Emitted when a response is received to this request. This event is emitted only once. The **response** argument will be an instance of http.IncomingMessage.

Options:

- `host`: A domain name or IP address of the server to issue the request to.
- `port`: Port of remote server.
- `socketPath`: Unix Domain Socket (use one of host:port or socketPath)

Event: 'socket'

```
function (socket) { }
```

Emitted after a socket is assigned to this request.

Event: 'connect'

```
function (response, socket, head) { }
```

Emitted each time a server responds to a request with a CONNECT method. If this event isn't being listened for, clients receiving a CONNECT method will have their connections closed.

A client server pair that show you how to listen for the **connect** event.

```
var http = require('http');
var net = require('net');
var url = require('url');

// Create an HTTP tunneling proxy
var proxy = http.createServer(function (req, res) {
  res.writeHead(200, {'Content-Type': 'text/plain'});
  res.end('okay');
});
proxy.on('connect', function(req, cltSocket, head) {
  // connect to an origin server
  var srvUrl = url.parse('http://' + req.url);
  var srvSocket = net.connect(srvUrl.port, srvUrl.hostname, function() {
    cltSocket.write('HTTP/1.1 200 Connection Established\r\n' +
                    'Proxy-agent: Node.js-Proxy\r\n' +
                    '\r\n');
    srvSocket.write(head);
    srvSocket.pipe(cltSocket);
    cltSocket.pipe(srvSocket);
  });
});

// now that proxy is running
proxy.listen(1337, '127.0.0.1', function() {

  // make a request to a tunneling proxy
  var options = {
    port: 1337,
    hostname: '127.0.0.1',
    method: 'CONNECT',
    path: 'www.google.com:80'
  };

  var req = http.request(options);
  req.end();

  req.on('connect', function(res, socket, head) {
    console.log('got connected!');

    // make a request over an HTTP tunnel
    socket.write('GET / HTTP/1.1\r\n' +
                 'Host: www.google.com:80\r\n' +
                 'Connection: close\r\n' +
```

```
                        '\r\n');
    socket.on('data', function(chunk) {
      console.log(chunk.toString());
    });
    socket.on('end', function() {
      proxy.close();
    });
  });
});
```

Event: 'upgrade'

```
function (response, socket, head) { }
```

Emitted each time a server responds to a request with an upgrade. If this event isn't being listened for, clients receiving an upgrade header will have their connections closed.

A client server pair that show you how to listen for the `upgrade` event.

```
var http = require('http');

// Create an HTTP server
var srv = http.createServer(function (req, res) {
  res.writeHead(200, {'Content-Type': 'text/plain'});
  res.end('okay');
});
srv.on('upgrade', function(req, socket, head) {
  socket.write('HTTP/1.1 101 Web Socket Protocol Handshake\r\n' +
               'Upgrade: WebSocket\r\n' +
               'Connection: Upgrade\r\n' +
               '\r\n');

  socket.pipe(socket); // echo back
});

// now that server is running
srv.listen(1337, '127.0.0.1', function() {

  // make a request
  var options = {
    port: 1337,
    hostname: '127.0.0.1',
    headers: {
      'Connection': 'Upgrade',
      'Upgrade': 'websocket'
    }
  };

  var req = http.request(options);
  req.end();

  req.on('upgrade', function(res, socket, upgradeHead) {
    console.log('got upgraded!');
    socket.end();
    process.exit(0);
  });
});
```

Event: 'continue'

```
function () { }
```

Emitted when the server sends a '100 Continue' HTTP response, usually because the request contained 'Expect: 100-continue'. This is an instruction that the client should send the request body.

Event: 'abort'

```
function () { }
```

Emitted when the request has been aborted by the client. This event is only emitted on the first call to `abort()`.

request.flushHeaders()

Flush the request headers.

For efficiency reasons, Node.js normally buffers the request headers until you call `request.end()` or write the first chunk of request data. It then tries hard to pack the request headers and data into a single TCP packet.

That's usually what you want (it saves a TCP round-trip) but not when the first data isn't sent until possibly much later. `request.flushHeaders()` lets you bypass the optimization and kickstart the request.

request.write(chunk[, encoding][, callback])

Sends a chunk of the body. By calling this method many times, the user can stream a request body to a server–in that case it is suggested to use the `['Transfer-Encoding', 'chunked']` header line when creating the request.

The `chunk` argument should be a Buffer or a string.

The `encoding` argument is optional and only applies when `chunk` is a string. Defaults to `'utf8'`.

The `callback` argument is optional and will be called when this chunk of data is flushed.

request.end([data][, encoding][, callback])

Finishes sending the request. If any parts of the body are unsent, it will flush them to the stream. If the request is chunked, this will send the terminating `'0\r\n\r\n'`.

If `data` is specified, it is equivalent to calling `request.write(data, encoding)` followed by `request.end(callback)`.

If `callback` is specified, it will be called when the request stream is finished.

request.abort()

Marks the request as aborting. Calling this will cause remaining data in the response to be dropped and the socket to be destroyed.

request.setTimeout(timeout[, callback])

Once a socket is assigned to this request and is connected socket.setTimeout() will be called.

Returns `request`.

request.setNoDelay([noDelay])

Once a socket is assigned to this request and is connected socket.setNoDelay() will be called.

request.setSocketKeepAlive([enable][, initialDelay])

Once a socket is assigned to this request and is connected socket.setKeepAlive() will be called.

http.IncomingMessage

An `IncomingMessage` object is created by http.Server or http.ClientRequest and passed as the first argument to the `'request'` and `'response'` event respectively. It may be used to access response status, headers and data.

It implements the Readable Stream interface, as well as the following additional events, methods, and properties.

Event: 'close'

```
function () { }
```

Indicates that the underlying connection was closed. Just like `'end'`, this event occurs only once per response.

message.httpVersion

In case of server request, the HTTP version sent by the client. In the case of client response, the HTTP version of the connected-to server. Probably either `'1.1'` or `'1.0'`.

Also `response.httpVersionMajor` is the first integer and `response.httpVersionMinor` is the second.

message.headers

The request/response headers object.

Read only map of header names and values. Header names are lower-cased. Example:

```
// Prints something like:
//
// { 'user-agent': 'curl/7.22.0',
//   host: '127.0.0.1:8000',
//   accept: '*/*' }
console.log(request.headers);
```

message.rawHeaders

The raw request/response headers list exactly as they were received.

Note that the keys and values are in the same list. It is *not* a list of tuples. So, the even-numbered offsets are key values, and the odd-numbered offsets are the associated values.

Header names are not lowercased, and duplicates are not merged.

```
// Prints something like:
//
// [ 'user-agent',
//   'this is invalid because there can be only one',
//   'User-Agent',
```

```
//    'curl/7.22.0',
//    'Host',
//    '127.0.0.1:8000',
//    'ACCEPT',
//    '*/*' ]
console.log(request.rawHeaders);
```

message.trailers

The request/response trailers object. Only populated at the 'end' event.

message.rawTrailers

The raw request/response trailer keys and values exactly as they were received. Only populated at the 'end' event.

message.setTimeout(msecs, callback)

- msecs {Number}
- callback {Function}

Calls `message.connection.setTimeout(msecs, callback)`.

Returns `message`.

message.method

Only valid for request obtained from http.Server.

The request method as a string. Read only. Example: `'GET'`, `'DELETE'`.

message.url

Only valid for request obtained from http.Server.

Request URL string. This contains only the URL that is present in the actual HTTP request. If the request is:

```
GET /status?name=ryan HTTP/1.1\r\n
Accept: text/plain\r\n
\r\n
```

Then `request.url` will be:

```
'/status?name=ryan'
```

If you would like to parse the URL into its parts, you can use `require('url').parse(request.url)`. Example:

```
node> require('url').parse('/status?name=ryan')
{ href: '/status?name=ryan',
  search: '?name=ryan',
  query: 'name=ryan',
  pathname: '/status' }
```

If you would like to extract the params from the query string, you can use the `require('querystring').parse` function, or pass **true** as the second argument to `require('url').parse`. Example:

```
node> require('url').parse('/status?name=ryan', true)
{ href: '/status?name=ryan',
  search: '?name=ryan',
  query: { name: 'ryan' },
  pathname: '/status' }
```

message.statusCode

Only valid for response obtained from `http.ClientRequest`.

The 3-digit HTTP response status code. E.G. 404.

message.statusMessage

Only valid for response obtained from `http.ClientRequest`.

The HTTP response status message (reason phrase). E.G. `OK` or `Internal Server Error`.

message.socket

The `net.Socket` object associated with the connection.

With HTTPS support, use request.socket.getPeerCertificate() to obtain the client's authentication details.

HTTPS

```
Stability: 2 - Stable
```

HTTPS is the HTTP protocol over TLS/SSL. In Node.js this is implemented as a separate module.

Class: https.Server

This class is a subclass of `tls.Server` and emits events same as `http.Server`. See `http.Server` for more information.

server.setTimeout(msecs, callback)

See http.Server#setTimeout().

server.timeout

See http.Server#timeout.

https.createServer(options[, requestListener])

Returns a new HTTPS web server object. The `options` is similar to tls.createServer(). The `requestListener` is a function which is automatically added to the `'request'` event.

Example:

```js
// curl -k https://localhost:8000/
var https = require('https');
var fs = require('fs');

var options = {
  key: fs.readFileSync('test/fixtures/keys/agent2-key.pem'),
  cert: fs.readFileSync('test/fixtures/keys/agent2-cert.pem')
};

https.createServer(options, function (req, res) {
  res.writeHead(200);
  res.end("hello world\n");
}).listen(8000);
```

Or

```js
var https = require('https');
var fs = require('fs');

var options = {
  pfx: fs.readFileSync('server.pfx')
};

https.createServer(options, function (req, res) {
  res.writeHead(200);
  res.end("hello world\n");
}).listen(8000);
```

server.listen(port[, host][, backlog][, callback])

server.listen(path[, callback])

server.listen(handle[, callback])

See http.listen() for details.

server.close([callback])

See http.close() for details.

https.request(options, callback)

Makes a request to a secure web server.

`options` can be an object or a string. If `options` is a string, it is automatically parsed with url.parse().

All options from http.request() are valid.

Example:

```
var https = require('https');

var options = {
  hostname: 'encrypted.google.com',
  port: 443,
  path: '/',
  method: 'GET'
};

var req = https.request(options, function(res) {
  console.log("statusCode: ", res.statusCode);
  console.log("headers: ", res.headers);

  res.on('data', function(d) {
    process.stdout.write(d);
  });
});
req.end();

req.on('error', function(e) {
  console.error(e);
});
```

The options argument has the following options

- `host`: A domain name or IP address of the server to issue the request to. Defaults to `'localhost'`.
- `hostname`: Alias for `host`. To support `url.parse()` `hostname` is preferred over `host`.
- `family`: IP address family to use when resolving `host` and `hostname`. Valid values are 4 or 6. When unspecified, both IP v4 and v6 will be used.
- `port`: Port of remote server. Defaults to 443.
- `localAddress`: Local interface to bind for network connections.
- `socketPath`: Unix Domain Socket (use one of host:port or socketPath).
- `method`: A string specifying the HTTP request method. Defaults to `'GET'`.
- `path`: Request path. Defaults to `'/'`. Should include query string if any. E.G. `'/index.html?page=12'`. An exception is thrown when the request path contains illegal characters. Currently, only spaces are rejected but that may change in the future.

- `headers`: An object containing request headers.
- `auth`: Basic authentication i.e. `'user:password'` to compute an Authorization header.
- `agent`: Controls Agent behavior. When an Agent is used request will default to `Connection: keep-alive`. Possible values:
- `undefined` (default): use globalAgent for this host and port.
- `Agent` object: explicitly use the passed in `Agent`.
- `false`: opts out of connection pooling with an Agent, defaults request to `Connection: close`.

The following options from tls.connect() can also be specified. However, a globalAgent silently ignores these.

- `pfx`: Certificate, Private key and CA certificates to use for SSL. Default `null`.
- `key`: Private key to use for SSL. Default `null`.
- `passphrase`: A string of passphrase for the private key or pfx. Default `null`.
- `cert`: Public x509 certificate to use. Default `null`.
- `ca`: An authority certificate or array of authority certificates to check the remote host against.
- `ciphers`: A string describing the ciphers to use or exclude. Consult `http://www.openssl.org/docs/apps/ciphers.html#CIPHER_LIST_FORMAT` for details on the format.
- `rejectUnauthorized`: If `true`, the server certificate is verified against the list of supplied CAs. An `'error'` event is emitted if verification fails. Verification happens at the connection level, *before* the HTTP request is sent. Default `true`.
- `secureProtocol`: The SSL method to use, e.g. `SSLv3_method` to force SSL version 3. The possible values depend on your installation of OpenSSL and are defined in the constant SSL_METHODS.

In order to specify these options, use a custom `Agent`.

Example:

```
var options = {
  hostname: 'encrypted.google.com',
  port: 443,
  path: '/',
  method: 'GET',
  key: fs.readFileSync('test/fixtures/keys/agent2-key.pem'),
  cert: fs.readFileSync('test/fixtures/keys/agent2-cert.pem')
};
options.agent = new https.Agent(options);

var req = https.request(options, function(res) {
  ...
}
```

Or does not use an `Agent`.

Example:

```
var options = {
  hostname: 'encrypted.google.com',
  port: 443,
  path: '/',
  method: 'GET',
  key: fs.readFileSync('test/fixtures/keys/agent2-key.pem'),
  cert: fs.readFileSync('test/fixtures/keys/agent2-cert.pem'),
  agent: false
};

var req = https.request(options, function(res) {
  ...
}
```

https.get(options, callback)

Like `http.get()` but for HTTPS.

`options` can be an object or a string. If `options` is a string, it is automatically parsed with url.parse().

Example:

```
var https = require('https');

https.get('https://encrypted.google.com/', function(res) {
  console.log("statusCode: ", res.statusCode);
  console.log("headers: ", res.headers);

  res.on('data', function(d) {
    process.stdout.write(d);
  });

}).on('error', function(e) {
  console.error(e);
});
```

Class: https.Agent

An Agent object for HTTPS similar to http.Agent. See https.request() for more information.

https.globalAgent

Global instance of https.Agent for all HTTPS client requests.

Modules

Stability: 3 - Locked

Node.js has a simple module loading system. In Node.js, files and modules are in one-to-one correspondence. As an example, `foo.js` loads the module `circle.js` in the same directory.

The contents of `foo.js`:

```
var circle = require('./circle.js');
console.log( 'The area of a circle of radius 4 is '
            + circle.area(4));
```

The contents of `circle.js`:

```
var PI = Math.PI;

exports.area = function (r) {
  return PI * r * r;
};

exports.circumference = function (r) {
  return 2 * PI * r;
};
```

The module `circle.js` has exported the functions `area()` and `circumference()`. To add functions and objects to the root of your module, you can add them to the special `exports` object.

Variables local to the module will be private, as though the module was wrapped in a function. In this example the variable `PI` is private to `circle.js`.

If you want the root of your module's export to be a function (such as a constructor) or if you want to export a complete object in one assignment instead of building it one property at a time, assign it to `module.exports` instead of `exports`.

Below, `bar.js` makes use of the `square` module, which exports a constructor:

```
var square = require('./square.js');
var mySquare = square(2);
console.log('The area of my square is ' + mySquare.area());
```

The `square` module is defined in `square.js`:

```
// assigning to exports will not modify module, must use module.exports
module.exports = function(width) {
  return {
    area: function() {
      return width * width;
    }
  };
}
```

The module system is implemented in the `require("module")` module.

Cycles

When there are circular `require()` calls, a module might not have finished executing when it is returned.

Consider this situation:

`a.js`:

```
console.log('a starting');
exports.done = false;
var b = require('./b.js');
console.log('in a, b.done = %j', b.done);
exports.done = true;
console.log('a done');
```

b.js:

```
console.log('b starting');
exports.done = false;
var a = require('./a.js');
console.log('in b, a.done = %j', a.done);
exports.done = true;
console.log('b done');
```

main.js:

```
console.log('main starting');
var a = require('./a.js');
var b = require('./b.js');
console.log('in main, a.done=%j, b.done=%j', a.done, b.done);
```

When main.js loads a.js, then a.js in turn loads b.js. At that point, b.js tries to load a.js. In order to prevent an infinite loop, an **unfinished copy** of the a.js exports object is returned to the b.js module. b.js then finishes loading, and its exports object is provided to the a.js module.

By the time main.js has loaded both modules, they're both finished. The output of this program would thus be:

```
$ node main.js
main starting
a starting
b starting
in b, a.done = false
b done
in a, b.done = true
a done
in main, a.done=true, b.done=true
```

If you have cyclic module dependencies in your program, make sure to plan accordingly.

Core Modules

Node.js has several modules compiled into the binary. These modules are described in greater detail elsewhere in this documentation.

The core modules are defined within Node.js's source and are located in the lib/ folder.

Core modules are always preferentially loaded if their identifier is passed to require(). For instance, require('http') will always return the built in HTTP module, even if there is a file by that name.

File Modules

If the exact filename is not found, then Node.js will attempt to load the required filename with the added extensions: .js, .json, and finally .node.

.js files are interpreted as JavaScript text files, and .json files are parsed as JSON text files. .node files are interpreted as compiled addon modules loaded with dlopen.

A required module prefixed with '/' is an absolute path to the file. For example, `require('/home/marco/foo.js')` will load the file at `/home/marco/foo.js`.

A required module prefixed with './' is relative to the file calling `require()`. That is, `circle.js` must be in the same directory as `foo.js` for `require('./circle')` to find it.

Without a leading '/', './', or '../' to indicate a file, the module must either be a core module or is loaded from a `node_modules` folder.

If the given path does not exist, `require()` will throw an Error with its `code` property set to `'MODULE_NOT_FOUND'`.

Loading from `node_modules` Folders

If the module identifier passed to `require()` is not a native module, and does not begin with '/', '../', or './', then Node.js starts at the parent directory of the current module, and adds `/node_modules`, and attempts to load the module from that location.

If it is not found there, then it moves to the parent directory, and so on, until the root of the file system is reached.

For example, if the file at '/home/ry/projects/foo.js' called `require('bar.js')`, then Node.js would look in the following locations, in this order:

- `/home/ry/projects/node_modules/bar.js`
- `/home/ry/node_modules/bar.js`
- `/home/node_modules/bar.js`
- `/node_modules/bar.js`

This allows programs to localize their dependencies, so that they do not clash.

You can require specific files or sub modules distributed with a module by including a path suffix after the module name. For instance `require('example-module/path/to/file')` would resolve `path/to/file` relative to where `example-module` is located. The suffixed path follows the same module resolution semantics.

Folders as Modules

It is convenient to organize programs and libraries into self-contained directories, and then provide a single entry point to that library. There are three ways in which a folder may be passed to `require()` as an argument.

The first is to create a `package.json` file in the root of the folder, which specifies a **main** module. An example package.json file might look like this:

```
{ "name" : "some-library",
  "main" : "./lib/some-library.js" }
```

If this was in a folder at ./some-library, then `require('./some-library')` would attempt to load `./some-library/lib/some-library.js`.

This is the extent of Node.js's awareness of package.json files.

If there is no package.json file present in the directory, then Node.js will attempt to load an `index.js` or `index.node` file out of that directory. For example, if there was no package.json file in the above example, then `require('./some-library')` would attempt to load:

- `./some-library/index.js`
- `./some-library/index.node`

Caching

Modules are cached after the first time they are loaded. This means (among other things) that every call to `require('foo')` will get exactly the same object returned, if it would resolve to the same file.

Multiple calls to `require('foo')` may not cause the module code to be executed multiple times. This is an important feature. With it, "partially done" objects can be returned, thus allowing transitive dependencies to be loaded even when they would cause cycles.

If you want to have a module execute code multiple times, then export a function, and call that function.

Module Caching Caveats

Modules are cached based on their resolved filename. Since modules may resolve to a different filename based on the location of the calling module (loading from `node_modules` folders), it is not a *guarantee* that `require('foo')` will always return the exact same object, if it would resolve to different files.

The `module` Object

- {Object}

In each module, the `module` free variable is a reference to the object representing the current module. For convenience, `module.exports` is also accessible via the `exports` module-global. `module` isn't actually a global but rather local to each module.

module.exports

- {Object}

The `module.exports` object is created by the Module system. Sometimes this is not acceptable; many want their module to be an instance of some class. To do this, assign the desired export object to `module.exports`. Note that assigning the desired object to `exports` will simply rebind the local `exports` variable, which is probably not what you want to do.

For example suppose we were making a module called `a.js`

```
var EventEmitter = require('events');

module.exports = new EventEmitter();

// Do some work, and after some time emit
// the 'ready' event from the module itself.
setTimeout(function() {
  module.exports.emit('ready');
}, 1000);
```

Then in another file we could do

```
var a = require('./a');
a.on('ready', function() {
  console.log('module a is ready');
});
```

Note that assignment to `module.exports` must be done immediately. It cannot be done in any callbacks. This does not work:

x.js:

```
setTimeout(function() {
  module.exports = { a: "hello" };
}, 0);
```

y.js:

```
var x = require('./x');
console.log(x.a);
```

exports alias   The `exports` variable that is available within a module starts as a reference to `module.exports`. As with any variable, if you assign a new value to it, it is no longer bound to the previous value.

To illustrate the behavior, imagine this hypothetical implementation of `require()`:

```
function require(...) {
  // ...
  function (module, exports) {
    // Your module code here
    exports = some_func;        // re-assigns exports, exports is no longer
                                // a shortcut, and nothing is exported.
    module.exports = some_func; // makes your module export 0
  } (module, module.exports);
  return module;
}
```

As a guideline, if the relationship between `exports` and `module.exports` seems like magic to you, ignore `exports` and only use `module.exports`.

module.require(id)

- id {String}
- Return: {Object} `module.exports` from the resolved module

The `module.require` method provides a way to load a module as if `require()` was called from the original module.

Note that in order to do this, you must get a reference to the `module` object. Since `require()` returns the `module.exports`, and the `module` is typically *only* available within a specific module's code, it must be explicitly exported in order to be used.

module.id

- {String}

The identifier for the module. Typically this is the fully resolved filename.

module.filename

- {String}

The fully resolved filename to the module.

module.loaded

- {Boolean}

Whether or not the module is done loading, or is in the process of loading.

module.parent

- {Module Object}

The module that first required this one.

module.children

- {Array}

The module objects required by this one.

All Together...

To get the exact filename that will be loaded when **require()** is called, use the **require.resolve()** function.

Putting together all of the above, here is the high-level algorithm in pseudocode of what require.resolve does:

```
require(X) from module at path Y
1. If X is a core module,
   a. return the core module
   b. STOP
2. If X begins with './' or '/' or '../'
   a. LOAD_AS_FILE(Y + X)
   b. LOAD_AS_DIRECTORY(Y + X)
3. LOAD_NODE_MODULES(X, dirname(Y))
4. THROW "not found"

LOAD_AS_FILE(X)
1. If X is a file, load X as JavaScript text.  STOP
2. If X.js is a file, load X.js as JavaScript text.  STOP
3. If X.json is a file, parse X.json to a JavaScript Object.  STOP
4. If X.node is a file, load X.node as binary addon.  STOP

LOAD_AS_DIRECTORY(X)
1. If X/package.json is a file,
   a. Parse X/package.json, and look for "main" field.
   b. let M = X + (json main field)
   c. LOAD_AS_FILE(M)
2. If X/index.js is a file, load X/index.js as JavaScript text.  STOP
3. If X/index.json is a file, parse X/index.json to a JavaScript object. STOP
4. If X/index.node is a file, load X/index.node as binary addon.  STOP

LOAD_NODE_MODULES(X, START)
1. let DIRS=NODE_MODULES_PATHS(START)
2. for each DIR in DIRS:
   a. LOAD_AS_FILE(DIR/X)
   b. LOAD_AS_DIRECTORY(DIR/X)

NODE_MODULES_PATHS(START)
1. let PARTS = path split(START)
2. let I = count of PARTS - 1
3. let DIRS = []
4. while I >= 0,
   a. if PARTS[I] = "node_modules" CONTINUE
   c. DIR = path join(PARTS[0 .. I] + "node_modules")
   b. DIRS = DIRS + DIR
```

```
     c. let I = I - 1
5. return DIRS
```

Loading from the global folders

If the NODE_PATH environment variable is set to a colon-delimited list of absolute paths, then Node.js will search those paths for modules if they are not found elsewhere. (Note: On Windows, NODE_PATH is delimited by semicolons instead of colons.)

NODE_PATH was originally created to support loading modules from varying paths before the current module resolution algorithm was frozen.

NODE_PATH is still supported, but is less necessary now that the Node.js ecosystem has settled on a convention for locating dependent modules. Sometimes deployments that rely on NODE_PATH show surprising behavior when people are unaware that NODE_PATH must be set. Sometimes a module's dependencies change, causing a different version (or even a different module) to be loaded as the NODE_PATH is searched.

Additionally, Node.js will search in the following locations:

- 1: $HOME/.node_modules
- 2: $HOME/.node_libraries
- 3: $PREFIX/lib/node

Where $HOME is the user's home directory, and $PREFIX is Node.js's configured node_prefix.

These are mostly for historic reasons. **You are highly encouraged to place your dependencies locally in node_modules folders.** They will be loaded faster, and more reliably.

Accessing the main module

When a file is run directly from Node.js, require.main is set to its module. That means that you can determine whether a file has been run directly by testing

```
require.main === module
```

For a file foo.js, this will be true if run via node foo.js, but false if run by require('./foo').

Because module provides a filename property (normally equivalent to __filename), the entry point of the current application can be obtained by checking require.main.filename.

Addenda: Package Manager Tips

The semantics of Node.js's require() function were designed to be general enough to support a number of sane directory structures. Package manager programs such as dpkg, rpm, and npm will hopefully find it possible to build native packages from Node.js modules without modification.

Below we give a suggested directory structure that could work:

Let's say that we wanted to have the folder at /usr/lib/node/<some-package>/<some-version> hold the contents of a specific version of a package.

Packages can depend on one another. In order to install package foo, you may have to install a specific version of package bar. The bar package may itself have dependencies, and in some cases, these dependencies may even collide or form cycles.

Since Node.js looks up the realpath of any modules it loads (that is, resolves symlinks), and then looks for their dependencies in the node_modules folders as described above, this situation is very simple to resolve with the following architecture:

- /usr/lib/node/foo/1.2.3/ - Contents of the foo package, version 1.2.3.

- `/usr/lib/node/bar/4.3.2/` - Contents of the `bar` package that `foo` depends on.
- `/usr/lib/node/foo/1.2.3/node_modules/bar` - Symbolic link to `/usr/lib/node/bar/4.3.2/`.
- `/usr/lib/node/bar/4.3.2/node_modules/*` - Symbolic links to the packages that `bar` depends on.

Thus, even if a cycle is encountered, or if there are dependency conflicts, every module will be able to get a version of its dependency that it can use.

When the code in the `foo` package does `require('bar')`, it will get the version that is symlinked into `/usr/lib/node/foo/1.2.3/node_modules/bar`. Then, when the code in the `bar` package calls `require('quux')`, it'll get the version that is symlinked into `/usr/lib/node/bar/4.3.2/node_modules/quux`.

Furthermore, to make the module lookup process even more optimal, rather than putting packages directly in `/usr/lib/node`, we could put them in `/usr/lib/node_modules/<name>/<version>`. Then Node.js will not bother looking for missing dependencies in `/usr/node_modules` or `/node_modules`.

In order to make modules available to the Node.js REPL, it might be useful to also add the `/usr/lib/node_modules` folder to the `$NODE_PATH` environment variable. Since the module lookups using `node_modules` folders are all relative, and based on the real path of the files making the calls to `require()`, the packages themselves can be anywhere.

net

Stability: 2 - Stable

The `net` module provides you with an asynchronous network wrapper. It contains functions for creating both servers and clients (called streams). You can include this module with `require('net');`.

net.createServer([options][, connectionListener])

Creates a new server. The `connectionListener` argument is automatically set as a listener for the 'connection' event.

`options` is an object with the following defaults:

```
{
  allowHalfOpen: false,
  pauseOnConnect: false
}
```

If `allowHalfOpen` is `true`, then the socket won't automatically send a FIN packet when the other end of the socket sends a FIN packet. The socket becomes non-readable, but still writable. You should call the `end()` method explicitly. See 'end' event for more information.

If `pauseOnConnect` is `true`, then the socket associated with each incoming connection will be paused, and no data will be read from its handle. This allows connections to be passed between processes without any data being read by the original process. To begin reading data from a paused socket, call `resume()`.

Here is an example of an echo server which listens for connections on port 8124:

```
var net = require('net');
var server = net.createServer(function(c) { //'connection' listener
  console.log('client connected');
  c.on('end', function() {
    console.log('client disconnected');
  });
  c.write('hello\r\n');
  c.pipe(c);
});
server.listen(8124, function() { //'listening' listener
  console.log('server bound');
});
```

Test this by using `telnet`:

```
telnet localhost 8124
```

To listen on the socket `/tmp/echo.sock` the third line from the last would just be changed to

```
server.listen('/tmp/echo.sock', function() { //'listening' listener
```

Use `nc` to connect to a UNIX domain socket server:

```
nc -U /tmp/echo.sock
```

net.connect(options[, connectListener])

net.createConnection(options[, connectListener])

A factory function, which returns a new 'net.Socket' and automatically connects with the supplied `options`.

The options are passed to both the 'net.Socket' constructor and the 'socket.connect' method.

The `connectListener` parameter will be added as a listener for the 'connect' event once.

Here is an example of a client of the previously described echo server:

```
var net = require('net');
var client = net.connect({port: 8124},
    function() { //'connect' listener
  console.log('connected to server!');
  client.write('world!\r\n');
});
client.on('data', function(data) {
  console.log(data.toString());
  client.end();
});
client.on('end', function() {
  console.log('disconnected from server');
});
```

To connect on the socket /tmp/echo.sock the second line would just be changed to

```
var client = net.connect({path: '/tmp/echo.sock'});
```

net.connect(port[, host][, connectListener])

net.createConnection(port[, host][, connectListener])

A factory function, which returns a new 'net.Socket' and automatically connects to the supplied `port` and `host`.

If `host` is omitted, `'localhost'` will be assumed.

The `connectListener` parameter will be added as a listener for the 'connect' event once.

net.connect(path[, connectListener])

net.createConnection(path[, connectListener])

A factory function, which returns a new unix 'net.Socket' and automatically connects to the supplied `path`.

The `connectListener` parameter will be added as a listener for the 'connect' event once.

Class: net.Server

This class is used to create a TCP or local server.

server.listen(port[, hostname][, backlog][, callback])

Begin accepting connections on the specified `port` and `hostname`. If the `hostname` is omitted, the server will accept connections on any IPv6 address (::) when IPv6 is available, or any IPv4 address (0.0.0.0) otherwise. A port value of zero will assign a random port.

Backlog is the maximum length of the queue of pending connections. The actual length will be determined by your OS through sysctl settings such as `tcp_max_syn_backlog` and `somaxconn` on linux. The default value of this parameter is 511 (not 512).

This function is asynchronous. When the server has been bound, 'listening' event will be emitted. The last parameter `callback` will be added as a listener for the 'listening' event.

One issue some users run into is getting `EADDRINUSE` errors. This means that another server is already running on the requested port. One way of handling this would be to wait a second and then try again. This can be done with

```
server.on('error', function (e) {
  if (e.code == 'EADDRINUSE') {
    console.log('Address in use, retrying...');
    setTimeout(function () {
      server.close();
      server.listen(PORT, HOST);
    }, 1000);
  }
});
```

(Note: All sockets in Node.js set `SO_REUSEADDR` already)

server.listen(path[, callback])

- `path` {String}
- `callback` {Function}

Start a local socket server listening for connections on the given `path`.

This function is asynchronous. When the server has been bound, 'listening' event will be emitted. The last parameter `callback` will be added as a listener for the 'listening' event.

On UNIX, the local domain is usually known as the UNIX domain. The path is a filesystem path name. It is subject to the same naming conventions and permissions checks as would be done on file creation, will be visible in the filesystem, and will *persist until unlinked*.

On Windows, the local domain is implemented using a named pipe. The path *must* refer to an entry in `\\?\pipe\` or `\\.\pipe\`. Any characters are permitted, but the latter may do some processing of pipe names, such as resolving `..` sequences. Despite appearances, the pipe name space is flat. Pipes will *not persist*, they are removed when the last reference to them is closed. Do not forget JavaScript string escaping requires paths to be specified with double-backslashes, such as:

```
net.createServer().listen(
    path.join('\\\\?\\pipe', process.cwd(), 'myctl'))
```

server.listen(handle[, callback])

- `handle` {Object}
- `callback` {Function}

The `handle` object can be set to either a server or socket (anything with an underlying `_handle` member), or a `{fd: <n>}` object.

This will cause the server to accept connections on the specified handle, but it is presumed that the file descriptor or handle has already been bound to a port or domain socket.

Listening on a file descriptor is not supported on Windows.

This function is asynchronous. When the server has been bound, 'listening' event will be emitted. The last parameter `callback` will be added as a listener for the 'listening' event.

server.listen(options[, callback])

- `options` {Object} - Required. Supports the following properties:
- `port` {Number} - Optional.
- `host` {String} - Optional.
- `backlog` {Number} - Optional.
- `path` {String} - Optional.
- `exclusive` {Boolean} - Optional.
- `callback` {Function} - Optional.

The `port`, `host`, and `backlog` properties of `options`, as well as the optional callback function, behave as they do on a call to server.listen(port, [host], [backlog], [callback]). Alternatively, the `path` option can be used to specify a UNIX socket.

If `exclusive` is `false` (default), then cluster workers will use the same underlying handle, allowing connection handling duties to be shared. When `exclusive` is `true`, the handle is not shared, and attempted port sharing results in an error. An example which listens on an exclusive port is shown below.

```
server.listen({
  host: 'localhost',
  port: 80,
  exclusive: true
});
```

server.close([callback])

Stops the server from accepting new connections and keeps existing connections. This function is asynchronous, the server is finally closed when all connections are ended and the server emits a 'close' event. The optional `callback` will be called once the `'close'` event occurs. Unlike that event, it will be called with an Error as its only argument if the server was not open when it was closed.

server.address()

Returns the bound address, the address family name and port of the server as reported by the operating system. Useful to find which port was assigned when giving getting an OS-assigned address. Returns an object with three properties, e.g. `{ port: 12346, family: 'IPv4', address: '127.0.0.1' }`

Example:

```
var server = net.createServer(function (socket) {
  socket.end("goodbye\n");
});

// grab a random port.
server.listen(function() {
  address = server.address();
  console.log("opened server on %j", address);
});
```

Don't call `server.address()` until the `'listening'` event has been emitted.

server.unref()

Calling `unref` on a server will allow the program to exit if this is the only active server in the event system. If the server is already `unref`d calling `unref` again will have no effect.

Returns `server`.

server.ref()

Opposite of `unref`, calling `ref` on a previously `unref`d server will *not* let the program exit if it's the only server left (the default behavior). If the server is `ref`d calling `ref` again will have no effect.

Returns `server`.

server.maxConnections

Set this property to reject connections when the server's connection count gets high.

It is not recommended to use this option once a socket has been sent to a child with `child_process.fork()`.

server.connections

Stability: 0 - Deprecated: Use [server.getConnections][] instead.

The number of concurrent connections on the server.

This becomes `null` when sending a socket to a child with `child_process.fork()`. To poll forks and get current number of active connections use asynchronous `server.getConnections` instead.

server.getConnections(callback)

Asynchronously get the number of concurrent connections on the server. Works when sockets were sent to forks.

Callback should take two arguments `err` and `count`.

`net.Server` is an EventEmitter with the following events:

Event: 'listening'

Emitted when the server has been bound after calling `server.listen`.

Event: 'connection'

- {Socket object} The connection object

Emitted when a new connection is made. `socket` is an instance of `net.Socket`.

Event: 'close'

Emitted when the server closes. Note that if connections exist, this event is not emitted until all connections are ended.

Event: 'error'

- {Error Object}

Emitted when an error occurs. The 'close' event will be called directly following this event. See example in discussion of `server.listen`.

Class: net.Socket

This object is an abstraction of a TCP or local socket. `net.Socket` instances implement a duplex Stream interface. They can be created by the user and used as a client (with `connect()`) or they can be created by Node.js and passed to the user through the `'connection'` event of a server.

new net.Socket([options])

Construct a new socket object.

`options` is an object with the following defaults:

```
{ fd: null,
  allowHalfOpen: false,
  readable: false,
  writable: false
}
```

`fd` allows you to specify the existing file descriptor of socket. Set `readable` and/or `writable` to `true` to allow reads and/or writes on this socket (NOTE: Works only when `fd` is passed). About `allowHalfOpen`, refer to `createServer()` and `'end'` event.

socket.connect(options[, connectListener])

Opens the connection for a given socket.

For TCP sockets, `options` argument should be an object which specifies:

- `port`: Port the client should connect to (Required).
- `host`: Host the client should connect to. Defaults to `'localhost'`.
- `localAddress`: Local interface to bind to for network connections.
- `localPort`: Local port to bind to for network connections.
- `family` : Version of IP stack. Defaults to 4.
- `lookup` : Custom lookup function. Defaults to `dns.lookup`.

For local domain sockets, `options` argument should be an object which specifies:

- `path`: Path the client should connect to (Required).

Normally this method is not needed, as `net.createConnection` opens the socket. Use this only if you are implementing a custom Socket.

This function is asynchronous. When the 'connect' event is emitted the socket is established. If there is a problem connecting, the `'connect'` event will not be emitted, the `'error'` event will be emitted with the exception.

The `connectListener` parameter will be added as a listener for the 'connect' event.

socket.connect(port[, host][, connectListener])

socket.connect(path[, connectListener])

As socket.connect(options[, connectListener]), with options either as either {port: port, host: host} or {path: path}.

socket.bufferSize

`net.Socket` has the property that `socket.write()` always works. This is to help users get up and running quickly. The computer cannot always keep up with the amount of data that is written to a socket - the network connection simply might be too slow. Node.js will internally queue up the data written to a socket and send it out over the wire when it is possible. (Internally it is polling on the socket's file descriptor for being writable).

The consequence of this internal buffering is that memory may grow. This property shows the number of characters currently buffered to be written. (Number of characters is approximately equal to the number of bytes to be written, but the buffer may contain strings, and the strings are lazily encoded, so the exact number of bytes is not known.)

Users who experience large or growing `bufferSize` should attempt to "throttle" the data flows in their program with `pause()` and `resume()`.

socket.setEncoding([encoding])

Set the encoding for the socket as a Readable Stream. See stream.setEncoding() for more information.

socket.write(data[, encoding][, callback])

Sends data on the socket. The second parameter specifies the encoding in the case of a string–it defaults to UTF8 encoding.

Returns `true` if the entire data was flushed successfully to the kernel buffer. Returns `false` if all or part of the data was queued in user memory. `'drain'` will be emitted when the buffer is again free.

The optional `callback` parameter will be executed when the data is finally written out - this may not be immediately.

socket.end([data][, encoding])

Half-closes the socket. i.e., it sends a FIN packet. It is possible the server will still send some data.

If `data` is specified, it is equivalent to calling `socket.write(data, encoding)` followed by `socket.end()`.

socket.destroy()

Ensures that no more I/O activity happens on this socket. Only necessary in case of errors (parse error or so).

socket.pause()

Pauses the reading of data. That is, `'data'` events will not be emitted. Useful to throttle back an upload.

socket.resume()

Resumes reading after a call to `pause()`.

socket.setTimeout(timeout[, callback])

Sets the socket to timeout after `timeout` milliseconds of inactivity on the socket. By default `net.Socket` do not have a timeout.

When an idle timeout is triggered the socket will receive a `'timeout'` event but the connection will not be severed. The user must manually `end()` or `destroy()` the socket.

If `timeout` is 0, then the existing idle timeout is disabled.

The optional `callback` parameter will be added as a one time listener for the `'timeout'` event.

Returns `socket`.

socket.setNoDelay([noDelay])

Disables the Nagle algorithm. By default TCP connections use the Nagle algorithm, they buffer data before sending it off. Setting `true` for `noDelay` will immediately fire off data each time `socket.write()` is called. `noDelay` defaults to `true`.

Returns `socket`.

socket.setKeepAlive([enable][, initialDelay])

Enable/disable keep-alive functionality, and optionally set the initial delay before the first keepalive probe is sent on an idle socket. `enable` defaults to `false`.

Set `initialDelay` (in milliseconds) to set the delay between the last data packet received and the first keepalive probe. Setting 0 for initialDelay will leave the value unchanged from the default (or previous) setting. Defaults to 0.

Returns `socket`.

socket.address()

Returns the bound address, the address family name and port of the socket as reported by the operating system. Returns an object with three properties, e.g. `{ port: 12346, family: 'IPv4', address: '127.0.0.1' }`

socket.unref()

Calling `unref` on a socket will allow the program to exit if this is the only active socket in the event system. If the socket is already `unref`d calling `unref` again will have no effect.

Returns `socket`.

socket.ref()

Opposite of `unref`, calling `ref` on a previously `unref`d socket will *not* let the program exit if it's the only socket left (the default behavior). If the socket is `ref`d calling `ref` again will have no effect.

Returns `socket`.

socket.remoteAddress

The string representation of the remote IP address. For example, `'74.125.127.100'` or `'2001:4860:a005::68'`.

socket.remoteFamily

The string representation of the remote IP family. 'IPv4' or 'IPv6'.

socket.remotePort

The numeric representation of the remote port. For example, 80 or 21.

socket.localAddress

The string representation of the local IP address the remote client is connecting on. For example, if you are listening on '0.0.0.0' and the client connects on '192.168.1.1', the value would be '192.168.1.1'.

socket.localPort

The numeric representation of the local port. For example, 80 or 21.

socket.bytesRead

The amount of received bytes.

socket.bytesWritten

The amount of bytes sent.

`net.Socket` instances are EventEmitter with the following events:

Event: 'lookup'

Emitted after resolving the hostname but before connecting. Not applicable to UNIX sockets.

- `err` {Error | Null} The error object. See dns.lookup().
- `address` {String} The IP address.
- `family` {String | Null} The address type. See dns.lookup().

Event: 'connect'

Emitted when a socket connection is successfully established. See `connect()`.

Event: 'data'

- {Buffer object}

Emitted when data is received. The argument `data` will be a `Buffer` or `String`. Encoding of data is set by `socket.setEncoding()`. (See the Readable Stream section for more information.)

Note that the **data will be lost** if there is no listener when a `Socket` emits a 'data' event.

Event: 'end'

Emitted when the other end of the socket sends a FIN packet.

By default (`allowHalfOpen == false`) the socket will destroy its file descriptor once it has written out its pending write queue. However, by setting `allowHalfOpen == true` the socket will not automatically `end()` its side allowing the user to write arbitrary amounts of data, with the caveat that the user is required to `end()` their side now.

Event: 'timeout'

Emitted if the socket times out from inactivity. This is only to notify that the socket has been idle. The user must manually close the connection.

See also: `socket.setTimeout()`

Event: 'drain'

Emitted when the write buffer becomes empty. Can be used to throttle uploads.

See also: the return values of `socket.write()`

Event: 'error'

- {Error object}

Emitted when an error occurs. The `'close'` event will be called directly following this event.

Event: 'close'

- `had_error` {Boolean} `true` if the socket had a transmission error.

Emitted once the socket is fully closed. The argument `had_error` is a boolean which says if the socket was closed due to a transmission error.

net.isIP(input)

Tests if input is an IP address. Returns 0 for invalid strings, returns 4 for IP version 4 addresses, and returns 6 for IP version 6 addresses.

net.isIPv4(input)

Returns true if input is a version 4 IP address, otherwise returns false.

net.isIPv6(input)

Returns true if input is a version 6 IP address, otherwise returns false.

OS

`Stability: 2 - Stable`

Provides a few basic operating-system related utility functions.

Use `require('os')` to access this module.

os.tmpdir()

Returns the operating system's default directory for temporary files.

os.homedir()

Returns the home directory of the current user.

os.endianness()

Returns the endianness of the CPU. Possible values are `'BE'` for big endian or `'LE'` for little endian.

os.hostname()

Returns the hostname of the operating system.

os.type()

Returns the operating system name. For example `'Linux'` on Linux, `'Darwin'` on OS X and `'Windows_NT'` on Windows.

os.platform()

Returns the operating system platform. Possible values are `'darwin'`, `'freebsd'`, `'linux'`, `'sunos'` or `'win32'`. Returns the value of `process.platform`.

os.arch()

Returns the operating system CPU architecture. Possible values are `'x64'`, `'arm'` and `'ia32'`. Returns the value of `process.arch`.

os.release()

Returns the operating system release.

os.uptime()

Returns the system uptime in seconds.

os.loadavg()

Returns an array containing the 1, 5, and 15 minute load averages.

The load average is a measure of system activity, calculated by the operating system and expressed as a fractional number. As a rule of thumb, the load average should ideally be less than the number of logical CPUs in the system.

The load average is a very UNIX-y concept; there is no real equivalent on Windows platforms. That is why this function always returns [0, 0, 0] on Windows.

os.totalmem()

Returns the total amount of system memory in bytes.

os.freemem()

Returns the amount of free system memory in bytes.

os.cpus()

Returns an array of objects containing information about each CPU/core installed: model, speed (in MHz), and times (an object containing the number of milliseconds the CPU/core spent in: user, nice, sys, idle, and irq).

Example inspection of os.cpus:

```
[ { model: 'Intel(R) Core(TM) i7 CPU         860  @ 2.80GHz',
    speed: 2926,
    times:
     { user: 252020,
       nice: 0,
       sys: 30340,
       idle: 1070356870,
       irq: 0 } },
  { model: 'Intel(R) Core(TM) i7 CPU         860  @ 2.80GHz',
    speed: 2926,
    times:
     { user: 306960,
       nice: 0,
       sys: 26980,
       idle: 1071569080,
       irq: 0 } },
  { model: 'Intel(R) Core(TM) i7 CPU         860  @ 2.80GHz',
    speed: 2926,
    times:
     { user: 248450,
       nice: 0,
       sys: 21750,
       idle: 1070919370,
       irq: 0 } },
  { model: 'Intel(R) Core(TM) i7 CPU         860  @ 2.80GHz',
    speed: 2926,
    times:
     { user: 256880,
       nice: 0,
```

```
      sys: 19430,
      idle: 1070905480,
      irq: 20 } },
  { model: 'Intel(R) Core(TM) i7 CPU        860  @ 2.80GHz',
    speed: 2926,
    times:
     { user: 511580,
       nice: 20,
       sys: 40900,
       idle: 1070842510,
       irq: 0 } },
  { model: 'Intel(R) Core(TM) i7 CPU        860  @ 2.80GHz',
    speed: 2926,
    times:
     { user: 291660,
       nice: 0,
       sys: 34360,
       idle: 1070888000,
       irq: 10 } },
  { model: 'Intel(R) Core(TM) i7 CPU        860  @ 2.80GHz',
    speed: 2926,
    times:
     { user: 308260,
       nice: 0,
       sys: 55410,
       idle: 1071129970,
       irq: 880 } },
  { model: 'Intel(R) Core(TM) i7 CPU        860  @ 2.80GHz',
    speed: 2926,
    times:
     { user: 266450,
       nice: 1480,
       sys: 34920,
       idle: 1072572010,
       irq: 30 } } ]
```

Note that since **nice** values are UNIX centric in Windows the **nice** values of all processors are always 0.

os.networkInterfaces()

Get a list of network interfaces:

```
{ lo:
   [ { address: '127.0.0.1',
       netmask: '255.0.0.0',
       family: 'IPv4',
       mac: '00:00:00:00:00:00',
       internal: true },
     { address: '::1',
       netmask: 'ffff:ffff:ffff:ffff:ffff:ffff:ffff:ffff',
       family: 'IPv6',
       mac: '00:00:00:00:00:00',
       internal: true } ],
  eth0:
   [ { address: '192.168.1.108',
       netmask: '255.255.255.0',
```

```
      family: 'IPv4',
      mac: '01:02:03:0a:0b:0c',
      internal: false },
    { address: 'fe80::a00:27ff:fe4e:66a1',
      netmask: 'ffff:ffff:ffff:ffff::',
      family: 'IPv6',
      mac: '01:02:03:0a:0b:0c',
      internal: false } ] }
```

Note that due to the underlying implementation this will only return network interfaces that have been assigned an address.

os.EOL

A constant defining the appropriate End-of-line marker for the operating system.

Path

Stability: 2 - Stable

This module contains utilities for handling and transforming file paths. Almost all these methods perform only string transformations. The file system is not consulted to check whether paths are valid.

Use `require('path')` to use this module. The following methods are provided:

path.normalize(p)

Normalize a string path, taking care of '..' and '.' parts.

When multiple slashes are found, they're replaced by a single one; when the path contains a trailing slash, it is preserved. On Windows backslashes are used.

Example:

```
path.normalize('/foo/bar//baz/asdf/quux/..')
// returns
'/foo/bar/baz/asdf'
```

Note: If the path string passed as argument is a zero-length string then '.' will be returned, which represents the current working directory.

path.join([path1][, path2][, ...])

Join all arguments together and normalize the resulting path.

Arguments must be strings. In v0.8, non-string arguments were silently ignored. In v0.10 and up, an exception is thrown.

Example:

```
path.join('/foo', 'bar', 'baz/asdf', 'quux', '..')
// returns
'/foo/bar/baz/asdf'
```

```
path.join('foo', {}, 'bar')
// throws exception
TypeError: Arguments to path.join must be strings
```

Note: If the arguments to `join` have zero-length strings, unlike other path module functions, they will be ignored. If the joined path string is a zero-length string then '.' will be returned, which represents the current working directory.

path.resolve([from ...], to)

Resolves `to` to an absolute path.

If `to` isn't already absolute `from` arguments are prepended in right to left order, until an absolute path is found. If after using all `from` paths still no absolute path is found, the current working directory is used as well. The resulting path is normalized, and trailing slashes are removed unless the path gets resolved to the root directory. Non-string `from` arguments are ignored.

Another way to think of it is as a sequence of `cd` commands in a shell.

```
path.resolve('foo/bar', '/tmp/file/', '..', 'a/../subfile')
```

Is similar to:

```
cd foo/bar
cd /tmp/file/
cd ..
cd a/../subfile
pwd
```

The difference is that the different paths don't need to exist and may also be files.

Examples:

```
path.resolve('/foo/bar', './baz')
// returns
'/foo/bar/baz'

path.resolve('/foo/bar', '/tmp/file/')
// returns
'/tmp/file'

path.resolve('wwwroot', 'static_files/png/', '../gif/image.gif')
// if currently in /home/myself/node, it returns
'/home/myself/node/wwwroot/static_files/gif/image.gif'
```

Note: If the arguments to `resolve` have zero-length strings then the current working directory will be used instead of them.

path.isAbsolute(path)

Determines whether `path` is an absolute path. An absolute path will always resolve to the same location, regardless of the working directory.

Posix examples:

```
path.isAbsolute('/foo/bar') // true
path.isAbsolute('/baz/..')  // true
path.isAbsolute('qux/')     // false
path.isAbsolute('.')        // false
```

Windows examples:

```
path.isAbsolute('//server')  // true
path.isAbsolute('C:/foo/..') // true
path.isAbsolute('bar\\baz')  // false
path.isAbsolute('.')         // false
```

Note: If the path string passed as parameter is a zero-length string, unlike other path module functions, it will be used as-is and `false` will be returned.

path.relative(from, to)

Solve the relative path from `from` to `to`.

At times we have two absolute paths, and we need to derive the relative path from one to the other. This is actually the reverse transform of `path.resolve`, which means we see that:

```
path.resolve(from, path.relative(from, to)) == path.resolve(to)
```

Examples:

```
path.relative('C:\\orandea\\test\\aaa', 'C:\\orandea\\impl\\bbb')
// returns
'..\\..\\impl\\bbb'
```

```
path.relative('/data/orandea/test/aaa', '/data/orandea/impl/bbb')
// returns
'../../impl/bbb'
```

Note: If the arguments to **relative** have zero-length strings then the current working directory will be used instead of the zero-length strings. If both the paths are the same then a zero-length string will be returned.

path.dirname(p)

Return the directory name of a path. Similar to the Unix **dirname** command.

Example:

```
path.dirname('/foo/bar/baz/asdf/quux')
// returns
'/foo/bar/baz/asdf'
```

path.basename(p[, ext])

Return the last portion of a path. Similar to the Unix **basename** command.

Example:

```
path.basename('/foo/bar/baz/asdf/quux.html')
// returns
'quux.html'
```

```
path.basename('/foo/bar/baz/asdf/quux.html', '.html')
// returns
'quux'
```

path.extname(p)

Return the extension of the path, from the last '.' to end of string in the last portion of the path. If there is no '.' in the last portion of the path or the first character of it is '.', then it returns an empty string. Examples:

```
path.extname('index.html')
// returns
'.html'
```

```
path.extname('index.coffee.md')
// returns
'.md'
```

```
path.extname('index.')
// returns
'.'
```

```
path.extname('index')
// returns
''
```

```
path.extname('.index')
// returns
''
```

path.sep

The platform-specific file separator. '\\' or '/'.

An example on *nix:

```
'foo/bar/baz'.split(path.sep)
// returns
['foo', 'bar', 'baz']
```

An example on Windows:

```
'foo\\bar\\baz'.split(path.sep)
// returns
['foo', 'bar', 'baz']
```

path.delimiter

The platform-specific path delimiter, ; or ':'.

An example on *nix:

```
console.log(process.env.PATH)
// '/usr/bin:/bin:/usr/sbin:/sbin:/usr/local/bin'

process.env.PATH.split(path.delimiter)
// returns
['/usr/bin', '/bin', '/usr/sbin', '/sbin', '/usr/local/bin']
```

An example on Windows:

```
console.log(process.env.PATH)
// 'C:\Windows\system32;C:\Windows;C:\Program Files\node\'

process.env.PATH.split(path.delimiter)
// returns
['C:\\Windows\\system32', 'C:\\Windows', 'C:\\Program Files\\node\\']
```

path.parse(pathString)

Returns an object from a path string.

An example on *nix:

```
path.parse('/home/user/dir/file.txt')
// returns
{
    root : "/",
    dir : "/home/user/dir",
    base : "file.txt",
    ext : ".txt",
    name : "file"
}
```

An example on Windows:

```
path.parse('C:\\path\\dir\\index.html')
// returns
{
    root : "C:\\",
    dir : "C:\\path\\dir",
    base : "index.html",
    ext : ".html",
    name : "index"
}
```

path.format(pathObject)

Returns a path string from an object, the opposite of `path.parse` above.

```
path.format({
    root : "/",
    dir : "/home/user/dir",
    base : "file.txt",
    ext : ".txt",
    name : "file"
})
// returns
'/home/user/dir/file.txt'
```

path.posix

Provide access to aforementioned `path` methods but always interact in a posix compatible way.

path.win32

Provide access to aforementioned `path` methods but always interact in a win32 compatible way.

process

The `process` object is a global object and can be accessed from anywhere. It is an instance of EventEmitter.

Exit Codes

Node.js will normally exit with a 0 status code when no more async operations are pending. The following status codes are used in other cases:

- **1 Uncaught Fatal Exception** - There was an uncaught exception, and it was not handled by a domain or an `uncaughtException` event handler.
- **2** - Unused (reserved by Bash for builtin misuse)
- **3 Internal JavaScript Parse Error** - The JavaScript source code internal in Node.js's bootstrapping process caused a parse error. This is extremely rare, and generally can only happen during development of Node.js itself.
- **4 Internal JavaScript Evaluation Failure** - The JavaScript source code internal in Node.js's bootstrapping process failed to return a function value when evaluated. This is extremely rare, and generally can only happen during development of Node.js itself.
- **5 Fatal Error** - There was a fatal unrecoverable error in V8. Typically a message will be printed to stderr with the prefix `FATAL ERROR`.
- **6 Non-function Internal Exception Handler** - There was an uncaught exception, but the internal fatal exception handler function was somehow set to a non-function, and could not be called.
- **7 Internal Exception Handler Run-Time Failure** - There was an uncaught exception, and the internal fatal exception handler function itself threw an error while attempting to handle it. This can happen, for example, if a `process.on('uncaughtException')` or `domain.on('error')` handler throws an error.
- **8** - Unused. In previous versions of Node.js, exit code 8 sometimes indicated an uncaught exception.
- **9 - Invalid Argument** - Either an unknown option was specified, or an option requiring a value was provided without a value.
- **10 Internal JavaScript Run-Time Failure** - The JavaScript source code internal in Node.js's bootstrapping process threw an error when the bootstrapping function was called. This is extremely rare, and generally can only happen during development of Node.js itself.
- **12 Invalid Debug Argument** - The `--debug` and/or `--debug-brk` options were set, but an invalid port number was chosen.
- **>128 Signal Exits** - If Node.js receives a fatal signal such as `SIGKILL` or `SIGHUP`, then its exit code will be `128` plus the value of the signal code. This is a standard Unix practice, since exit codes are defined to be 7-bit integers, and signal exits set the high-order bit, and then contain the value of the signal code.

Event: 'exit'

Emitted when the process is about to exit. There is no way to prevent the exiting of the event loop at this point, and once all **exit** listeners have finished running the process will exit. Therefore you **must** only perform **synchronous** operations in this handler. This is a good hook to perform checks on the module's state (like for unit tests). The callback takes one argument, the code the process is exiting with.

This event is only emitted when node exits explicitly by process.exit() or implicitly by the event loop draining.

Example of listening for `exit`:

```
process.on('exit', function(code) {
  // do *NOT* do this
  setTimeout(function() {
    console.log('This will not run');
  }, 0);
  console.log('About to exit with code:', code);
});
```

Event: 'message'

- `message` {Object} a parsed JSON object or primitive value
- `sendHandle` {Handle object} a net.Socket or net.Server object, or undefined.

Messages sent by ChildProcess.send() are obtained using the `'message'` event on the child's process object.

Event: 'beforeExit'

This event is emitted when Node.js empties its event loop and has nothing else to schedule. Normally, Node.js exits when there is no work scheduled, but a listener for 'beforeExit' can make asynchronous calls, and cause Node.js to continue.

'beforeExit' is not emitted for conditions causing explicit termination, such as `process.exit()` or uncaught exceptions, and should not be used as an alternative to the 'exit' event unless the intention is to schedule more work.

Event: 'uncaughtException'

Emitted when an exception bubbles all the way back to the event loop. If a listener is added for this exception, the default action (which is to print a stack trace and exit) will not occur.

Example of listening for uncaughtException:

```
process.on('uncaughtException', function(err) {
  console.log('Caught exception: ' + err);
});

setTimeout(function() {
  console.log('This will still run.');
}, 500);

// Intentionally cause an exception, but don't catch it.
nonexistentFunc();
console.log('This will not run.');
```

Note that uncaughtException is a very crude mechanism for exception handling.

Do *not* use it as the Node.js equivalent of `On Error Resume Next`. An unhandled exception means your application - and by extension Node.js itself - is in an undefined state. Blindly resuming means *anything* could happen.

Think of resuming as pulling the power cord when you are upgrading your system. Nine out of ten times nothing happens - but the 10th time, your system is bust.

uncaughtException should be used to perform synchronous cleanup before shutting down the process. It is not safe to resume normal operation after uncaughtException. If you do use it, restart your application after every unhandled exception!

You have been warned.

Event: 'unhandledRejection'

Emitted whenever a `Promise` is rejected and no error handler is attached to the promise within a turn of the event loop. When programming with promises exceptions are encapsulated as rejected promises. Such promises can be caught and handled using `promise.catch(...)` and rejections are propagated through a promise chain. This event is useful for detecting and keeping track of promises that were rejected whose rejections were not handled yet. This event is emitted with the following arguments:

- **reason** the object with which the promise was rejected (usually an **Error** instance).
- **p** the promise that was rejected.

Here is an example that logs every unhandled rejection to the console

```
process.on('unhandledRejection', function(reason, p) {
    console.log("Unhandled Rejection at: Promise ", p, " reason: ", reason);
    // application specific logging, throwing an error, or other logic here
});
```

For example, here is a rejection that will trigger the **'unhandledRejection'** event:

```
somePromise.then(function(res) {
  return reportToUser(JSON.pasre(res)); // note the typo
}); // no '.catch' or '.then'
```

Here is an example of a coding pattern that will also trigger **'unhandledRejection'**:

```
function SomeResource() {
  // Initially set the loaded status to a rejected promise
  this.loaded = Promise.reject(new Error('Resource not yet loaded!'));
}
```

```
var resource = new SomeResource();
// no .catch or .then on resource.loaded for at least a turn
```

In cases like this, you may not want to track the rejection as a developer error like you would for other **'unhandledRejection'** events. To address this, you can either attach a dummy **.catch(function() { })** handler to **resource.loaded**, preventing the **'unhandledRejection'** event from being emitted, or you can use the **'rejectionHandled'** event. Below is an explanation of how to do that.

Event: 'rejectionHandled'

Emitted whenever a Promise was rejected and an error handler was attached to it (for example with **.catch()**) later than after an event loop turn. This event is emitted with the following arguments:

- **p** the promise that was previously emitted in an **'unhandledRejection'** event, but which has now gained a rejection handler.

There is no notion of a top level for a promise chain at which rejections can always be handled. Being inherently asynchronous in nature, a promise rejection can be be handled at a future point in time — possibly much later than the event loop turn it takes for the **'unhandledRejection'** event to be emitted.

Another way of stating this is that, unlike in synchronous code where there is an ever-growing list of unhandled exceptions, with promises there is a growing-and-shrinking list of unhandled rejections. In synchronous code, the 'uncaughtException' event tells you when the list of unhandled exceptions grows. And in asynchronous code, the **'unhandledRejection'** event tells you when the list of unhandled rejections grows, while the 'rejectionHandled' event tells you when the list of unhandled rejections shrinks.

For example using the rejection detection hooks in order to keep a map of all the rejected promise reasons at a given time:

```
var unhandledRejections = new Map();
process.on('unhandledRejection', function(reason, p) {
  unhandledRejections.set(p, reason);
});
process.on('rejectionHandled', function(p) {
  unhandledRejections.delete(p);
});
```

This map will grow and shrink over time, reflecting rejections that start unhandled and then become handled. You could record the errors in some error log, either periodically (probably best for long-running programs, allowing you to clear the map, which in the case of a very buggy program could grow indefinitely) or upon process exit (more convenient for scripts).

Signal Events

Emitted when the processes receives a signal. See sigaction(2) for a list of standard POSIX signal names such as SIGINT, SIGHUP, etc.

Example of listening for `SIGINT`:

```
// Start reading from stdin so we don't exit.
process.stdin.resume();

process.on('SIGINT', function() {
  console.log('Got SIGINT.  Press Control-D to exit.');
});
```

An easy way to send the `SIGINT` signal is with `Control-C` in most terminal programs.

Note:

- `SIGUSR1` is reserved by Node.js to start the debugger. It's possible to install a listener but that won't stop the debugger from starting.
- `SIGTERM` and `SIGINT` have default handlers on non-Windows platforms that resets the terminal mode before exiting with code `128 + signal number`. If one of these signals has a listener installed, its default behavior will be removed (Node.js will no longer exit).
- `SIGPIPE` is ignored by default. It can have a listener installed.
- `SIGHUP` is generated on Windows when the console window is closed, and on other platforms under various similar conditions, see signal(7). It can have a listener installed, however Node.js will be unconditionally terminated by Windows about 10 seconds later. On non-Windows platforms, the default behavior of `SIGHUP` is to terminate Node.js, but once a listener has been installed its default behavior will be removed.
- `SIGTERM` is not supported on Windows, it can be listened on.
- `SIGINT` from the terminal is supported on all platforms, and can usually be generated with `CTRL+C` (though this may be configurable). It is not generated when terminal raw mode is enabled.
- `SIGBREAK` is delivered on Windows when `CTRL+BREAK` is pressed, on non-Windows platforms it can be listened on, but there is no way to send or generate it.
- `SIGWINCH` is delivered when the console has been resized. On Windows, this will only happen on write to the console when the cursor is being moved, or when a readable tty is used in raw mode.
- `SIGKILL` cannot have a listener installed, it will unconditionally terminate Node.js on all platforms.
- `SIGSTOP` cannot have a listener installed.

Note that Windows does not support sending Signals, but Node.js offers some emulation with `process.kill()`, and `child_process.kill()`. Sending signal 0 can be used to test for the existence of a process. Sending `SIGINT`, `SIGTERM`, and `SIGKILL` cause the unconditional termination of the target process.

process.stdout

A `Writable Stream` to `stdout` (on fd 1).

For example, a `console.log` equivalent could look like this:

```
console.log = function(msg) {
  process.stdout.write(msg + '\n');
};
```

`process.stderr` and `process.stdout` are unlike other streams in Node.js in that they cannot be closed (`end()` will throw), they never emit the `finish` event and that writes can block when output is redirected to a file (although disks are fast and operating systems normally employ write-back caching so it should be a very rare occurrence indeed.)

To check if Node.js is being run in a TTY context, read the isTTY property on process.stderr, process.stdout, or process.stdin:

```
$ node -p "Boolean(process.stdin.isTTY)"
true
$ echo "foo" | node -p "Boolean(process.stdin.isTTY)"
false

$ node -p "Boolean(process.stdout.isTTY)"
true
$ node -p "Boolean(process.stdout.isTTY)" | cat
false
```

See the tty docs for more information.

process.stderr

A writable stream to stderr (on fd 2).

process.stderr and process.stdout are unlike other streams in Node.js in that they cannot be closed (end() will throw), they never emit the finish event and that writes can block when output is redirected to a file (although disks are fast and operating systems normally employ write-back caching so it should be a very rare occurrence indeed.)

process.stdin

A Readable Stream for stdin (on fd 0).

Example of opening standard input and listening for both events:

```
process.stdin.setEncoding('utf8');

process.stdin.on('readable', function() {
  var chunk = process.stdin.read();
  if (chunk !== null) {
    process.stdout.write('data: ' + chunk);
  }
});

process.stdin.on('end', function() {
  process.stdout.write('end');
});
```

As a Stream, process.stdin can also be used in "old" mode that is compatible with scripts written for node.js prior to v0.10. For more information see Stream compatibility.

In "old" Streams mode the stdin stream is paused by default, so one must call process.stdin.resume() to read from it. Note also that calling process.stdin.resume() itself would switch stream to "old" mode.

If you are starting a new project you should prefer a more recent "new" Streams mode over "old" one.

process.argv

An array containing the command line arguments. The first element will be 'node', the second element will be the name of the JavaScript file. The next elements will be any additional command line arguments.

```
// print process.argv
process.argv.forEach(function(val, index, array) {
  console.log(index + ': ' + val);
});
```

This will generate:

```
$ node process-2.js one two=three four
0: node
1: /Users/mjr/work/node/process-2.js
2: one
3: two=three
4: four
```

process.execPath

This is the absolute pathname of the executable that started the process.

Example:

```
/usr/local/bin/node
```

process.execArgv

This is the set of Node.js-specific command line options from the executable that started the process. These options do not show up in `process.argv`, and do not include the Node.js executable, the name of the script, or any options following the script name. These options are useful in order to spawn child processes with the same execution environment as the parent.

Example:

```
$ node --harmony script.js --version
```

results in process.execArgv:

```
['--harmony']
```

and process.argv:

```
['/usr/local/bin/node', 'script.js', '--version']
```

process.abort()

This causes Node.js to emit an abort. This will cause Node.js to exit and generate a core file.

process.chdir(directory)

Changes the current working directory of the process or throws an exception if that fails.

```
console.log('Starting directory: ' + process.cwd());
try {
  process.chdir('/tmp');
  console.log('New directory: ' + process.cwd());
}
catch (err) {
  console.log('chdir: ' + err);
}
```

process.cwd()

Returns the current working directory of the process.

```
console.log('Current directory: ' + process.cwd());
```

process.env

An object containing the user environment. See environ(7).

An example of this object looks like:

```
{ TERM: 'xterm-256color',
  SHELL: '/usr/local/bin/bash',
  USER: 'maciej',
  PATH: '~/.bin/:/usr/bin:/bin:/usr/sbin:/sbin:/usr/local/bin',
  PWD: '/Users/maciej',
  EDITOR: 'vim',
  SHLVL: '1',
  HOME: '/Users/maciej',
  LOGNAME: 'maciej',
  _: '/usr/local/bin/node' }
```

You can write to this object, but changes won't be reflected outside of your process. That means that the following won't work:

```
$ node -e 'process.env.foo = "bar"' && echo $foo
```

But this will:

```
process.env.foo = 'bar';
console.log(process.env.foo);
```

process.exit([code])

Ends the process with the specified `code`. If omitted, exit uses the 'success' code 0.

To exit with a 'failure' code:

```
process.exit(1);
```

The shell that executed Node.js should see the exit code as 1.

process.exitCode

A number which will be the process exit code, when the process either exits gracefully, or is exited via `process.exit()` without specifying a code.

Specifying a code to `process.exit(code)` will override any previous setting of `process.exitCode`.

process.getgid()

Note: this function is only available on POSIX platforms (i.e. not Windows, Android)

Gets the group identity of the process. (See getgid(2).) This is the numerical group id, not the group name.

```
if (process.getgid) {
  console.log('Current gid: ' + process.getgid());
}
```

process.getegid()

Note: this function is only available on POSIX platforms (i.e. not Windows, Android)

Gets the effective group identity of the process. (See getegid(2).) This is the numerical group id, not the group name.

```
if (process.getegid) {
  console.log('Current gid: ' + process.getegid());
}
```

process.setgid(id)

Note: this function is only available on POSIX platforms (i.e. not Windows, Android)

Sets the group identity of the process. (See setgid(2).) This accepts either a numerical ID or a groupname string. If a groupname is specified, this method blocks while resolving it to a numerical ID.

```
if (process.getgid && process.setgid) {
  console.log('Current gid: ' + process.getgid());
  try {
    process.setgid(501);
    console.log('New gid: ' + process.getgid());
  }
  catch (err) {
    console.log('Failed to set gid: ' + err);
  }
}
```

process.setegid(id)

Note: this function is only available on POSIX platforms (i.e. not Windows, Android)

Sets the effective group identity of the process. (See setegid(2).) This accepts either a numerical ID or a groupname string. If a groupname is specified, this method blocks while resolving it to a numerical ID.

```
if (process.getegid && process.setegid) {
  console.log('Current gid: ' + process.getegid());
  try {
    process.setegid(501);
    console.log('New gid: ' + process.getegid());
  }
  catch (err) {
    console.log('Failed to set gid: ' + err);
  }
}
```

process.getuid()

Note: this function is only available on POSIX platforms (i.e. not Windows, Android)

Gets the user identity of the process. (See getuid(2).) This is the numerical userid, not the username.

```
if (process.getuid) {
  console.log('Current uid: ' + process.getuid());
}
```

process.geteuid()

Note: this function is only available on POSIX platforms (i.e. not Windows, Android)

Gets the effective user identity of the process. (See geteuid(2).) This is the numerical userid, not the username.

```
if (process.geteuid) {
  console.log('Current uid: ' + process.geteuid());
}
```

process.setuid(id)

Note: this function is only available on POSIX platforms (i.e. not Windows, Android)

Sets the user identity of the process. (See setuid(2).) This accepts either a numerical ID or a username string. If a username is specified, this method blocks while resolving it to a numerical ID.

```
if (process.getuid && process.setuid) {
  console.log('Current uid: ' + process.getuid());
  try {
    process.setuid(501);
    console.log('New uid: ' + process.getuid());
  }
  catch (err) {
    console.log('Failed to set uid: ' + err);
  }
}
```

process.seteuid(id)

Note: this function is only available on POSIX platforms (i.e. not Windows, Android)

Sets the effective user identity of the process. (See seteuid(2).) This accepts either a numerical ID or a username string. If a username is specified, this method blocks while resolving it to a numerical ID.

```
if (process.geteuid && process.seteuid) {
  console.log('Current uid: ' + process.geteuid());
  try {
    process.seteuid(501);
    console.log('New uid: ' + process.geteuid());
  }
  catch (err) {
    console.log('Failed to set uid: ' + err);
  }
}
```

process.getgroups()

Note: this function is only available on POSIX platforms (i.e. not Windows, Android)

Returns an array with the supplementary group IDs. POSIX leaves it unspecified if the effective group ID is included but Node.js ensures it always is.

process.setgroups(groups)

Note: this function is only available on POSIX platforms (i.e. not Windows, Android)

Sets the supplementary group IDs. This is a privileged operation, meaning you need to be root or have the CAP_SETGID capability.

The list can contain group IDs, group names or both.

process.initgroups(user, extra_group)

Note: this function is only available on POSIX platforms (i.e. not Windows, Android)

Reads /etc/group and initializes the group access list, using all groups of which the user is a member. This is a privileged operation, meaning you need to be root or have the CAP_SETGID capability.

user is a user name or user ID. extra_group is a group name or group ID.

Some care needs to be taken when dropping privileges. Example:

```
console.log(process.getgroups());        // [ 0 ]
process.initgroups('bnoordhuis', 1000);   // switch user
console.log(process.getgroups());        // [ 27, 30, 46, 1000, 0 ]
process.setgid(1000);                     // drop root gid
console.log(process.getgroups());        // [ 27, 30, 46, 1000 ]
```

process.version

A compiled-in property that exposes NODE_VERSION.

```
console.log('Version: ' + process.version);
```

process.versions

A property exposing version strings of Node.js and its dependencies.

```
console.log(process.versions);
```

Will print something like:

```
{ http_parser: '2.3.0',
  node: '1.1.1',
  v8: '4.1.0.14',
  uv: '1.3.0',
  zlib: '1.2.8',
  ares: '1.10.0-DEV',
  modules: '43',
  icu: '55.1',
  openssl: '1.0.1k' }
```

process.config

An Object containing the JavaScript representation of the configure options that were used to compile the current Node.js executable. This is the same as the "config.gypi" file that was produced when running the ./configure script.

An example of the possible output looks like:

```
{ target_defaults:
   { cflags: [],
     default_configuration: 'Release',
```

```
      defines: [],
      include_dirs: [],
      libraries: [] },
   variables:
    { host_arch: 'x64',
      node_install_npm: 'true',
      node_prefix: '',
      node_shared_cares: 'false',
      node_shared_http_parser: 'false',
      node_shared_libuv: 'false',
      node_shared_zlib: 'false',
      node_use_dtrace: 'false',
      node_use_openssl: 'true',
      node_shared_openssl: 'false',
      strict_aliasing: 'true',
      target_arch: 'x64',
      v8_use_snapshot: 'true' } }
```

process.release

An Object containing metadata related to the current release, including URLs for the source tarball and headers-only tarball.

`process.release` contains the following properties:

- **name**: a string with a value that will always be **"node"** for Node.js. For legacy io.js releases, this will be **"io.js"**.
- **sourceUrl**: a complete URL pointing to a *.tar.gz* file containing the source of the current release.
- **headersUrl**: a complete URL pointing to a *.tar.gz* file containing only the header files for the current release. This file is significantly smaller than the full source file and can be used for compiling add-ons against Node.js.
- **libUrl**: a complete URL pointing to an *node.lib* file matching the architecture and version of the current release. This file is used for compiling add-ons against Node.js. *This property is only present on Windows builds of Node.js and will be missing on all other platforms.*

e.g.

```
{ name: 'node',
  sourceUrl: 'https://nodejs.org/download/release/v4.0.0/node-v4.0.0.tar.gz',
  headersUrl: 'https://nodejs.org/download/release/v4.0.0/node-v4.0.0-headers.tar.gz',
  libUrl: 'https://nodejs.org/download/release/v4.0.0/win-x64/node.lib' }
```

In custom builds from non-release versions of the source tree, only the **name** property may be present. The additional properties should not be relied upon to exist.

process.kill(pid[, signal])

Send a signal to a process. **pid** is the process id and **signal** is the string describing the signal to send. Signal names are strings like 'SIGINT' or 'SIGHUP'. If omitted, the signal will be 'SIGTERM'. See Signal Events and kill(2) for more information.

Will throw an error if target does not exist, and as a special case, a signal of 0 can be used to test for the existence of a process.

Note that even though the name of this function is **process.kill**, it is really just a signal sender, like the **kill** system call. The signal sent may do something other than kill the target process.

Example of sending a signal to yourself:

```
process.on('SIGHUP', function() {
  console.log('Got SIGHUP signal.');
});

setTimeout(function() {
  console.log('Exiting.');
  process.exit(0);
}, 100);

process.kill(process.pid, 'SIGHUP');
```

Note: When SIGUSR1 is received by Node.js it starts the debugger, see Signal Events.

process.pid

The PID of the process.

```
console.log('This process is pid ' + process.pid);
```

process.title

Getter/setter to set what is displayed in 'ps'.

When used as a setter, the maximum length is platform-specific and probably short.

On Linux and OS X, it's limited to the size of the binary name plus the length of the command line arguments because it overwrites the argv memory.

v0.8 allowed for longer process title strings by also overwriting the environ memory but that was potentially insecure/confusing in some (rather obscure) cases.

process.arch

What processor architecture you're running on: 'arm', 'ia32', or 'x64'.

```
console.log('This processor architecture is ' + process.arch);
```

process.platform

What platform you're running on: 'darwin', 'freebsd', 'linux', 'sunos' or 'win32'

```
console.log('This platform is ' + process.platform);
```

process.memoryUsage()

Returns an object describing the memory usage of the Node.js process measured in bytes.

```
var util = require('util');

console.log(util.inspect(process.memoryUsage()));
```

This will generate:

```
{ rss: 4935680,
  heapTotal: 1826816,
  heapUsed: 650472 }
```

heapTotal and heapUsed refer to V8's memory usage.

process.nextTick(callback[, arg][, ...])

- callback {Function}

Once the current event loop turn runs to completion, call the callback function.

This is *not* a simple alias to setTimeout(fn, 0), it's much more efficient. It runs before any additional I/O events (including timers) fire in subsequent ticks of the event loop.

```
console.log('start');
process.nextTick(function() {
  console.log('nextTick callback');
});
console.log('scheduled');
// Output:
// start
// scheduled
// nextTick callback
```

This is important in developing APIs where you want to give the user the chance to assign event handlers after an object has been constructed, but before any I/O has occurred.

```
function MyThing(options) {
  this.setupOptions(options);

  process.nextTick(function() {
    this.startDoingStuff();
  }.bind(this));
}

var thing = new MyThing();
thing.getReadyForStuff();

// thing.startDoingStuff() gets called now, not before.
```

It is very important for APIs to be either 100% synchronous or 100% asynchronous. Consider this example:

```
// WARNING!  DO NOT USE!  BAD UNSAFE HAZARD!
function maybeSync(arg, cb) {
  if (arg) {
    cb();
    return;
  }

  fs.stat('file', cb);
}
```

This API is hazardous. If you do this:

```
maybeSync(true, function() {
  foo();
});
bar();
```

then it's not clear whether foo() or bar() will be called first.

This approach is much better:

```
function definitelyAsync(arg, cb) {
  if (arg) {
    process.nextTick(cb);
    return;
  }

  fs.stat('file', cb);
}
```

Note: the nextTick queue is completely drained on each pass of the event loop **before** additional I/O is processed. As a result, recursively setting nextTick callbacks will block any I/O from happening, just like a `while(true);` loop.

process.umask([mask])

Sets or reads the process's file mode creation mask. Child processes inherit the mask from the parent process. Returns the old mask if `mask` argument is given, otherwise returns the current mask.

```
var oldmask, newmask = 0022;

oldmask = process.umask(newmask);
console.log('Changed umask from: ' + oldmask.toString(8) +
            ' to ' + newmask.toString(8));
```

process.uptime()

Number of seconds Node.js has been running.

process.hrtime()

Returns the current high-resolution real time in a `[seconds, nanoseconds]` tuple Array. It is relative to an arbitrary time in the past. It is not related to the time of day and therefore not subject to clock drift. The primary use is for measuring performance between intervals.

You may pass in the result of a previous call to `process.hrtime()` to get a diff reading, useful for benchmarks and measuring intervals:

```
var time = process.hrtime();
// [ 1800216, 25 ]

setTimeout(function() {
  var diff = process.hrtime(time);
  // [ 1, 552 ]

  console.log('benchmark took %d nanoseconds', diff[0] * 1e9 + diff[1]);
  // benchmark took 1000000527 nanoseconds
}, 1000);
```

process.send(message[, sendHandle][, callback])

- message {Object}
- sendHandle {Handle object}

When Node.js is spawned with an IPC channel attached, it can send messages to its parent process using `process.send()`. Each will be received as a 'message' event on the parent's `ChildProcess` object.

If Node.js was not spawned with an IPC channel, `process.send()` will be undefined.

process.disconnect()

Close the IPC channel to the parent process, allowing this child to exit gracefully once there are no other connections keeping it alive.

Identical to the parent process's ChildProcess.disconnect().

If Node.js was not spawned with an IPC channel, `process.disconnect()` will be undefined.

process.connected

- {Boolean} Set to false after `process.disconnect()` is called

If `process.connected` is false, it is no longer possible to send messages.

process.mainModule

Alternate way to retrieve `require.main`. The difference is that if the main module changes at runtime, `require.main` might still refer to the original main module in modules that were required before the change occurred. Generally it's safe to assume that the two refer to the same module.

As with `require.main`, it will be `undefined` if there was no entry script.

punycode

`Stability: 2 - Stable`

Punycode.js is bundled with Node.js v0.6.2+. Use `require('punycode')` to access it. (To use it with other Node.js versions, use npm to install the `punycode` module first.)

punycode.decode(string)

Converts a Punycode string of ASCII-only symbols to a string of Unicode symbols.

```
// decode domain name parts
punycode.decode('maana-pta'); // 'maÃśana'
punycode.decode('--dqo34k'); // 'âŸČ-âŃŸ'
```

punycode.encode(string)

Converts a string of Unicode symbols to a Punycode string of ASCII-only symbols.

```
// encode domain name parts
punycode.encode('maÃśana'); // 'maana-pta'
punycode.encode('âŸČ-âŃŸ'); // '--dqo34k'
```

punycode.toUnicode(domain)

Converts a Punycode string representing a domain name to Unicode. Only the Punycoded parts of the domain name will be converted, i.e. it doesn't matter if you call it on a string that has already been converted to Unicode.

```
// decode domain names
punycode.toUnicode('xn--maana-pta.com'); // 'maÃśana.com'
punycode.toUnicode('xn----dqo34k.com'); // 'âŸČ-âŃŸ.com'
```

punycode.toASCII(domain)

Converts a Unicode string representing a domain name to Punycode. Only the non-ASCII parts of the domain name will be converted, i.e. it doesn't matter if you call it with a domain that's already in ASCII.

```
// encode domain names
punycode.toASCII('maÃśana.com'); // 'xn--maana-pta.com'
punycode.toASCII('âŸČ-âŃŸ.com'); // 'xn----dqo34k.com'
```

punycode.ucs2

punycode.ucs2.decode(string)

Creates an array containing the numeric code point values of each Unicode symbol in the string. While JavaScript uses UCS-2 internally, this function will convert a pair of surrogate halves (each of which UCS-2 exposes as separate characters) into a single code point, matching UTF-16.

```
punycode.ucs2.decode('abc'); // [0x61, 0x62, 0x63]
// surrogate pair for U+1D306 tetragram for centre:
punycode.ucs2.decode('\uD834\uDF06'); // [0x1D306]
```

punycode.ucs2.encode(codePoints)

Creates a string based on an array of numeric code point values.

```
punycode.ucs2.encode([0x61, 0x62, 0x63]); // 'abc'
punycode.ucs2.encode([0x1D306]); // '\uD834\uDF06'
```

punycode.version

A string representing the current Punycode.js version number.

Query String

Stability: 2 - Stable

This module provides utilities for dealing with query strings. It provides the following methods:

querystring.stringify(obj[, sep][, eq][, options])

Serialize an object to a query string. Optionally override the default separator ('&') and assignment ('=') characters.

Options object may contain encodeURIComponent property (querystring.escape by default), it can be used to encode string with non-utf8 encoding if necessary.

Example:

```
querystring.stringify({ foo: 'bar', baz: ['qux', 'quux'], corge: '' })
// returns
'foo=bar&baz=qux&baz=quux&corge='

querystring.stringify({foo: 'bar', baz: 'qux'}, ';', ':')
// returns
'foo:bar;baz:qux'


// Suppose gbkEncodeURIComponent function already exists,
// it can encode string with 'gbk' encoding
querystring.stringify({ w: 'äÿŋæŰĞ', foo: 'bar' }, null, null,
  { encodeURIComponent: gbkEncodeURIComponent })
// returns
'w=%D6%D0%CE%C4&foo=bar'
```

querystring.parse(str[, sep][, eq][, options])

Deserialize a query string to an object. Optionally override the default separator ('&') and assignment ('=') characters.

Options object may contain maxKeys property (equal to 1000 by default), it'll be used to limit processed keys. Set it to 0 to remove key count limitation.

Options object may contain decodeURIComponent property (querystring.unescape by default), it can be used to decode a non-utf8 encoding string if necessary.

Example:

```
querystring.parse('foo=bar&baz=qux&baz=quux&corge')
// returns
{ foo: 'bar', baz: ['qux', 'quux'], corge: '' }


// Suppose gbkDecodeURIComponent function already exists,
// it can decode 'gbk' encoding string
querystring.parse('w=%D6%D0%CE%C4&foo=bar', null, null,
  { decodeURIComponent: gbkDecodeURIComponent })
// returns
{ w: 'äÿŋæŰĞ', foo: 'bar' }
```

querystring.escape

The escape function used by `querystring.stringify`, provided so that it could be overridden if necessary.

querystring.unescape

The unescape function used by `querystring.parse`, provided so that it could be overridden if necessary.

It will try to use `decodeURIComponent` in the first place, but if that fails it falls back to a safer equivalent that doesn't throw on malformed URLs.

Readline

Stability: 2 - Stable

To use this module, do `require('readline')`. Readline allows reading of a stream (such as `process.stdin`) on a line-by-line basis.

Note that once you've invoked this module, your Node.js program will not terminate until you've closed the interface. Here's how to allow your program to gracefully exit:

```
var readline = require('readline');

var rl = readline.createInterface({
  input: process.stdin,
  output: process.stdout
});

rl.question("What do you think of Node.js? ", function(answer) {
  // TODO: Log the answer in a database
  console.log("Thank you for your valuable feedback:", answer);

  rl.close();
});
```

readline.createInterface(options)

Creates a readline `Interface` instance. Accepts an "options" Object that takes the following values:

- `input` - the readable stream to listen to (Required).

- `output` - the writable stream to write readline data to (Optional).

- `completer` - an optional function that is used for Tab autocompletion. See below for an example of using this.

- `terminal` - pass `true` if the `input` and `output` streams should be treated like a TTY, and have ANSI/VT100 escape codes written to it. Defaults to checking `isTTY` on the `output` stream upon instantiation.

- `historySize` - maximum number of history lines retained. Defaults to 30.

The `completer` function is given the current line entered by the user, and is supposed to return an Array with 2 entries:

1. An Array with matching entries for the completion.

2. The substring that was used for the matching.

Which ends up looking something like: `[[substr1, substr2, ...], originalsubstring]`.

Example:

```
function completer(line) {
  var completions = '.help .error .exit .quit .q'.split(' ')
  var hits = completions.filter(function(c) { return c.indexOf(line) == 0 })
  // show all completions if none found
  return [hits.length ? hits : completions, line]
}
```

Also `completer` can be run in async mode if it accepts two arguments:

```
function completer(linePartial, callback) {
  callback(null, [['123'], linePartial]);
}
```

createInterface is commonly used with process.stdin and process.stdout in order to accept user input:

```
var readline = require('readline');
var rl = readline.createInterface({
  input: process.stdin,
  output: process.stdout
});
```

Once you have a readline instance, you most commonly listen for the "line" event.

If terminal is true for this instance then the output stream will get the best compatibility if it defines an output.columns property, and fires a "resize" event on the output if/when the columns ever change (process.stdout does this automatically when it is a TTY).

Class: Interface

The class that represents a readline interface with an input and output stream.

rl.setPrompt(prompt)

Sets the prompt, for example when you run node on the command line, you see >, which is node.js's prompt.

rl.prompt([preserveCursor])

Readies readline for input from the user, putting the current setPrompt options on a new line, giving the user a new spot to write. Set preserveCursor to true to prevent the cursor placement being reset to 0.

This will also resume the input stream used with createInterface if it has been paused.

If output is set to null or undefined when calling createInterface, the prompt is not written.

rl.question(query, callback)

Prepends the prompt with query and invokes callback with the user's response. Displays the query to the user, and then invokes callback with the user's response after it has been typed.

This will also resume the input stream used with createInterface if it has been paused.

If output is set to null or undefined when calling createInterface, nothing is displayed.

Example usage:

```
interface.question('What is your favorite food?', function(answer) {
  console.log('Oh, so your favorite food is ' + answer);
});
```

rl.pause()

Pauses the readline input stream, allowing it to be resumed later if needed.

Note that this doesn't immediately pause the stream of events. Several events may be emitted after calling pause, including line.

rl.resume()

Resumes the readline **input** stream.

rl.close()

Closes the **Interface** instance, relinquishing control on the **input** and **output** streams. The "close" event will also be emitted.

rl.write(data[, key])

Writes **data** to **output** stream, unless **output** is set to **null** or **undefined** when calling **createInterface**. **key** is an object literal to represent a key sequence; available if the terminal is a TTY.

This will also resume the **input** stream if it has been paused.

Example:

```
rl.write('Delete me!');
// Simulate ctrl+u to delete the line written previously
rl.write(null, {ctrl: true, name: 'u'});
```

Events

Event: 'line'

```
function (line) {}
```

Emitted whenever the **input** stream receives a \n, usually received when the user hits enter, or return. This is a good hook to listen for user input.

Example of listening for **line**:

```
rl.on('line', function (cmd) {
  console.log('You just typed: '+cmd);
});
```

Event: 'pause'

```
function () {}
```

Emitted whenever the **input** stream is paused.

Also emitted whenever the **input** stream is not paused and receives the **SIGCONT** event. (See events **SIGTSTP** and **SIGCONT**)

Example of listening for **pause**:

```
rl.on('pause', function() {
  console.log('Readline paused.');
});
```

Event: 'resume'

```
function () {}
```

Emitted whenever the **input** stream is resumed.

Example of listening for **resume**:

```
rl.on('resume', function() {
  console.log('Readline resumed.');
});
```

Event: 'close'

```
function () {}
```

Emitted when `close()` is called.

Also emitted when the `input` stream receives its "end" event. The `Interface` instance should be considered "finished" once this is emitted. For example, when the `input` stream receives ^D, respectively known as EOT.

This event is also called if there is no `SIGINT` event listener present when the `input` stream receives a ^C, respectively known as `SIGINT`.

Event: 'SIGINT'

```
function () {}
```

Emitted whenever the `input` stream receives a ^C, respectively known as `SIGINT`. If there is no `SIGINT` event listener present when the `input` stream receives a `SIGINT`, `pause` will be triggered.

Example of listening for `SIGINT`:

```
rl.on('SIGINT', function() {
  rl.question('Are you sure you want to exit?', function(answer) {
    if (answer.match(/^y(es)?$/i)) rl.pause();
  });
});
```

Event: 'SIGTSTP'

```
function () {}
```

This does not work on Windows.

Emitted whenever the `input` stream receives a ^Z, respectively known as `SIGTSTP`. If there is no `SIGTSTP` event listener present when the `input` stream receives a `SIGTSTP`, the program will be sent to the background.

When the program is resumed with `fg`, the `pause` and `SIGCONT` events will be emitted. You can use either to resume the stream.

The `pause` and `SIGCONT` events will not be triggered if the stream was paused before the program was sent to the background.

Example of listening for `SIGTSTP`:

```
rl.on('SIGTSTP', function() {
  // This will override SIGTSTP and prevent the program from going to the
  // background.
  console.log('Caught SIGTSTP.');
});
```

Event: 'SIGCONT'

```
function () {}
```

This does not work on Windows.

Emitted whenever the `input` stream is sent to the background with ^Z, respectively known as `SIGTSTP`, and then continued with `fg(1)`. This event only emits if the stream was not paused before sending the program to the background.

Example of listening for `SIGCONT`:

```
rl.on('SIGCONT', function() {
  // 'prompt' will automatically resume the stream
  rl.prompt();
});
```

Example: Tiny CLI

Here's an example of how to use all these together to craft a tiny command line interface:

```
var readline = require('readline'),
    rl = readline.createInterface(process.stdin, process.stdout);

rl.setPrompt('OHAI> ');
rl.prompt();

rl.on('line', function(line) {
  switch(line.trim()) {
    case 'hello':
      console.log('world!');
      break;
    default:
      console.log('Say what? I might have heard '' + line.trim() + '''');
      break;
  }
  rl.prompt();
}).on('close', function() {
  console.log('Have a great day!');
  process.exit(0);
});
```

readline.cursorTo(stream, x, y)

Move cursor to the specified position in a given TTY stream.

readline.moveCursor(stream, dx, dy)

Move cursor relative to it's current position in a given TTY stream.

readline.clearLine(stream, dir)

Clears current line of given TTY stream in a specified direction. `dir` should have one of following values:

- `-1` - to the left from cursor
- `1` - to the right from cursor
- `0` - the entire line

readline.clearScreenDown(stream)

Clears the screen from the current position of the cursor down.

REPL

```
Stability: 2 - Stable
```

A Read-Eval-Print-Loop (REPL) is available both as a standalone program and easily includable in other programs. The REPL provides a way to interactively run JavaScript and see the results. It can be used for debugging, testing, or just trying things out.

By executing **node** without any arguments from the command-line you will be dropped into the REPL. It has simplistic emacs line-editing.

```
mjr:~$ node
Type '.help' for options.
> a = [ 1, 2, 3];
[ 1, 2, 3 ]
> a.forEach(function (v) {
...   console.log(v);
...   });
1
2
3
```

For advanced line-editors, start Node.js with the environmental variable `NODE_NO_READLINE=1`. This will start the main and debugger REPL in canonical terminal settings which will allow you to use with `rlwrap`.

For example, you could add this to your bashrc file:

```
alias node="env NODE_NO_READLINE=1 rlwrap node"
```

Persistent History

By default, the REPL will persist history between **node** REPL sessions by saving to a `.node_repl_history` file in the user's home directory. This can be disabled by setting the environment variable `NODE_REPL_HISTORY=""`.

NODE_REPL_HISTORY_FILE

```
Stability: 0 - Deprecated: Use 'NODE_REPL_HISTORY' instead.
```

Previously in Node.js/io.js v2.x, REPL history was controlled by using a `NODE_REPL_HISTORY_FILE` environment variable, and the history was saved in JSON format. This variable has now been deprecated, and your REPL history will automatically be converted to using plain text. The new file will be saved to either your home directory, or a directory defined by the `NODE_REPL_HISTORY` variable, as documented below.

Environment Variable Options

The built-in repl (invoked by running **node** or **node -i**) may be controlled via the following environment variables:

- `NODE_REPL_HISTORY` - When a valid path is given, persistent REPL history will be saved to the specified file rather than `.node_repl_history` in the user's home directory. Setting this value to "" will disable persistent REPL history.
- `NODE_REPL_HISTORY_SIZE` - defaults to 1000. Controls how many lines of history will be persisted if history is available. Must be a positive number.
- `NODE_REPL_MODE` - may be any of `sloppy`, `strict`, or `magic`. Defaults to `magic`, which will automatically run "strict mode only" statements in strict mode.

repl.start(options)

Returns and starts a `REPLServer` instance, that inherits from Readline Interface. Accepts an "options" Object that takes the following values:

- `prompt` - the prompt and `stream` for all I/O. Defaults to `>`.

- `input` - the readable stream to listen to. Defaults to `process.stdin`.

- `output` - the writable stream to write readline data to. Defaults to `process.stdout`.

- `terminal` - pass `true` if the `stream` should be treated like a TTY, and have ANSI/VT100 escape codes written to it. Defaults to checking `isTTY` on the `output` stream upon instantiation.

- `eval` - function that will be used to eval each given line. Defaults to an async wrapper for `eval()`. See below for an example of a custom `eval`.

- `useColors` - a boolean which specifies whether or not the `writer` function should output colors. If a different `writer` function is set then this does nothing. Defaults to the repl's `terminal` value.

- `useGlobal` - if set to `true`, then the repl will use the `global` object, instead of running scripts in a separate context. Defaults to `false`.

- `ignoreUndefined` - if set to `true`, then the repl will not output the return value of command if it's `undefined`. Defaults to `false`.

- `writer` - the function to invoke for each command that gets evaluated which returns the formatting (including coloring) to display. Defaults to `util.inspect`.

- `replMode` - controls whether the repl runs all commands in strict mode, default mode, or a hybrid mode ("magic" mode.) Acceptable values are:

- `repl.REPL_MODE_SLOPPY` - run commands in sloppy mode.

- `repl.REPL_MODE_STRICT` - run commands in strict mode. This is equivalent to prefacing every repl statement with `'use strict'`.

- `repl.REPL_MODE_MAGIC` - attempt to run commands in default mode. If they fail to parse, re-try in strict mode.

You can use your own `eval` function if it has following signature:

```
function eval(cmd, context, filename, callback) {
  callback(null, result);
}
```

On tab completion - `eval` will be called with `.scope` as an input string. It is expected to return an array of scope names to be used for the auto-completion.

Multiple REPLs may be started against the same running instance of Node.js. Each will share the same global object but will have unique I/O.

Here is an example that starts a REPL on stdin, a Unix socket, and a TCP socket:

```
var net = require('net'),
    repl = require('repl'),
    connections = 0;

repl.start({
  prompt: 'Node.js via stdin> ',
  input: process.stdin,
  output: process.stdout
});

net.createServer(function (socket) {
  connections += 1;
```

```
  repl.start({
    prompt: 'Node.js via Unix socket> ',
    input: socket,
    output: socket
  }).on('exit', function() {
    socket.end();
  })
}).listen('/tmp/node-repl-sock');

net.createServer(function (socket) {
  connections += 1;
  repl.start({
    prompt: 'Node.js via TCP socket> ',
    input: socket,
    output: socket
  }).on('exit', function() {
    socket.end();
  });
}).listen(5001);
```

Running this program from the command line will start a REPL on stdin. Other REPL clients may connect through the Unix socket or TCP socket. `telnet` is useful for connecting to TCP sockets, and `socat` can be used to connect to both Unix and TCP sockets.

By starting a REPL from a Unix socket-based server instead of stdin, you can connect to a long-running Node.js process without restarting it.

For an example of running a "full-featured" (`terminal`) REPL over a `net.Server` and `net.Socket` instance, see: https://gist.github.com/2209310

For an example of running a REPL instance over `curl(1)`, see: https://gist.github.com/2053342

Event: 'exit'

```
function () {}
```

Emitted when the user exits the REPL in any of the defined ways. Namely, typing `.exit` at the repl, pressing Ctrl+C twice to signal SIGINT, or pressing Ctrl+D to signal "end" on the `input` stream.

Example of listening for `exit`:

```
r.on('exit', function () {
  console.log('Got "exit" event from repl!');
  process.exit();
});
```

Event: 'reset'

```
function (context) {}
```

Emitted when the REPL's context is reset. This happens when you type `.clear`. If you start the repl with { `useGlobal:   true` } then this event will never be emitted.

Example of listening for `reset`:

```
// Extend the initial repl context.
var r = repl.start({ options ... });
someExtension.extend(r.context);
```

```
// When a new context is created extend it as well.
r.on('reset', function (context) {
  console.log('repl has a new context');
  someExtension.extend(context);
});
```

REPL Features

Inside the REPL, Control+D will exit. Multi-line expressions can be input. Tab completion is supported for both global and local variables.

Core modules will be loaded on-demand into the environment. For example, accessing **fs** will **require()** the **fs** module as **global.fs**.

The special variable **_** (underscore) contains the result of the last expression.

```
> [ 'a', 'b', 'c' ]
[ 'a', 'b', 'c' ]
> _.length
3
> _ += 1
4
```

The REPL provides access to any variables in the global scope. You can expose a variable to the REPL explicitly by assigning it to the **context** object associated with each **REPLServer**. For example:

```
// repl_test.js
var repl = require('repl'),
    msg = 'message';

repl.start('> ').context.m = msg;
```

Things in the **context** object appear as local within the REPL:

```
mjr:~$ node repl_test.js
> m
'message'
```

There are a few special REPL commands:

- **.break** - While inputting a multi-line expression, sometimes you get lost or just don't care about completing it. **.break** will start over.
- **.clear** - Resets the **context** object to an empty object and clears any multi-line expression.
- **.exit** - Close the I/O stream, which will cause the REPL to exit.
- **.help** - Show this list of special commands.
- **.save** - Save the current REPL session to a file >.save ./file/to/save.js
- **.load** - Load a file into the current REPL session. >.load ./file/to/load.js

The following key combinations in the REPL have these special effects:

- **<ctrl>C** - Similar to the **.break** keyword. Terminates the current command. Press twice on a blank line to forcibly exit.
- **<ctrl>D** - Similar to the **.exit** keyword.
- **<tab>** - Show both global and local(scope) variables

Customizing Object displays in the REPL

The REPL module internally uses util.inspect(), when printing values. However, **util.inspect** delegates the call to the object's **inspect()** function, if it has one. You can read more about this delegation here.

For example, if you have defined an **inspect()** function on an object, like this:

```
> var obj = { foo: 'this will not show up in the inspect() output' };
undefined
> obj.inspect = function() {
...    return { bar: 'baz' };
... };
[Function]
```

and try to print **obj** in REPL, it will invoke the custom **inspect()** function:

```
> obj
{ bar: 'baz' }
```

Smalloc

Stability: 1 - Experimental

Class: smalloc

Buffers are backed by a simple allocator that only handles the assignation of external raw memory. Smalloc exposes that functionality.

smalloc.alloc(length[, receiver][, type])

- `length` {Number} <= `smalloc.kMaxLength`
- `receiver` {Object} Default: `new Object`
- `type` {Enum} Default: `Uint8`

Returns `receiver` with allocated external array data. If no `receiver` is passed then a new Object will be created and returned.

This can be used to create your own Buffer-like classes. No other properties are set, so the user will need to keep track of other necessary information (e.g. `length` of the allocation).

```
function SimpleData(n) {
  this.length = n;
  smalloc.alloc(this.length, this);
}

SimpleData.prototype = { /* ... */ };
```

It only checks if the `receiver` is an Object, and also not an Array. Because of this it is possible to allocate external array data to more than a plain Object.

```
function allocMe() { }
smalloc.alloc(3, allocMe);

// { [Function allocMe] '0': 0, '1': 0, '2': 0 }
```

v8 does not support allocating external array data to an Array, and if passed will throw.

It's possible to specify the type of external array data you would like. All possible options are listed in `smalloc.Types`. Example usage:

```
var doubleArr = smalloc.alloc(3, smalloc.Types.Double);

for (var i = 0; i < 3; i++)
  doubleArr = i / 10;

// { '0': 0, '1': 0.1, '2': 0.2 }
```

It is not possible to freeze, seal and prevent extensions of objects with external data using `Object.freeze`, `Object.seal` and `Object.preventExtensions` respectively.

smalloc.copyOnto(source, sourceStart, dest, destStart, copyLength);

- `source` {Object} with external array allocation
- `sourceStart` {Number} Position to begin copying from
- `dest` {Object} with external array allocation
- `destStart` {Number} Position to begin copying onto

- copyLength {Number} Length of copy

Copy memory from one external array allocation to another. No arguments are optional, and any violation will throw.

```
var a = smalloc.alloc(4);
var b = smalloc.alloc(4);

for (var i = 0; i < 4; i++) {
  a[i] = i;
  b[i] = i * 2;
}

// { '0': 0, '1': 1, '2': 2, '3': 3 }
// { '0': 0, '1': 2, '2': 4, '3': 6 }

smalloc.copyOnto(b, 2, a, 0, 2);

// { '0': 4, '1': 6, '2': 2, '3': 3 }
```

copyOnto automatically detects the length of the allocation internally, so no need to set any additional properties for this to work.

smalloc.dispose(obj)

- obj Object

Free memory that has been allocated to an object via `smalloc.alloc`.

```
var a = {};
smalloc.alloc(3, a);

// { '0': 0, '1': 0, '2': 0 }

smalloc.dispose(a);

// {}
```

This is useful to reduce strain on the garbage collector, but developers must be careful. Cryptic errors may arise in applications that are difficult to trace.

```
var a = smalloc.alloc(4);
var b = smalloc.alloc(4);

// perform this somewhere along the line
smalloc.dispose(b);

// now trying to copy some data out
smalloc.copyOnto(b, 2, a, 0, 2);

// now results in:
// RangeError: copy_length > source_length
```

After `dispose()` is called object still behaves as one with external data, for example `smalloc.hasExternalData()` returns `true`. `dispose()` does not support Buffers, and will throw if passed.

smalloc.hasExternalData(obj)

- obj {Object}

Returns `true` if the `obj` has externally allocated memory.

smalloc.kMaxLength

Size of maximum allocation. This is also applicable to Buffer creation.

smalloc.Types

Enum of possible external array types. Contains:

- `Int8`
- `Uint8`
- `Int16`
- `Uint16`
- `Int32`
- `Uint32`
- `Float`
- `Double`
- `Uint8Clamped`

Stream

Stability: 2 - Stable

A stream is an abstract interface implemented by various objects in Node.js. For example a request to an HTTP server is a stream, as is stdout. Streams are readable, writable, or both. All streams are instances of EventEmitter

You can load the Stream base classes by doing `require('stream')`. There are base classes provided for Readable streams, Writable streams, Duplex streams, and Transform streams.

This document is split up into 3 sections. The first explains the parts of the API that you need to be aware of to use streams in your programs. If you never implement a streaming API yourself, you can stop there.

The second section explains the parts of the API that you need to use if you implement your own custom streams yourself. The API is designed to make this easy for you to do.

The third section goes into more depth about how streams work, including some of the internal mechanisms and functions that you should probably not modify unless you definitely know what you are doing.

API for Stream Consumers

Streams can be either Readable, Writable, or both (Duplex).

All streams are EventEmitters, but they also have other custom methods and properties depending on whether they are Readable, Writable, or Duplex.

If a stream is both Readable and Writable, then it implements all of the methods and events below. So, a Duplex or Transform stream is fully described by this API, though their implementation may be somewhat different.

It is not necessary to implement Stream interfaces in order to consume streams in your programs. If you **are** implementing streaming interfaces in your own program, please also refer to API for Stream Implementors below.

Almost all Node.js programs, no matter how simple, use Streams in some way. Here is an example of using Streams in an Node.js program:

```
var http = require('http');

var server = http.createServer(function (req, res) {
  // req is an http.IncomingMessage, which is a Readable Stream
  // res is an http.ServerResponse, which is a Writable Stream

  var body = '';
  // we want to get the data as utf8 strings
  // If you don't set an encoding, then you'll get Buffer objects
  req.setEncoding('utf8');

  // Readable streams emit 'data' events once a listener is added
  req.on('data', function (chunk) {
    body += chunk;
  });

  // the end event tells you that you have entire body
  req.on('end', function () {
    try {
      var data = JSON.parse(body);
    } catch (er) {
      // uh oh!  bad json!
```

```
        res.statusCode = 400;
        return res.end('error: ' + er.message);
    }

    // write back something interesting to the user:
    res.write(typeof data);
    res.end();
  });
});

server.listen(1337);

// $ curl localhost:1337 -d '{}'
// object
// $ curl localhost:1337 -d '"foo"'
// string
// $ curl localhost:1337 -d 'not json'
// error: Unexpected token o
```

Class: stream.Readable

The Readable stream interface is the abstraction for a *source* of data that you are reading from. In other words, data comes *out* of a Readable stream.

A Readable stream will not start emitting data until you indicate that you are ready to receive it.

Readable streams have two "modes": a **flowing mode** and a **paused mode**. When in flowing mode, data is read from the underlying system and provided to your program as fast as possible. In paused mode, you must explicitly call **stream.read()** to get chunks of data out. Streams start out in paused mode.

Note: If no data event handlers are attached, and there are no **pipe()** destinations, and the stream is switched into flowing mode, then data will be lost.

You can switch to flowing mode by doing any of the following:

- Adding a **'data'** event handler to listen for data.
- Calling the **resume()** method to explicitly open the flow.
- Calling the **pipe()** method to send the data to a Writable.

You can switch back to paused mode by doing either of the following:

- If there are no pipe destinations, by calling the **pause()** method.
- If there are pipe destinations, by removing any **'data'** event handlers, and removing all pipe destinations by calling the **unpipe()** method.

Note that, for backwards compatibility reasons, removing **'data'** event handlers will **not** automatically pause the stream. Also, if there are piped destinations, then calling **pause()** will not guarantee that the stream will *remain* paused once those destinations drain and ask for more data.

Examples of readable streams include:

- http responses, on the client
- http requests, on the server
- fs read streams
- zlib streams
- crypto streams
- tcp sockets
- child process stdout and stderr
- process.stdin

Event: 'readable'   When a chunk of data can be read from the stream, it will emit a `'readable'` event.

In some cases, listening for a `'readable'` event will cause some data to be read into the internal buffer from the underlying system, if it hadn't already.

```
var readable = getReadableStreamSomehow();
readable.on('readable', function() {
  // there is some data to read now
});
```

Once the internal buffer is drained, a `readable` event will fire again when more data is available.

The `readable` event is not emitted in the "flowing" mode with the sole exception of the last one, on end-of-stream.

The 'readable' event indicates that the stream has new information: either new data is available or the end of the stream has been reached. In the former case, `.read()` will return that data. In the latter case, `.read()` will return null. For instance, in the following example, `foo.txt` is an empty file:

```
var fs = require('fs');
var rr = fs.createReadStream('foo.txt');
rr.on('readable', function() {
  console.log('readable:', rr.read());
});
rr.on('end', function() {
  console.log('end');
});
```

The output of running this script is:

```
bash-3.2$ node test.js
readable: null
end
```

Event: 'data'

- chunk {Buffer | String} The chunk of data.

Attaching a `data` event listener to a stream that has not been explicitly paused will switch the stream into flowing mode. Data will then be passed as soon as it is available.

If you just want to get all the data out of the stream as fast as possible, this is the best way to do so.

```
var readable = getReadableStreamSomehow();
readable.on('data', function(chunk) {
  console.log('got %d bytes of data', chunk.length);
});
```

Event: 'end'   This event fires when there will be no more data to read.

Note that the `end` event **will not fire** unless the data is completely consumed. This can be done by switching into flowing mode, or by calling `read()` repeatedly until you get to the end.

```
var readable = getReadableStreamSomehow();
readable.on('data', function(chunk) {
  console.log('got %d bytes of data', chunk.length);
});
readable.on('end', function() {
  console.log('there will be no more data.');
});
```

Event: 'close'   Emitted when the stream and any of its underlying resources (a file descriptor, for example) have been closed. The event indicates that no more events will be emitted, and no further computation will occur.

Not all streams will emit the 'close' event.

Event: 'error'

- {Error Object}

Emitted if there was an error receiving data.

readable.read([size])

- `size` {Number} Optional argument to specify how much data to read.
- Return {String | Buffer | null}

The `read()` method pulls some data out of the internal buffer and returns it. If there is no data available, then it will return `null`.

If you pass in a `size` argument, then it will return that many bytes. If `size` bytes are not available, then it will return `null`, unless we've ended, in which case it will return the data remaining in the buffer.

If you do not specify a `size` argument, then it will return all the data in the internal buffer.

This method should only be called in paused mode. In flowing mode, this method is called automatically until the internal buffer is drained.

```
var readable = getReadableStreamSomehow();
readable.on('readable', function() {
  var chunk;
  while (null !== (chunk = readable.read())) {
    console.log('got %d bytes of data', chunk.length);
  }
});
```

If this method returns a data chunk, then it will also trigger the emission of a `'data'` event.

Note that calling `readable.read([size])` after the `end` event has been triggered will return `null`. No runtime error will be raised.

readable.setEncoding(encoding)

- `encoding` {String} The encoding to use.
- Return: `this`

Call this function to cause the stream to return strings of the specified encoding instead of Buffer objects. For example, if you do `readable.setEncoding('utf8')`, then the output data will be interpreted as UTF-8 data, and returned as strings. If you do `readable.setEncoding('hex')`, then the data will be encoded in hexadecimal string format.

This properly handles multi-byte characters that would otherwise be potentially mangled if you simply pulled the Buffers directly and called `buf.toString(encoding)` on them. If you want to read the data as strings, always use this method.

```
var readable = getReadableStreamSomehow();
readable.setEncoding('utf8');
readable.on('data', function(chunk) {
  assert.equal(typeof chunk, 'string');
  console.log('got %d characters of string data', chunk.length);
});
```

readable.resume()

- Return: `this`

This method will cause the readable stream to resume emitting `data` events.

This method will switch the stream into flowing mode. If you do *not* want to consume the data from a stream, but you *do* want to get to its `end` event, you can call `readable.resume()` to open the flow of data.

```
var readable = getReadableStreamSomehow();
readable.resume();
readable.on('end', function() {
  console.log('got to the end, but did not read anything');
});
```

readable.pause()

- Return: `this`

This method will cause a stream in flowing mode to stop emitting `data` events, switching out of flowing mode. Any data that becomes available will remain in the internal buffer.

```
var readable = getReadableStreamSomehow();
readable.on('data', function(chunk) {
  console.log('got %d bytes of data', chunk.length);
  readable.pause();
  console.log('there will be no more data for 1 second');
  setTimeout(function() {
    console.log('now data will start flowing again');
    readable.resume();
  }, 1000);
});
```

readable.isPaused()

- Return: `Boolean`

This method returns whether or not the `readable` has been **explicitly** paused by client code (using `readable.pause()` without a corresponding `readable.resume()`).

```
var readable = new stream.Readable

readable.isPaused() // === false
readable.pause()
readable.isPaused() // === true
readable.resume()
readable.isPaused() // === false
```

readable.pipe(destination[, options])

- `destination` {Writable Stream} The destination for writing data
- `options` {Object} Pipe options
- `end` {Boolean} End the writer when the reader ends. Default = `true`

This method pulls all the data out of a readable stream, and writes it to the supplied destination, automatically managing the flow so that the destination is not overwhelmed by a fast readable stream.

Multiple destinations can be piped to safely.

```
var readable = getReadableStreamSomehow();
var writable = fs.createWriteStream('file.txt');
// All the data from readable goes into 'file.txt'
readable.pipe(writable);
```

This function returns the destination stream, so you can set up pipe chains like so:

```
var r = fs.createReadStream('file.txt');
var z = zlib.createGzip();
var w = fs.createWriteStream('file.txt.gz');
r.pipe(z).pipe(w);
```

For example, emulating the Unix `cat` command:

```
process.stdin.pipe(process.stdout);
```

By default `end()` is called on the destination when the source stream emits `end`, so that `destination` is no longer writable. Pass `{ end:  false }` as `options` to keep the destination stream open.

This keeps `writer` open so that "Goodbye" can be written at the end.

```
reader.pipe(writer, { end: false });
reader.on('end', function() {
  writer.end('Goodbye\n');
});
```

Note that `process.stderr` and `process.stdout` are never closed until the process exits, regardless of the specified options.

readable.unpipe([destination])

- `destination` {Writable Stream} Optional specific stream to unpipe

This method will remove the hooks set up for a previous `pipe()` call.

If the destination is not specified, then all pipes are removed.

If the destination is specified, but no pipe is set up for it, then this is a no-op.

```
var readable = getReadableStreamSomehow();
var writable = fs.createWriteStream('file.txt');
// All the data from readable goes into 'file.txt',
// but only for the first second
readable.pipe(writable);
setTimeout(function() {
  console.log('stop writing to file.txt');
  readable.unpipe(writable);
  console.log('manually close the file stream');
  writable.end();
}, 1000);
```

readable.unshift(chunk)

- `chunk` {Buffer | String} Chunk of data to unshift onto the read queue

This is useful in certain cases where a stream is being consumed by a parser, which needs to "un-consume" some data that it has optimistically pulled out of the source, so that the stream can be passed on to some other party.

Note that `stream.unshift(chunk)` cannot be called after the `end` event has been triggered; a runtime error will be raised.

If you find that you must often call `stream.unshift(chunk)` in your programs, consider implementing a Transform stream instead. (See API for Stream Implementors, below.)

```
// Pull off a header delimited by \n\n
// use unshift() if we get too much
// Call the callback with (error, header, stream)
var StringDecoder = require('string_decoder').StringDecoder;
function parseHeader(stream, callback) {
  stream.on('error', callback);
  stream.on('readable', onReadable);
  var decoder = new StringDecoder('utf8');
  var header = '';
  function onReadable() {
    var chunk;
    while (null !== (chunk = stream.read())) {
      var str = decoder.write(chunk);
      if (str.match(/\n\n/)) {
        // found the header boundary
        var split = str.split(/\n\n/);
        header += split.shift();
        var remaining = split.join('\n\n');
        var buf = new Buffer(remaining, 'utf8');
        if (buf.length)
          stream.unshift(buf);
        stream.removeListener('error', callback);
        stream.removeListener('readable', onReadable);
        // now the body of the message can be read from the stream.
        callback(null, header, stream);
      } else {
        // still reading the header.
        header += str;
      }
    }
  }
}
```

Note that, unlike `stream.push(chunk)`, `stream.unshift(chunk)` will not end the reading process by resetting the internal reading state of the stream. This can cause unexpected results if `unshift` is called during a read (i.e. from within a `_read` implementation on a custom stream). Following the call to `unshift` with an immediate `stream.push(")` will reset the reading state appropriately, however it is best to simply avoid calling `unshift` while in the process of performing a read.

readable.wrap(stream)

- `stream` {Stream} An "old style" readable stream

Versions of Node.js prior to v0.10 had streams that did not implement the entire Streams API as it is today. (See "Compatibility" below for more information.)

If you are using an older Node.js library that emits `'data'` events and has a `pause()` method that is advisory only, then you can use the `wrap()` method to create a Readable stream that uses the old stream as its data source.

You will very rarely ever need to call this function, but it exists as a convenience for interacting with old Node.js programs and libraries.

For example:

```
var OldReader = require('./old-api-module.js').OldReader;
var oreader = new OldReader;
var Readable = require('stream').Readable;
var myReader = new Readable().wrap(oreader);

myReader.on('readable', function() {
  myReader.read(); // etc.
});
```

Class: stream.Writable

The Writable stream interface is an abstraction for a *destination* that you are writing data *to*.

Examples of writable streams include:

- http requests, on the client
- http responses, on the server
- fs write streams
- zlib streams
- crypto streams
- tcp sockets
- child process stdin
- process.stdout, process.stderr

writable.write(chunk[, encoding][, callback])

- chunk {String | Buffer} The data to write
- encoding {String} The encoding, if chunk is a String
- callback {Function} Callback for when this chunk of data is flushed
- Returns: {Boolean} True if the data was handled completely.

This method writes some data to the underlying system, and calls the supplied callback once the data has been fully handled.

The return value indicates if you should continue writing right now. If the data had to be buffered internally, then it will return false. Otherwise, it will return true.

This return value is strictly advisory. You MAY continue to write, even if it returns false. However, writes will be buffered in memory, so it is best not to do this excessively. Instead, wait for the drain event before writing more data.

Event: 'drain'
If a writable.write(chunk) call returns false, then the drain event will indicate when it is appropriate to begin writing more data to the stream.

```
// Write the data to the supplied writable stream one million times.
// Be attentive to back-pressure.
function writeOneMillionTimes(writer, data, encoding, callback) {
  var i = 1000000;
  write();
  function write() {
    var ok = true;
    do {
      i -= 1;
      if (i === 0) {
        // last time!
        writer.write(data, encoding, callback);
```

```
      } else {
        // see if we should continue, or wait
        // don't pass the callback, because we're not done yet.
        ok = writer.write(data, encoding);
      }
    } while (i > 0 && ok);
    if (i > 0) {
      // had to stop early!
      // write some more once it drains
      writer.once('drain', write);
    }
  }
}
```

writable.cork()   Forces buffering of all writes.

Buffered data will be flushed either at .uncork() or at .end() call.

writable.uncork()   Flush all data, buffered since .cork() call.

writable.setDefaultEncoding(encoding)

- encoding {String} The new default encoding

Sets the default encoding for a writable stream.

writable.end([chunk][, encoding][, callback])

- chunk {String | Buffer} Optional data to write
- encoding {String} The encoding, if chunk is a String
- callback {Function} Optional callback for when the stream is finished

Call this method when no more data will be written to the stream. If supplied, the callback is attached as a listener on the **finish** event.

Calling write() after calling end() will raise an error.

```
// write 'hello, ' and then end with 'world!'
var file = fs.createWriteStream('example.txt');
file.write('hello, ');
file.end('world!');
// writing more now is not allowed!
```

Event: 'finish'   When the end() method has been called, and all data has been flushed to the underlying system, this event is emitted.

```
var writer = getWritableStreamSomehow();
for (var i = 0; i < 100; i ++) {
  writer.write('hello, #' + i + '!\n');
}
writer.end('this is the end\n');
writer.on('finish', function() {
  console.error('all writes are now complete.');
});
```

Event: 'pipe'

- `src` {Readable Stream} source stream that is piping to this writable

This is emitted whenever the `pipe()` method is called on a readable stream, adding this writable to its set of destinations.

```
var writer = getWritableStreamSomehow();
var reader = getReadableStreamSomehow();
writer.on('pipe', function(src) {
  console.error('something is piping into the writer');
  assert.equal(src, reader);
});
reader.pipe(writer);
```

Event: 'unpipe'

- `src` {Readable Stream} The source stream that unpiped this writable

This is emitted whenever the `unpipe()` method is called on a readable stream, removing this writable from its set of destinations.

```
var writer = getWritableStreamSomehow();
var reader = getReadableStreamSomehow();
writer.on('unpipe', function(src) {
  console.error('something has stopped piping into the writer');
  assert.equal(src, reader);
});
reader.pipe(writer);
reader.unpipe(writer);
```

Event: 'error'

- {Error object}

Emitted if there was an error when writing or piping data.

Class: stream.Duplex

Duplex streams are streams that implement both the Readable and Writable interfaces. See above for usage.

Examples of Duplex streams include:

- tcp sockets
- zlib streams
- crypto streams

Class: stream.Transform

Transform streams are Duplex streams where the output is in some way computed from the input. They implement both the Readable and Writable interfaces. See above for usage.

Examples of Transform streams include:

- zlib streams
- crypto streams

API for Stream Implementors

To implement any sort of stream, the pattern is the same:

1. Extend the appropriate parent class in your own subclass. (The `util.inherits` method is particularly helpful for this.)
2. Call the appropriate parent class constructor in your constructor, to be sure that the internal mechanisms are set up properly.
3. Implement one or more specific methods, as detailed below.

The class to extend and the method(s) to implement depend on the sort of stream class you are writing:

Use-case

Class

Method(s) to implement

Reading only

Readable

_read

Writing only

Writable

_write, _writev

Reading and writing

Duplex

_read, _write, _writev

Operate on written data, then read the result

Transform

transform, flush

In your implementation code, it is very important to never call the methods described in API for Stream Consumers above. Otherwise, you can potentially cause adverse side effects in programs that consume your streaming interfaces.

Class: stream.Readable

`stream.Readable` is an abstract class designed to be extended with an underlying implementation of the `_read(size)` method.

Please see above under API for Stream Consumers for how to consume streams in your programs. What follows is an explanation of how to implement Readable streams in your programs.

Example: A Counting Stream This is a basic example of a Readable stream. It emits the numerals from 1 to 1,000,000 in ascending order, and then ends.

```
var Readable = require('stream').Readable;
var util = require('util');
util.inherits(Counter, Readable);

function Counter(opt) {
  Readable.call(this, opt);
  this._max = 1000000;
  this._index = 1;
```

```
}

Counter.prototype._read = function() {
  var i = this._index++;
  if (i > this._max)
    this.push(null);
  else {
    var str = '' + i;
    var buf = new Buffer(str, 'ascii');
    this.push(buf);
  }
};
```

Example: SimpleProtocol v1 (Sub-optimal)   This is similar to the `parseHeader` function described above, but implemented as a custom stream. Also, note that this implementation does not convert the incoming data to a string.

However, this would be better implemented as a Transform stream. See below for a better implementation.

```
// A parser for a simple data protocol.
// The "header" is a JSON object, followed by 2 \n characters, and
// then a message body.
//
// NOTE: This can be done more simply as a Transform stream!
// Using Readable directly for this is sub-optimal.  See the
// alternative example below under the Transform section.

var Readable = require('stream').Readable;
var util = require('util');

util.inherits(SimpleProtocol, Readable);

function SimpleProtocol(source, options) {
  if (!(this instanceof SimpleProtocol))
    return new SimpleProtocol(source, options);

  Readable.call(this, options);
  this._inBody = false;
  this._sawFirstCr = false;

  // source is a readable stream, such as a socket or file
  this._source = source;

  var self = this;
  source.on('end', function() {
    self.push(null);
  });

  // give it a kick whenever the source is readable
  // read(0) will not consume any bytes
  source.on('readable', function() {
    self.read(0);
  });

  this._rawHeader = [];
  this.header = null;
```

```
}

SimpleProtocol.prototype._read = function(n) {
  if (!this._inBody) {
    var chunk = this._source.read();

    // if the source doesn't have data, we don't have data yet.
    if (chunk === null)
      return this.push('');

    // check if the chunk has a \n\n
    var split = -1;
    for (var i = 0; i < chunk.length; i++) {
      if (chunk[i] === 10) { // '\n'
        if (this._sawFirstCr) {
          split = i;
          break;
        } else {
          this._sawFirstCr = true;
        }
      } else {
        this._sawFirstCr = false;
      }
    }

    if (split === -1) {
      // still waiting for the \n\n
      // stash the chunk, and try again.
      this._rawHeader.push(chunk);
      this.push('');
    } else {
      this._inBody = true;
      var h = chunk.slice(0, split);
      this._rawHeader.push(h);
      var header = Buffer.concat(this._rawHeader).toString();
      try {
        this.header = JSON.parse(header);
      } catch (er) {
        this.emit('error', new Error('invalid simple protocol data'));
        return;
      }
      // now, because we got some extra data, unshift the rest
      // back into the read queue so that our consumer will see it.
      var b = chunk.slice(split);
      this.unshift(b);
      // calling unshift by itself does not reset the reading state
      // of the stream; since we're inside _read, doing an additional
      // push('') will reset the state appropriately.
      this.push('');

      // and let them know that we are done parsing the header.
      this.emit('header', this.header);
    }
  } else {
    // from there on, just provide the data to our consumer.
    // careful not to push(null), since that would indicate EOF.
```

```
      var chunk = this._source.read();
      if (chunk) this.push(chunk);
  }
};

// Usage:
// var parser = new SimpleProtocol(source);
// Now parser is a readable stream that will emit 'header'
// with the parsed header data.
```

new stream.Readable([options])

- `options` {Object}
- `highWaterMark` {Number} The maximum number of bytes to store in the internal buffer before ceasing to read from the underlying resource. Default=16kb, or 16 for `objectMode` streams
- `encoding` {String} If specified, then buffers will be decoded to strings using the specified encoding. Default=null
- `objectMode` {Boolean} Whether this stream should behave as a stream of objects. Meaning that stream.read(n) returns a single value instead of a Buffer of size n. Default=false

In classes that extend the Readable class, make sure to call the Readable constructor so that the buffering settings can be properly initialized.

readable._read(size)

- `size` {Number} Number of bytes to read asynchronously

Note: **Implement this method, but do NOT call it directly.**

This method is prefixed with an underscore because it is internal to the class that defines it and should only be called by the internal Readable class methods. All Readable stream implementations must provide a _read method to fetch data from the underlying resource.

When *read is called, if data is available from the resource, **_read** should start pushing that data into the read queue by calling **this.push(dataChunk)**. _read should continue reading from the resource and pushing data until push returns false, at which point it should stop reading from the resource. Only when* read is called again after it has stopped should it start reading more data from the resource and pushing that data onto the queue.

Note: once the `_read()` method is called, it will not be called again until the **push** method is called.

The `size` argument is advisory. Implementations where a "read" is a single call that returns data can use this to know how much data to fetch. Implementations where that is not relevant, such as TCP or TLS, may ignore this argument, and simply provide data whenever it becomes available. There is no need, for example to "wait" until `size` bytes are available before calling `stream.push(chunk)`.

readable.push(chunk[, encoding])

- `chunk` {Buffer | null | String} Chunk of data to push into the read queue
- `encoding` {String} Encoding of String chunks. Must be a valid Buffer encoding, such as `'utf8'` or `'ascii'`
- `return` {Boolean} Whether or not more pushes should be performed

Note: **This method should be called by Readable implementors, NOT by consumers of Readable streams.**

If a value other than null is passed, The **push()** method adds a chunk of data into the queue for subsequent stream processors to consume. If **null** is passed, it signals the end of the stream (EOF), after which no more data can be written.

The data added with **push** can be pulled out by calling the **read()** method when the `'readable'` event fires.

This API is designed to be as flexible as possible. For example, you may be wrapping a lower-level source which has some sort of pause/resume mechanism, and a data callback. In those cases, you could wrap the low-level source object by doing something like this:

```
// source is an object with readStop() and readStart() methods,
// and an 'ondata' member that gets called when it has data, and
// an 'onend' member that gets called when the data is over.

util.inherits(SourceWrapper, Readable);

function SourceWrapper(options) {
  Readable.call(this, options);

  this._source = getLowlevelSourceObject();
  var self = this;

  // Every time there's data, we push it into the internal buffer.
  this._source.ondata = function(chunk) {
    // if push() returns false, then we need to stop reading from source
    if (!self.push(chunk))
      self._source.readStop();
  };

  // When the source ends, we push the EOF-signaling 'null' chunk
  this._source.onend = function() {
    self.push(null);
  };
}

// _read will be called when the stream wants to pull more data in
// the advisory size argument is ignored in this case.
SourceWrapper.prototype._read = function(size) {
  this._source.readStart();
};
```

Class: stream.Writable

`stream.Writable` is an abstract class designed to be extended with an underlying implementation of the `_write(chunk, encoding, callback)` method.

Please see above under API for Stream Consumers for how to consume writable streams in your programs. What follows is an explanation of how to implement Writable streams in your programs.

new stream.Writable([options])

- options {Object}
- highWaterMark {Number} Buffer level when write() starts returning false. Default=16kb, or 16 for objectMode streams
- decodeStrings {Boolean} Whether or not to decode strings into Buffers before passing them to _write(). Default=true
- objectMode {Boolean} Whether or not the write(anyObj) is a valid operation. If set you can write arbitrary data instead of only Buffer / String data. Default=false

In classes that extend the Writable class, make sure to call the constructor so that the buffering settings can be properly initialized.

writable._write(chunk, encoding, callback)

- chunk {Buffer | String} The chunk to be written. Will **always** be a buffer unless the `decodeStrings` option was set to `false`.
- encoding {String} If the chunk is a string, then this is the encoding type. If chunk is a buffer, then this is the special value - 'buffer', ignore it in this case.
- callback {Function} Call this function (optionally with an error argument) when you are done processing the supplied chunk.

All Writable stream implementations must provide a `_write()` method to send data to the underlying resource.

Note: **This function MUST NOT be called directly.** It should be implemented by child classes, and called by the internal Writable class methods only.

Call the callback using the standard `callback(error)` pattern to signal that the write completed successfully or with an error.

If the `decodeStrings` flag is set in the constructor options, then `chunk` may be a string rather than a Buffer, and `encoding` will indicate the sort of string that it is. This is to support implementations that have an optimized handling for certain string data encodings. If you do not explicitly set the `decodeStrings` option to `false`, then you can safely ignore the `encoding` argument, and assume that `chunk` will always be a Buffer.

This method is prefixed with an underscore because it is internal to the class that defines it, and should not be called directly by user programs. However, you **are** expected to override this method in your own extension classes.

writable._writev(chunks, callback)

- chunks {Array} The chunks to be written. Each chunk has following format: `{ chunk: ..., encoding: ... }`.
- callback {Function} Call this function (optionally with an error argument) when you are done processing the supplied chunks.

Note: **This function MUST NOT be called directly.** It may be implemented by child classes, and called by the internal Writable class methods only.

This function is completely optional to implement. In most cases it is unnecessary. If implemented, it will be called with all the chunks that are buffered in the write queue.

Class: stream.Duplex

A "duplex" stream is one that is both Readable and Writable, such as a TCP socket connection.

Note that `stream.Duplex` is an abstract class designed to be extended with an underlying implementation of the `_read(size)` and `_write(chunk, encoding, callback)` methods as you would with a Readable or Writable stream class.

Since JavaScript doesn't have multiple prototypal inheritance, this class prototypally inherits from Readable, and then parasitically from Writable. It is thus up to the user to implement both the lowlevel `_read(n)` method as well as the lowlevel `_write(chunk, encoding, callback)` method on extension duplex classes.

new stream.Duplex(options)

- options {Object} Passed to both Writable and Readable constructors. Also has the following fields:
- allowHalfOpen {Boolean} Default=true. If set to `false`, then the stream will automatically end the readable side when the writable side ends and vice versa.
- readableObjectMode {Boolean} Default=false. Sets `objectMode` for readable side of the stream. Has no effect if `objectMode` is true.
- writableObjectMode {Boolean} Default=false. Sets `objectMode` for writable side of the stream. Has no effect if `objectMode` is true.

In classes that extend the Duplex class, make sure to call the constructor so that the buffering settings can be properly initialized.

Class: stream.Transform

A "transform" stream is a duplex stream where the output is causally connected in some way to the input, such as a zlib stream or a crypto stream.

There is no requirement that the output be the same size as the input, the same number of chunks, or arrive at the same time. For example, a Hash stream will only ever have a single chunk of output which is provided when the input is ended. A zlib stream will produce output that is either much smaller or much larger than its input.

Rather than implement the `_read()` and `_write()` methods, Transform classes must implement the `_transform()` method, and may optionally also implement the `_flush()` method. (See below.)

new stream.Transform([options])

- `options` {Object} Passed to both Writable and Readable constructors.

In classes that extend the Transform class, make sure to call the constructor so that the buffering settings can be properly initialized.

transform._transform(chunk, encoding, callback)

- `chunk` {Buffer | String} The chunk to be transformed. Will **always** be a buffer unless the `decodeStrings` option was set to `false`.
- `encoding` {String} If the chunk is a string, then this is the encoding type. If chunk is a buffer, then this is the special value - 'buffer', ignore it in this case.
- `callback` {Function} Call this function (optionally with an error argument and data) when you are done processing the supplied chunk.

Note: **This function MUST NOT be called directly.** It should be implemented by child classes, and called by the internal Transform class methods only.

All Transform stream implementations must provide a `_transform` method to accept input and produce output.

`_transform` should do whatever has to be done in this specific Transform class, to handle the bytes being written, and pass them off to the readable portion of the interface. Do asynchronous I/O, process things, and so on.

Call `transform.push(outputChunk)` 0 or more times to generate output from this input chunk, depending on how much data you want to output as a result of this chunk.

Call the callback function only when the current chunk is completely consumed. Note that there may or may not be output as a result of any particular input chunk. If you supply a second argument to the callback it will be passed to the push method. In other words the following are equivalent:

```
transform.prototype._transform = function (data, encoding, callback) {
  this.push(data);
  callback();
};
```

```
transform.prototype._transform = function (data, encoding, callback) {
  callback(null, data);
};
```

This method is prefixed with an underscore because it is internal to the class that defines it, and should not be called directly by user programs. However, you **are** expected to override this method in your own extension classes.

transform._flush(callback)

- `callback` {Function} Call this function (optionally with an error argument) when you are done flushing any remaining data.

Note: **This function MUST NOT be called directly.** It MAY be implemented by child classes, and if so, will be called by the internal Transform class methods only.

In some cases, your transform operation may need to emit a bit more data at the end of the stream. For example, a `Zlib` compression stream will store up some internal state so that it can optimally compress the output. At the end, however, it needs to do the best it can with what is left, so that the data will be complete.

In those cases, you can implement a `_flush` method, which will be called at the very end, after all the written data is consumed, but before emitting `end` to signal the end of the readable side. Just like with `_transform`, call `transform.push(chunk)` zero or more times, as appropriate, and call `callback` when the flush operation is complete.

This method is prefixed with an underscore because it is internal to the class that defines it, and should not be called directly by user programs. However, you **are** expected to override this method in your own extension classes.

Events: 'finish' and 'end'   The `finish` and `end` events are from the parent Writable and Readable classes respectively. The `finish` event is fired after `.end()` is called and all chunks have been processed by `_transform`, `end` is fired after all data has been output which is after the callback in `_flush` has been called.

Example: `SimpleProtocol` parser v2   The example above of a simple protocol parser can be implemented simply by using the higher level Transform stream class, similar to the `parseHeader` and `SimpleProtocol v1` examples above.

In this example, rather than providing the input as an argument, it would be piped into the parser, which is a more idiomatic Node.js stream approach.

```
var util = require('util');
var Transform = require('stream').Transform;
util.inherits(SimpleProtocol, Transform);

function SimpleProtocol(options) {
  if (!(this instanceof SimpleProtocol))
    return new SimpleProtocol(options);

  Transform.call(this, options);
  this._inBody = false;
  this._sawFirstCr = false;
  this._rawHeader = [];
  this.header = null;
}

SimpleProtocol.prototype._transform = function(chunk, encoding, done) {
  if (!this._inBody) {
    // check if the chunk has a \n\n
    var split = -1;
    for (var i = 0; i < chunk.length; i++) {
      if (chunk[i] === 10) { // '\n'
        if (this._sawFirstCr) {
          split = i;
          break;
        } else {
          this._sawFirstCr = true;
        }
      }
```

```
      } else {
        this._sawFirstCr = false;
      }
    }

    if (split === -1) {
      // still waiting for the \n\n
      // stash the chunk, and try again.
      this._rawHeader.push(chunk);
    } else {
      this._inBody = true;
      var h = chunk.slice(0, split);
      this._rawHeader.push(h);
      var header = Buffer.concat(this._rawHeader).toString();
      try {
        this.header = JSON.parse(header);
      } catch (er) {
        this.emit('error', new Error('invalid simple protocol data'));
        return;
      }
      // and let them know that we are done parsing the header.
      this.emit('header', this.header);

      // now, because we got some extra data, emit this first.
      this.push(chunk.slice(split));
    }
  } else {
    // from there on, just provide the data to our consumer as-is.
    this.push(chunk);
  }
  done();
};

// Usage:
// var parser = new SimpleProtocol();
// source.pipe(parser)
// Now parser is a readable stream that will emit 'header'
// with the parsed header data.
```

Class: stream.PassThrough

This is a trivial implementation of a Transform stream that simply passes the input bytes across to the output. Its purpose is mainly for examples and testing, but there are occasionally use cases where it can come in handy as a building block for novel sorts of streams.

Simplified Constructor API

In simple cases there is now the added benefit of being able to construct a stream without inheritance.

This can be done by passing the appropriate methods as constructor options:

Examples:

Readable

```
var readable = new stream.Readable({
  read: function(n) {
    // sets this._read under the hood
  }
});
```

Writable

```
var writable = new stream.Writable({
  write: function(chunk, encoding, next) {
    // sets this._write under the hood
  }
});

// or

var writable = new stream.Writable({
  writev: function(chunks, next) {
    // sets this._writev under the hood
  }
});
```

Duplex

```
var duplex = new stream.Duplex({
  read: function(n) {
    // sets this._read under the hood
  },
  write: function(chunk, encoding, next) {
    // sets this._write under the hood
  }
});

// or

var duplex = new stream.Duplex({
  read: function(n) {
    // sets this._read under the hood
  },
  writev: function(chunks, next) {
    // sets this._writev under the hood
  }
});
```

Transform

```
var transform = new stream.Transform({
  transform: function(chunk, encoding, next) {
    // sets this._transform under the hood
  },
```

```
  flush: function(done) {
    // sets this._flush under the hood
  }
});
```

Streams: Under the Hood

Buffering

Both Writable and Readable streams will buffer data on an internal object which can be retrieved from `_writableState.getBuffer()` or `_readableState.buffer`, respectively.

The amount of data that will potentially be buffered depends on the `highWaterMark` option which is passed into the constructor.

Buffering in Readable streams happens when the implementation calls `stream.push(chunk)`. If the consumer of the Stream does not call `stream.read()`, then the data will sit in the internal queue until it is consumed.

Buffering in Writable streams happens when the user calls `stream.write(chunk)` repeatedly, even when `write()` returns `false`.

The purpose of streams, especially with the `pipe()` method, is to limit the buffering of data to acceptable levels, so that sources and destinations of varying speed will not overwhelm the available memory.

stream.read(0)

There are some cases where you want to trigger a refresh of the underlying readable stream mechanisms, without actually consuming any data. In that case, you can call `stream.read(0)`, which will always return null.

If the internal read buffer is below the `highWaterMark`, and the stream is not currently reading, then calling `read(0)` will trigger a low-level `_read` call.

There is almost never a need to do this. However, you will see some cases in Node.js's internals where this is done, particularly in the Readable stream class internals.

stream.push(")

Pushing a zero-byte string or Buffer (when not in Object mode) has an interesting side effect. Because it *is* a call to `stream.push()`, it will end the `reading` process. However, it does *not* add any data to the readable buffer, so there's nothing for a user to consume.

Very rarely, there are cases where you have no data to provide now, but the consumer of your stream (or, perhaps, another bit of your own code) will know when to check again, by calling `stream.read(0)`. In those cases, you *may* call `stream.push(")`.

So far, the only use case for this functionality is in the tls.CryptoStream class, which is deprecated in Node.js/io.js v1.0. If you find that you have to use `stream.push(")`, please consider another approach, because it almost certainly indicates that something is horribly wrong.

Compatibility with Older Node.js Versions

In versions of Node.js prior to v0.10, the Readable stream interface was simpler, but also less powerful and less useful.

- Rather than waiting for you to call the `read()` method, 'data' events would start emitting immediately. If you needed to do some I/O to decide how to handle data, then you had to store the chunks in some kind of buffer so that they would not be lost.

- The `pause()` method was advisory, rather than guaranteed. This meant that you still had to be prepared to receive `'data'` events even when the stream was in a paused state.

In Node.js v0.10, the Readable class described below was added. For backwards compatibility with older Node.js programs, Readable streams switch into "flowing mode" when a `'data'` event handler is added, or when the `resume()` method is called. The effect is that, even if you are not using the new `read()` method and `'readable'` event, you no longer have to worry about losing `'data'` chunks.

Most programs will continue to function normally. However, this introduces an edge case in the following conditions:

- No `'data'` event handler is added.
- The `resume()` method is never called.
- The stream is not piped to any writable destination.

For example, consider the following code:

```
// WARNING!  BROKEN!
net.createServer(function(socket) {

  // we add an 'end' method, but never consume the data
  socket.on('end', function() {
    // It will never get here.
    socket.end('I got your message (but didnt read it)\n');
  });

}).listen(1337);
```

In versions of Node.js prior to v0.10, the incoming message data would be simply discarded. However, in Node.js v0.10 and beyond, the socket will remain paused forever.

The workaround in this situation is to call the `resume()` method to start the flow of data:

```
// Workaround
net.createServer(function(socket) {

  socket.on('end', function() {
    socket.end('I got your message (but didnt read it)\n');
  });

  // start the flow of data, discarding it.
  socket.resume();

}).listen(1337);
```

In addition to new Readable streams switching into flowing mode, pre-v0.10 style streams can be wrapped in a Readable class using the `wrap()` method.

Object Mode

Normally, Streams operate on Strings and Buffers exclusively.

Streams that are in **object mode** can emit generic JavaScript values other than Buffers and Strings.

A Readable stream in object mode will always return a single item from a call to `stream.read(size)`, regardless of what the size argument is.

A Writable stream in object mode will always ignore the `encoding` argument to `stream.write(data, encoding)`.

The special value `null` still retains its special value for object mode streams. That is, for object mode readable streams, `null` as a return value from `stream.read()` indicates that there is no more data, and `stream.push(null)` will signal the end of stream data (`EOF`).

No streams in Node.js core are object mode streams. This pattern is only used by userland streaming libraries.

You should set `objectMode` in your stream child class constructor on the options object. Setting `objectMode` mid-stream is not safe.

For Duplex streams `objectMode` can be set exclusively for readable or writable side with `readableObjectMode` and `writableObjectMode` respectively. These options can be used to implement parsers and serializers with Transform streams.

```javascript
var util = require('util');
var StringDecoder = require('string_decoder').StringDecoder;
var Transform = require('stream').Transform;
util.inherits(JSONParseStream, Transform);


// Gets \n-delimited JSON string data, and emits the parsed objects
function JSONParseStream() {
  if (!(this instanceof JSONParseStream))
    return new JSONParseStream();

  Transform.call(this, { readableObjectMode : true });

  this._buffer = '';
  this._decoder = new StringDecoder('utf8');
}


JSONParseStream.prototype._transform = function(chunk, encoding, cb) {
  this._buffer += this._decoder.write(chunk);
  // split on newlines
  var lines = this._buffer.split(/\r?\n/);
  // keep the last partial line buffered
  this._buffer = lines.pop();
  for (var l = 0; l < lines.length; l++) {
    var line = lines[l];
    try {
      var obj = JSON.parse(line);
    } catch (er) {
      this.emit('error', er);
      return;
    }
    // push the parsed object out to the readable consumer
    this.push(obj);
  }
  cb();
};


JSONParseStream.prototype._flush = function(cb) {
  // Just handle any leftover
  var rem = this._buffer.trim();
  if (rem) {
    try {
      var obj = JSON.parse(rem);
    } catch (er) {
      this.emit('error', er);
      return;
    }
    // push the parsed object out to the readable consumer
    this.push(obj);
  }
```

```
  cb();
};
```

StringDecoder

`Stability: 2 - Stable`

To use this module, do `require('string_decoder')`. StringDecoder decodes a buffer to a string. It is a simple interface to `buffer.toString()` but provides additional support for utf8.

```
var StringDecoder = require('string_decoder').StringDecoder;
var decoder = new StringDecoder('utf8');

var cent = new Buffer([0xC2, 0xA2]);
console.log(decoder.write(cent));

var euro = new Buffer([0xE2, 0x82, 0xAC]);
console.log(decoder.write(euro));
```

Class: StringDecoder

Accepts a single argument, `encoding` which defaults to `utf8`.

decoder.write(buffer)

Returns a decoded string.

decoder.end()

Returns any trailing bytes that were left in the buffer.

Timers

Stability: 3 - Locked

All of the timer functions are globals. You do not need to `require()` this module in order to use them.

setTimeout(callback, delay[, arg][, ...])

To schedule execution of a one-time `callback` after `delay` milliseconds. Returns a `timeoutObject` for possible use with `clearTimeout()`. Optionally you can also pass arguments to the callback.

It is important to note that your callback will probably not be called in exactly `delay` milliseconds - Node.js makes no guarantees about the exact timing of when the callback will fire, nor of the ordering things will fire in. The callback will be called as close as possible to the time specified.

To follow browser behavior, when using delays larger than 2147483647 milliseconds (approximately 25 days) or less than 1, the timeout is executed immediately, as if the `delay` was set to 1.

clearTimeout(timeoutObject)

Prevents a timeout from triggering.

setInterval(callback, delay[, arg][, ...])

To schedule the repeated execution of `callback` every `delay` milliseconds. Returns a `intervalObject` for possible use with `clearInterval()`. Optionally you can also pass arguments to the callback.

To follow browser behavior, when using delays larger than 2147483647 milliseconds (approximately 25 days) or less than 1, Node.js will use 1 as the `delay`.

clearInterval(intervalObject)

Stops an interval from triggering.

unref()

The opaque value returned by `setTimeout` and `setInterval` also has the method `timer.unref()` which will allow you to create a timer that is active but if it is the only item left in the event loop, it won't keep the program running. If the timer is already `unref`d calling `unref` again will have no effect.

In the case of `setTimeout` when you `unref` you create a separate timer that will wakeup the event loop, creating too many of these may adversely effect event loop performance – use wisely.

Returns the timer.

ref()

If you had previously `unref()`d a timer you can call `ref()` to explicitly request the timer hold the program open. If the timer is already `ref`d calling `ref` again will have no effect.

Returns the timer.

setImmediate(callback[, arg][, ...])

To schedule the "immediate" execution of `callback` after I/O events callbacks and before `setTimeout` and `setInterval` . Returns an `immediateObject` for possible use with `clearImmediate()`. Optionally you can also pass arguments to the callback.

Callbacks for immediates are queued in the order in which they were created. The entire callback queue is processed every event loop iteration. If you queue an immediate from inside an executing callback, that immediate won't fire until the next event loop iteration.

clearImmediate(immediateObject)

Stops an immediate from triggering.

TLS (SSL)

```
Stability: 2 - Stable
```

Use `require('tls')` to access this module.

The `tls` module uses OpenSSL to provide Transport Layer Security and/or Secure Socket Layer: encrypted stream communication.

TLS/SSL is a public/private key infrastructure. Each client and each server must have a private key. A private key is created like this:

```
openssl genrsa -out ryans-key.pem 2048
```

All servers and some clients need to have a certificate. Certificates are public keys signed by a Certificate Authority or self-signed. The first step to getting a certificate is to create a "Certificate Signing Request" (CSR) file. This is done with:

```
openssl req -new -sha256 -key ryans-key.pem -out ryans-csr.pem
```

To create a self-signed certificate with the CSR, do this:

```
openssl x509 -req -in ryans-csr.pem -signkey ryans-key.pem -out ryans-cert.pem
```

Alternatively you can send the CSR to a Certificate Authority for signing.

For Perfect Forward Secrecy, it is required to generate Diffie-Hellman parameters:

```
openssl dhparam -outform PEM -out dhparam.pem 2048
```

To create .pfx or .p12, do this:

```
openssl pkcs12 -export -in agent5-cert.pem -inkey agent5-key.pem \
   -certfile ca-cert.pem -out agent5.pfx
```

- `in`: certificate
- `inkey`: private key
- `certfile`: all CA certs concatenated in one file like `cat ca1-cert.pem ca2-cert.pem > ca-cert.pem`

Client-initiated renegotiation attack mitigation

The TLS protocol lets the client renegotiate certain aspects of the TLS session. Unfortunately, session renegotiation requires a disproportional amount of server-side resources, which makes it a potential vector for denial-of-service attacks.

To mitigate this, renegotiations are limited to three times every 10 minutes. An error is emitted on the tls.TLSSocket instance when the threshold is exceeded. The limits are configurable:

- `tls.CLIENT_RENEG_LIMIT`: renegotiation limit, default is 3.
- `tls.CLIENT_RENEG_WINDOW`: renegotiation window in seconds, default is 10 minutes.

Don't change the defaults unless you know what you are doing.

To test your server, connect to it with `openssl s_client -connect address:port` and tap R<CR> (that's the letter R followed by a carriage return) a few times.

ALPN, NPN and SNI

ALPN (Application-Layer Protocol Negotiation Extension), NPN (Next Protocol Negotiation) and SNI (Server Name Indication) are TLS handshake extensions allowing you:

- ALPN/NPN - to use one TLS server for multiple protocols (HTTP, SPDY, HTTP/2)
- SNI - to use one TLS server for multiple hostnames with different SSL certificates.

Modifying the Default TLS Cipher suite

Node.js is built with a default suite of enabled and disabled TLS ciphers. Currently, the default cipher suite is:

```
ECDHE-RSA-AES128-GCM-SHA256:
ECDHE-ECDSA-AES128-GCM-SHA256:
ECDHE-RSA-AES256-GCM-SHA384:
ECDHE-ECDSA-AES256-GCM-SHA384:
DHE-RSA-AES128-GCM-SHA256:
ECDHE-RSA-AES128-SHA256:
DHE-RSA-AES128-SHA256:
ECDHE-RSA-AES256-SHA384:
DHE-RSA-AES256-SHA384:
ECDHE-RSA-AES256-SHA256:
DHE-RSA-AES256-SHA256:
HIGH:
!aNULL:
!eNULL:
!EXPORT:
!DES:
!RC4:
!MD5:
!PSK:
!SRP:
!CAMELLIA
```

This default can be overriden entirely using the **--tls-cipher-list** command line switch. For instance, the following makes **ECDHE-RSA-AES128-GCM-SHA256:!RC4** the default TLS cipher suite:

```
node --tls-cipher-list="ECDHE-RSA-AES128-GCM-SHA256:!RC4"
```

Note that the default cipher suite included within Node.js has been carefully selected to reflect current security best practices and risk mitigation. Changing the default cipher suite can have a significant impact on the security of an application. The **--tls-cipher-list** switch should by used only if absolutely necessary.

Perfect Forward Secrecy

The term "Forward Secrecy" or "Perfect Forward Secrecy" describes a feature of key-agreement (i.e. key-exchange) methods. Practically it means that even if the private key of a (your) server is compromised, communication can only be decrypted by eavesdroppers if they manage to obtain the key-pair specifically generated for each session.

This is achieved by randomly generating a key pair for key-agreement on every handshake (in contrary to the same key for all sessions). Methods implementing this technique, thus offering Perfect Forward Secrecy, are called "ephemeral".

Currently two methods are commonly used to achieve Perfect Forward Secrecy (note the character "E" appended to the traditional abbreviations):

- DHE - An ephemeral version of the Diffie Hellman key-agreement protocol.
- ECDHE - An ephemeral version of the Elliptic Curve Diffie Hellman key-agreement protocol.

Ephemeral methods may have some performance drawbacks, because key generation is expensive.

tls.getCiphers()

Returns an array with the names of the supported SSL ciphers.

Example:

```
var ciphers = tls.getCiphers();
console.log(ciphers); // ['AES128-SHA', 'AES256-SHA', ...]
```

tls.createServer(options[, secureConnectionListener])

Creates a new tls.Server. The `connectionListener` argument is automatically set as a listener for the secureConnection event. The `options` object has these possibilities:

- `pfx`: A string or `Buffer` containing the private key, certificate and CA certs of the server in PFX or PKCS12 format. (Mutually exclusive with the `key`, `cert` and `ca` options.)

- `key`: A string or `Buffer` containing the private key of the server in PEM format. To support multiple keys using different algorithms, an array can be provided. It can either be a plain array of keys, or an array of objects in the format `{pem: key, passphrase: passphrase}`. (Required)

- `passphrase`: A string of passphrase for the private key or pfx.

- `cert`: A string or `Buffer` containing the certificate key of the server in PEM format. (Could be an array of certs). (Required)

- `ca`: An array of strings or `Buffer`s of trusted certificates in PEM format. If this is omitted several well known "root" CAs will be used, like VeriSign. These are used to authorize connections.

- `crl` : Either a string or list of strings of PEM encoded CRLs (Certificate Revocation List)

- `ciphers`: A string describing the ciphers to use or exclude, separated by :. The default cipher suite is:
  ```
  ECDHE-RSA-AES128-GCM-SHA256:
  ECDHE-ECDSA-AES128-GCM-SHA256:
  ECDHE-RSA-AES256-GCM-SHA384:
  ECDHE-ECDSA-AES256-GCM-SHA384:
  DHE-RSA-AES128-GCM-SHA256:
  ECDHE-RSA-AES128-SHA256:
  DHE-RSA-AES128-SHA256:
  ECDHE-RSA-AES256-SHA384:
  DHE-RSA-AES256-SHA384:
  ECDHE-RSA-AES256-SHA256:
  DHE-RSA-AES256-SHA256:
  HIGH:
  !aNULL:
  !eNULL:
  !EXPORT:
  !DES:
  !RC4:
  !MD5:
  !PSK:
  !SRP:
  !CAMELLIA
  ```

The default cipher suite prefers GCM ciphers for Chrome's 'modern cryptography' setting and also prefers ECDHE and DHE ciphers for Perfect Forward secrecy, while offering *some* backward compatibiltity.

128 bit AES is preferred over 192 and 256 bit AES in light of specific attacks affecting larger AES key sizes.

Old clients that rely on insecure and deprecated RC4 or DES-based ciphers (like Internet Explorer 6) aren't able to complete the handshake with the default configuration. If you absolutely must support these clients, the TLS recommendations may offer a compatible cipher suite. For more details on the format, see the OpenSSL cipher list format documentation.

- ecdhCurve: A string describing a named curve to use for ECDH key agreement or false to disable ECDH.

  Defaults to prime256v1 (NIST P-256). Use crypto.getCurves() to obtain a list of available curve names. On recent releases, openssl ecparam -list_curves will also display the name and description of each available elliptic curve.

- dhparam: A string or Buffer containing Diffie Hellman parameters, required for Perfect Forward Secrecy. Use openssl dhparam to create it. Its key length should be greater than or equal to 1024 bits, otherwise it throws an error. It is strongly recommended to use 2048 bits or more for stronger security. If omitted or invalid, it is silently discarded and DHE ciphers won't be available.

- handshakeTimeout: Abort the connection if the SSL/TLS handshake does not finish in this many milliseconds. The default is 120 seconds.

  A 'clientError' is emitted on the tls.Server object whenever a handshake times out.

- honorCipherOrder : When choosing a cipher, use the server's preferences instead of the client preferences. Default: true.

- requestCert: If true the server will request a certificate from clients that connect and attempt to verify that certificate. Default: false.

- rejectUnauthorized: If true the server will reject any connection which is not authorized with the list of supplied CAs. This option only has an effect if requestCert is true. Default: false.

- NPNProtocols: An array or Buffer of possible NPN protocols. (Protocols should be ordered by their priority).

- ALPNProtocols: An array or Buffer of possible ALPN protocols. (Protocols should be ordered by their priority). When the server receives both NPN and ALPN extensions from the client, ALPN takes precedence over NPN and the server does not send an NPN extension to the client.

- SNICallback(servername, cb): A function that will be called if client supports SNI TLS extension. Two argument will be passed to it: servername, and cb. SNICallback should invoke cb(null, ctx), where ctx is a SecureContext instance. (You can use tls.createSecureContext(...) to get proper SecureContext). If SNICallback wasn't provided - default callback with high-level API will be used (see below).

- sessionTimeout: An integer specifying the seconds after which TLS session identifiers and TLS session tickets created by the server are timed out. See SSL_CTX_set_timeout for more details.

- ticketKeys: A 48-byte Buffer instance consisting of 16-byte prefix, 16-byte hmac key, 16-byte AES key. You could use it to accept tls session tickets on multiple instances of tls server.

  NOTE: Automatically shared between cluster module workers.

- sessionIdContext: A string containing an opaque identifier for session resumption. If requestCert is true, the default is MD5 hash value generated from command-line. Otherwise, the default is not provided.

- secureProtocol: The SSL method to use, e.g. SSLv3_method to force SSL version 3. The possible values depend on your installation of OpenSSL and are defined in the constant SSL_METHODS.

Here is a simple example echo server:

```
var tls = require('tls');
var fs = require('fs');

var options = {
  key: fs.readFileSync('server-key.pem'),
  cert: fs.readFileSync('server-cert.pem'),

  // This is necessary only if using the client certificate authentication.
  requestCert: true,
```

```
  // This is necessary only if the client uses the self-signed certificate.
  ca: [ fs.readFileSync('client-cert.pem') ]
};

var server = tls.createServer(options, function(socket) {
  console.log('server connected',
              socket.authorized ? 'authorized' : 'unauthorized');
  socket.write("welcome!\n");
  socket.setEncoding('utf8');
  socket.pipe(socket);
});
server.listen(8000, function() {
  console.log('server bound');
});
```

Or

```
var tls = require('tls');
var fs = require('fs');

var options = {
  pfx: fs.readFileSync('server.pfx'),

  // This is necessary only if using the client certificate authentication.
  requestCert: true,

};

var server = tls.createServer(options, function(socket) {
  console.log('server connected',
              socket.authorized ? 'authorized' : 'unauthorized');
  socket.write("welcome!\n");
  socket.setEncoding('utf8');
  socket.pipe(socket);
});
server.listen(8000, function() {
  console.log('server bound');
});
```

You can test this server by connecting to it with `openssl s_client`:

```
openssl s_client -connect 127.0.0.1:8000
```

tls.connect(options[, callback])

tls.connect(port[, host][, options][, callback])

Creates a new client connection to the given `port` and `host` (old API) or `options.port` and `options.host`. (If `host` is omitted, it defaults to `localhost`.) `options` should be an object which specifies:

- `host`: Host the client should connect to

- `port`: Port the client should connect to

- `socket`: Establish secure connection on a given socket rather than creating a new socket. If this option is specified, `host` and `port` are ignored.

- `path`: Creates unix socket connection to path. If this option is specified, `host` and `port` are ignored.

- **pfx**: A string or `Buffer` containing the private key, certificate and CA certs of the client in PFX or PKCS12 format.

- **key**: A string or `Buffer` containing the private key of the client in PEM format. (Could be an array of keys).

- **passphrase**: A string of passphrase for the private key or pfx.

- **cert**: A string or `Buffer` containing the certificate key of the client in PEM format. (Could be an array of certs).

- **ca**: An array of strings or `Buffers` of trusted certificates in PEM format. If this is omitted several well known "root" CAs will be used, like VeriSign. These are used to authorize connections.

- **ciphers**: A string describing the ciphers to use or exclude, separated by :. Uses the same default cipher suite as `tls.createServer`.

- **rejectUnauthorized**: If `true`, the server certificate is verified against the list of supplied CAs. An `'error'` event is emitted if verification fails; `err.code` contains the OpenSSL error code. Default: `true`.

- **NPNProtocols**: An array of strings or `Buffers` containing supported NPN protocols. `Buffers` should have the following format: `0x05hello0x05world`, where first byte is next protocol name's length. (Passing array should usually be much simpler: `['hello', 'world']`.)

- **ALPNProtocols**: An array of strings or `Buffers` containing supported ALPN protocols. `Buffers` should have following format: `0x05hello0x05world`, where the first byte is the next protocol name's length. (Passing array should usually be much simpler: `['hello', 'world']`.)

- **servername**: Servername for SNI (Server Name Indication) TLS extension.

- **checkServerIdentity(servername, cert)**: Provide an override for checking server's hostname against the certificate. Should return an error if verification fails. Return `undefined` if passing.

- **secureProtocol**: The SSL method to use, e.g. `SSLv3_method` to force SSL version 3. The possible values depend on your installation of OpenSSL and are defined in the constant SSL_METHODS.

- **session**: A `Buffer` instance, containing TLS session.

- **minDHSize**: Minimum size of DH parameter in bits to accept a TLS connection. When a server offers DH parameter with a size less than this, the TLS connection is destroyed and throws an error. Default: 1024.

The `callback` parameter will be added as a listener for the 'secureConnect' event.

`tls.connect()` returns a tls.TLSSocket object.

Here is an example of a client of echo server as described previously:

```
var tls = require('tls');
var fs = require('fs');

var options = {
  // These are necessary only if using the client certificate authentication
  key: fs.readFileSync('client-key.pem'),
  cert: fs.readFileSync('client-cert.pem'),

  // This is necessary only if the server uses the self-signed certificate
  ca: [ fs.readFileSync('server-cert.pem') ]
};

var socket = tls.connect(8000, options, function() {
  console.log('client connected',
              socket.authorized ? 'authorized' : 'unauthorized');
  process.stdin.pipe(socket);
  process.stdin.resume();
});
```

```
socket.setEncoding('utf8');
socket.on('data', function(data) {
  console.log(data);
});
socket.on('end', function() {
  server.close();
});
```

Or

```
var tls = require('tls');
var fs = require('fs');

var options = {
  pfx: fs.readFileSync('client.pfx')
};

var socket = tls.connect(8000, options, function() {
  console.log('client connected',
              socket.authorized ? 'authorized' : 'unauthorized');
  process.stdin.pipe(socket);
  process.stdin.resume();
});
socket.setEncoding('utf8');
socket.on('data', function(data) {
  console.log(data);
});
socket.on('end', function() {
  server.close();
});
```

Class: tls.TLSSocket

Wrapper for instance of net.Socket, replaces internal socket read/write routines to perform transparent encryption/decryption of incoming/outgoing data.

new tls.TLSSocket(socket[, options])

Construct a new TLSSocket object from existing TCP socket.

`socket` is an instance of net.Socket

`options` is an optional object that might contain following properties:

- secureContext: An optional TLS context object from `tls.createSecureContext( ... )`
- isServer: If `true` - TLS socket will be instantiated in server-mode. Default: `false`
- server: An optional net.Server instance
- requestCert: Optional, see tls.createSecurePair
- rejectUnauthorized: Optional, see tls.createSecurePair
- NPNProtocols: Optional, see tls.createServer
- ALPNProtocols: Optional, see tls.createServer
- SNICallback: Optional, see tls.createServer
- session: Optional, a `Buffer` instance, containing TLS session

- `requestOCSP`: Optional, if `true` - OCSP status request extension would be added to client hello, and `OCSPResponse` event will be emitted on socket before establishing secure communication

tls.createSecureContext(details)

Creates a credentials object, with the optional details being a dictionary with keys:

- `pfx` : A string or buffer holding the PFX or PKCS12 encoded private key, certificate and CA certificates
- `key`: A string or `Buffer` containing the private key of the server in PEM format. To support multiple keys using different algorithms, an array can be provided. It can either be a plain array of keys, or an array of objects in the format `{pem:  key, passphrase:  passphrase}`. (Required)
- `passphrase` : A string of passphrase for the private key or pfx
- `cert` : A string holding the PEM encoded certificate
- `ca` : Either a string or list of strings of PEM encoded CA certificates to trust.
- `crl` : Either a string or list of strings of PEM encoded CRLs (Certificate Revocation List)
- `ciphers`: A string describing the ciphers to use or exclude. Consult `http://www.openssl.org/docs/apps/ciphers.html#CIPHER_LIST_FORMAT` for details on the format.
- `honorCipherOrder` : When choosing a cipher, use the server's preferences instead of the client preferences. For further details see `tls` module documentation.

If no 'ca' details are given, then Node.js will use the default publicly trusted list of CAs as given in `http://mxr.mozilla.org/mozilla/source/security/nss/lib/ckfw/builtins/certdata.txt`.

tls.createSecurePair([context][, isServer][, requestCert][, rejectUnauthorized][, options])

Creates a new secure pair object with two streams, one of which reads/writes encrypted data, and one reads/writes cleartext data. Generally the encrypted one is piped to/from an incoming encrypted data stream, and the cleartext one is used as a replacement for the initial encrypted stream.

- `credentials`: A secure context object from tls.createSecureContext(...)

- `isServer`: A boolean indicating whether this tls connection should be opened as a server or a client.

- `requestCert`: A boolean indicating whether a server should request a certificate from a connecting client. Only applies to server connections.

- `rejectUnauthorized`: A boolean indicating whether a server should automatically reject clients with invalid certificates. Only applies to servers with `requestCert` enabled.

- `options`: An object with common SSL options. See tls.TLSSocket.

`tls.createSecurePair()` returns a SecurePair object with `cleartext` and `encrypted` stream properties.

NOTE: `cleartext` has the same APIs as tls.TLSSocket

Class: SecurePair

Returned by tls.createSecurePair.

Event: 'secure'

The event is emitted from the SecurePair once the pair has successfully established a secure connection.

Similarly to the checking for the server 'secureConnection' event, pair.cleartext.authorized should be checked to confirm whether the certificate used properly authorized.

Class: tls.Server

This class is a subclass of `net.Server` and has the same methods on it. Instead of accepting just raw TCP connections, this accepts encrypted connections using TLS or SSL.

Event: 'secureConnection'

```
function (tlsSocket) {}
```

This event is emitted after a new connection has been successfully handshaked. The argument is an instance of tls.TLSSocket. It has all the common stream methods and events.

`socket.authorized` is a boolean value which indicates if the client has verified by one of the supplied certificate authorities for the server. If `socket.authorized` is false, then `socket.authorizationError` is set to describe how authorization failed. Implied but worth mentioning: depending on the settings of the TLS server, you unauthorized connections may be accepted.

`socket.npnProtocol` is a string containing the selected NPN protocol and `socket.alpnProtocol` is a string containing the selected ALPN protocol, When both NPN and ALPN extensions are received, ALPN takes precedence over NPN and the next protocol is selected by ALPN. When ALPN has no selected protocol, this returns false.

`socket.servername` is a string containing servername requested with SNI.

Event: 'clientError'

```
function (exception, tlsSocket) { }
```

When a client connection emits an 'error' event before secure connection is established - it will be forwarded here.

`tlsSocket` is the tls.TLSSocket that the error originated from.

Event: 'newSession'

```
function (sessionId, sessionData, callback) { }
```

Emitted on creation of TLS session. May be used to store sessions in external storage. `callback` must be invoked eventually, otherwise no data will be sent or received from secure connection.

NOTE: adding this event listener will have an effect only on connections established after addition of event listener.

Event: 'resumeSession'

```
function (sessionId, callback) { }
```

Emitted when client wants to resume previous TLS session. Event listener may perform lookup in external storage using given `sessionId`, and invoke `callback(null, sessionData)` once finished. If session can't be resumed (i.e. doesn't exist in storage) one may call `callback(null, null)`. Calling `callback(err)` will terminate incoming connection and destroy socket.

NOTE: adding this event listener will have an effect only on connections established after addition of event listener.

Here's an example for using TLS session resumption:

```
var tlsSessionStore = {};
server.on('newSession', function(id, data, cb) {
  tlsSessionStore[id.toString('hex')] = data;
  cb();
});
server.on('resumeSession', function(id, cb) {
  cb(null, tlsSessionStore[id.toString('hex')] || null);
});
```

Event: 'OCSPRequest'

```
function (certificate, issuer, callback) { }
```

Emitted when the client sends a certificate status request. You could parse server's current certificate to obtain OCSP url and certificate id, and after obtaining OCSP response invoke `callback(null, resp)`, where `resp` is a `Buffer` instance. Both `certificate` and `issuer` are a `Buffer` DER-representations of the primary and issuer's certificates. They could be used to obtain OCSP certificate id and OCSP endpoint url.

Alternatively, `callback(null, null)` could be called, meaning that there is no OCSP response.

Calling `callback(err)` will result in a `socket.destroy(err)` call.

Typical flow:

1. Client connects to server and sends `OCSPRequest` to it (via status info extension in ClientHello.)
2. Server receives request and invokes `OCSPRequest` event listener if present
3. Server grabs OCSP url from either `certificate` or `issuer` and performs an OCSP request to the CA
4. Server receives `OCSPResponse` from CA and sends it back to client via `callback` argument
5. Client validates the response and either destroys socket or performs a handshake.

NOTE: `issuer` could be null, if the certificate is self-signed or if the issuer is not in the root certificates list. (You could provide an issuer via `ca` option.)

NOTE: adding this event listener will have an effect only on connections established after addition of event listener.

NOTE: you may want to use some npm module like asn1.js to parse the certificates.

server.listen(port[, hostname][, callback])

Begin accepting connections on the specified `port` and `hostname`. If the `hostname` is omitted, the server will accept connections on any IPv6 address (`::`) when IPv6 is available, or any IPv4 address (`0.0.0.0`) otherwise. A port value of zero will assign a random port.

This function is asynchronous. The last parameter `callback` will be called when the server has been bound.

See `net.Server` for more information.

server.close([callback])

Stops the server from accepting new connections. This function is asynchronous, the server is finally closed when the server emits a `'close'` event. Optionally, you can pass a callback to listen for the `'close'` event.

server.address()

Returns the bound address, the address family name and port of the server as reported by the operating system. See net.Server.address() for more information.

server.getTicketKeys()

Returns `Buffer` instance holding the keys currently used for encryption/decryption of the TLS Session Tickets

server.setTicketKeys(keys)

Updates the keys for encryption/decryption of the TLS Session Tickets.

NOTE: the buffer should be 48 bytes long. See server `ticketKeys` option for more information oh how it is going to be used.

NOTE: the change is effective only for the future server connections. Existing or currently pending server connections will use previous keys.

server.addContext(hostname, context)

Add secure context that will be used if client request's SNI hostname is matching passed `hostname` (wildcards can be used). `context` can contain `key`, `cert`, `ca` and/or any other properties from `tls.createSecureContext` `options` argument.

server.maxConnections

Set this property to reject connections when the server's connection count gets high.

server.connections

The number of concurrent connections on the server.

Class: CryptoStream

Stability: 0 - Deprecated: Use [tls.TLSSocket][] instead.

This is an encrypted stream.

cryptoStream.bytesWritten

A proxy to the underlying socket's bytesWritten accessor, this will return the total bytes written to the socket, *including the TLS overhead.*

Class: tls.TLSSocket

This is a wrapped version of net.Socket that does transparent encryption of written data and all required TLS negotiation.

This instance implements a duplex Stream interfaces. It has all the common stream methods and events.

Event: 'secureConnect'

This event is emitted after a new connection has been successfully handshaked. The listener will be called no matter if the server's certificate was authorized or not. It is up to the user to test `tlsSocket.authorized` to see if the server certificate was signed by one of the specified CAs. If `tlsSocket.authorized === false` then the error can be found in `tlsSocket.authorizationError`. Also if ALPN or NPN was used - you can check `tlsSocket.alpnProtocol` or `tlsSocket.npnProtocol` for the negotiated protocol.

Event: 'OCSPResponse'

```
function (response) { }
```

This event will be emitted if `requestOCSP` option was set. `response` is a buffer object, containing server's OCSP response.

Traditionally, the `response` is a signed object from the server's CA that contains information about server's certificate revocation status.

tlsSocket.encrypted

Static boolean value, always `true`. May be used to distinguish TLS sockets from regular ones.

tlsSocket.authorized

A boolean that is `true` if the peer certificate was signed by one of the specified CAs, otherwise `false`

tlsSocket.authorizationError

The reason why the peer's certificate has not been verified. This property becomes available only when `tlsSocket.authorized === false`.

tlsSocket.getPeerCertificate([detailed])

Returns an object representing the peer's certificate. The returned object has some properties corresponding to the field of the certificate. If `detailed` argument is `true` - the full chain with `issuer` property will be returned, if `false` - only the top certificate without `issuer` property.

Example:
```
{ subject:
   { C: 'UK',
     ST: 'Acknack Ltd',
     L: 'Rhys Jones',
     O: 'node.js',
     OU: 'Test TLS Certificate',
     CN: 'localhost' },
  issuerInfo:
   { C: 'UK',
     ST: 'Acknack Ltd',
     L: 'Rhys Jones',
     O: 'node.js',
     OU: 'Test TLS Certificate',
     CN: 'localhost' },
  issuer:
   { ... another certificate ... },
  raw: < RAW DER buffer >,
  valid_from: 'Nov 11 09:52:22 2009 GMT',
  valid_to: 'Nov  6 09:52:22 2029 GMT',
  fingerprint: '2A:7A:C2:DD:E5:F9:CC:53:72:35:99:7A:02:5A:71:38:52:EC:8A:DF',
  serialNumber: 'B9B0D332A1AA5635' }
```

If the peer does not provide a certificate, it returns `null` or an empty object.

tlsSocket.getCipher()

Returns an object representing the cipher name and the SSL/TLS protocol version of the current connection.

Example: { name: 'AES256-SHA', version: 'TLSv1/SSLv3' }

See SSL_CIPHER_get_name() and SSL_CIPHER_get_version() in http://www.openssl.org/docs/ssl/ssl.html#DEALI for more information.

tlsSocket.getEphemeralKeyInfo()

Returns an object representing a type, name and size of parameter of an ephemeral key exchange in Perfect forward Secrecy on a client connection. It returns an empty object when the key exchange is not ephemeral. As it is only supported on a client socket, it returns null if this is called on a server socket. The supported types are 'DH' and 'ECDH'. The `name` property is only available in 'ECDH'.

Example:

`{ type: 'ECDH', name: 'prime256v1', size: 256 }`

tlsSocket.renegotiate(options, callback)

Initiate TLS renegotiation process. The `options` may contain the following fields: `rejectUnauthorized`, `requestCert` (See tls.createServer for details). `callback(err)` will be executed with `null` as `err`, once the renegotiation is successfully completed.

NOTE: Can be used to request peer's certificate after the secure connection has been established.

ANOTHER NOTE: When running as the server, socket will be destroyed with an error after `handshakeTimeout` timeout.

tlsSocket.setMaxSendFragment(size)

Set maximum TLS fragment size (default and maximum value is: `16384`, minimum is: `512`). Returns `true` on success, `false` otherwise.

Smaller fragment size decreases buffering latency on the client: large fragments are buffered by the TLS layer until the entire fragment is received and its integrity is verified; large fragments can span multiple roundtrips, and their processing can be delayed due to packet loss or reordering. However, smaller fragments add extra TLS framing bytes and CPU overhead, which may decrease overall server throughput.

tlsSocket.getSession()

Return ASN.1 encoded TLS session or `undefined` if none was negotiated. Could be used to speed up handshake establishment when reconnecting to the server.

tlsSocket.getTLSTicket()

NOTE: Works only with client TLS sockets. Useful only for debugging, for session reuse provide `session` option to `tls.connect`.

Return TLS session ticket or `undefined` if none was negotiated.

tlsSocket.address()

Returns the bound address, the address family name and port of the underlying socket as reported by the operating system. Returns an object with three properties, e.g. `{ port: 12346, family: 'IPv4', address: '127.0.0.1' }`

tlsSocket.remoteAddress

The string representation of the remote IP address. For example, '74.125.127.100' or '2001:4860:a005::68'.

tlsSocket.remoteFamily

The string representation of the remote IP family. 'IPv4' or 'IPv6'.

tlsSocket.remotePort

The numeric representation of the remote port. For example, 443.

tlsSocket.localAddress

The string representation of the local IP address.

tlsSocket.localPort

The numeric representation of the local port.

TTY

Stability: 2 - Stable

The `tty` module houses the `tty.ReadStream` and `tty.WriteStream` classes. In most cases, you will not need to use this module directly.

When Node.js detects that it is being run inside a TTY context, then `process.stdin` will be a `tty.ReadStream` instance and `process.stdout` will be a `tty.WriteStream` instance. The preferred way to check if Node.js is being run in a TTY context is to check `process.stdout.isTTY`:

```
$ node -p -e "Boolean(process.stdout.isTTY)"
true
$ node -p -e "Boolean(process.stdout.isTTY)" | cat
false
```

tty.isatty(fd)

Returns `true` or `false` depending on if the `fd` is associated with a terminal.

tty.setRawMode(mode)

Stability: 0 - Deprecated: Use [tty.ReadStream#setRawMode][] (i.e. process.stdin.setRawMode) instead

Class: ReadStream

A `net.Socket` subclass that represents the readable portion of a tty. In normal circumstances, `process.stdin` will be the only `tty.ReadStream` instance in any Node.js program (only when `isatty(0)` is true).

rs.isRaw

A `Boolean` that is initialized to `false`. It represents the current "raw" state of the `tty.ReadStream` instance.

rs.setRawMode(mode)

`mode` should be `true` or `false`. This sets the properties of the `tty.ReadStream` to act either as a raw device or default. `isRaw` will be set to the resulting mode.

Class: WriteStream

A `net.Socket` subclass that represents the writable portion of a tty. In normal circumstances, `process.stdout` will be the only `tty.WriteStream` instance ever created (and only when `isatty(1)` is true).

ws.columns

A `Number` that gives the number of columns the TTY currently has. This property gets updated on "resize" events.

ws.rows

A `Number` that gives the number of rows the TTY currently has. This property gets updated on "resize" events.

Event: 'resize'

```
function () {}
```

Emitted by **refreshSize()** when either of the **columns** or **rows** properties has changed.

```
process.stdout.on('resize', function() {
  console.log('screen size has changed!');
  console.log(process.stdout.columns + 'x' + process.stdout.rows);
});
```

UDP / Datagram Sockets

`Stability: 2 - Stable`

Datagram sockets are available through `require('dgram')`.

Important note: the behavior of `dgram.Socket#bind()` has changed in v0.10 and is always asynchronous now. If you have code that looks like this:

```
var s = dgram.createSocket('udp4');
s.bind(1234);
s.addMembership('224.0.0.114');
```

You have to change it to this:

```
var s = dgram.createSocket('udp4');
s.bind(1234, function() {
  s.addMembership('224.0.0.114');
});
```

dgram.createSocket(type[, callback])

- `type` String. Either 'udp4' or 'udp6'
- `callback` Function. Attached as a listener to `message` events. Optional
- Returns: Socket object

Creates a datagram Socket of the specified types. Valid types are `udp4` and `udp6`.

Takes an optional callback which is added as a listener for `message` events.

Call `socket.bind()` if you want to receive datagrams. `socket.bind()` will bind to the "all interfaces" address on a random port (it does the right thing for both `udp4` and `udp6` sockets). You can then retrieve the address and port with `socket.address().address` and `socket.address().port`.

dgram.createSocket(options[, callback])

- `options` Object
- `callback` Function. Attached as a listener to `message` events.
- Returns: Socket object

The `options` object should contain a `type` field of either `udp4` or `udp6` and an optional boolean `reuseAddr` field.

When `reuseAddr` is `true` `socket.bind()` will reuse the address, even if another process has already bound a socket on it. `reuseAddr` defaults to `false`.

Takes an optional callback which is added as a listener for `message` events.

Call `socket.bind()` if you want to receive datagrams. `socket.bind()` will bind to the "all interfaces" address on a random port (it does the right thing for both `udp4` and `udp6` sockets). You can then retrieve the address and port with `socket.address().address` and `socket.address().port`.

Class: dgram.Socket

The dgram Socket class encapsulates the datagram functionality. It should be created via `dgram.createSocket(...)`

Event: 'message'

- `msg` Buffer object. The message
- `rinfo` Object. Remote address information

Emitted when a new datagram is available on a socket. `msg` is a `Buffer` and `rinfo` is an object with the sender's address information:

```
socket.on('message', function(msg, rinfo) {
  console.log('Received %d bytes from %s:%d\n',
            msg.length, rinfo.address, rinfo.port);
});
```

Event: 'listening'

Emitted when a socket starts listening for datagrams. This happens as soon as UDP sockets are created.

Event: 'close'

Emitted after a socket is closed with `close()`. No new `message` events will be emitted on this socket.

Event: 'error'

- `exception` Error object

Emitted when an error occurs.

socket.send(buf, offset, length, port, address[, callback])

- `buf` Buffer object or string. Message to be sent
- `offset` Integer. Offset in the buffer where the message starts.
- `length` Integer. Number of bytes in the message.
- `port` Integer. Destination port.
- `address` String. Destination hostname or IP address.
- `callback` Function. Called when the message has been sent. Optional.

For UDP sockets, the destination port and address must be specified. A string may be supplied for the `address` parameter, and it will be resolved with DNS.

If the address is omitted or is an empty string, '0.0.0.0' or '::0' is used instead. Depending on the network configuration, those defaults may or may not work; it's best to be explicit about the destination address.

If the socket has not been previously bound with a call to `bind`, it gets assigned a random port number and is bound to the "all interfaces" address ('0.0.0.0' for `udp4` sockets, '::0' for `udp6` sockets.)

An optional callback may be specified to detect DNS errors or for determining when it's safe to reuse the `buf` object. Note that DNS lookups delay the time to send for at least one tick. The only way to know for sure that the datagram has been sent is by using a callback. If an error occurs and a callback is given, the error will be the first argument to the callback. If a callback is not given, the error is emitted as an `'error'` event on the `socket` object.

With consideration for multi-byte characters, `offset` and `length` will be calculated with respect to byte length and not the character position.

Example of sending a UDP packet to a random port on `localhost`;

```
var dgram = require('dgram');
var message = new Buffer("Some bytes");
var client = dgram.createSocket("udp4");
client.send(message, 0, message.length, 41234, "localhost", function(err) {
  client.close();
});
```

A Note about UDP datagram size

The maximum size of an `IPv4/v6` datagram depends on the `MTU` (*Maximum Transmission Unit*) and on the `Payload Length` field size.

- The `Payload Length` field is `16 bits` wide, which means that a normal payload cannot be larger than 64K octets including internet header and data (65,507 bytes = 65,535 âĹŠ 8 bytes UDP header âĹŠ 20 bytes IP header); this is generally true for loopback interfaces, but such long datagrams are impractical for most hosts and networks.

- The `MTU` is the largest size a given link layer technology can support for datagrams. For any link, `IPv4` mandates a minimum `MTU` of 68 octets, while the recommended `MTU` for IPv4 is 576 (typically recommended as the `MTU` for dial-up type applications), whether they arrive whole or in fragments.

For `IPv6`, the minimum `MTU` is 1280 octets, however, the mandatory minimum fragment reassembly buffer size is 1500 octets. The value of 68 octets is very small, since most current link layer technologies have a minimum `MTU` of 1500 (like Ethernet).

Note that it's impossible to know in advance the MTU of each link through which a packet might travel, and that generally sending a datagram greater than the (receiver) `MTU` won't work (the packet gets silently dropped, without informing the source that the data did not reach its intended recipient).

socket.bind([port][, address][, callback])

- `port` Integer, Optional
- `address` String, Optional
- `callback` Function with no parameters, Optional. Callback when binding is done.

For UDP sockets, listen for datagrams on a named `port` and optional `address`. If `port` is not specified, the OS will try to bind to a random port. If `address` is not specified, the OS will try to listen on all addresses. After binding is done, a "listening" event is emitted and the `callback`(if specified) is called. Specifying both a "listening" event listener and `callback` is not harmful but not very useful.

A bound datagram socket keeps the Node.js process running to receive datagrams.

If binding fails, an "error" event is generated. In rare case (e.g. binding a closed socket), an `Error` may be thrown by this method.

Example of a UDP server listening on port 41234:

```
var dgram = require("dgram");

var server = dgram.createSocket("udp4");

server.on("error", function (err) {
  console.log("server error:\n" + err.stack);
  server.close();
});

server.on("message", function (msg, rinfo) {
  console.log("server got: " + msg + " from " +
    rinfo.address + ":" + rinfo.port);
});
```

```
server.on("listening", function () {
  var address = server.address();
  console.log("server listening " +
      address.address + ":" + address.port);
});

server.bind(41234);
// server listening 0.0.0.0:41234
```

socket.bind(options[, callback])

- options {Object} - Required. Supports the following properties:
- port {Number} - Required.
- address {String} - Optional.
- exclusive {Boolean} - Optional.
- callback {Function} - Optional.

The port and address properties of options, as well as the optional callback function, behave as they do on a call to socket.bind(port, [address], [callback]).

If exclusive is false (default), then cluster workers will use the same underlying handle, allowing connection handling duties to be shared. When exclusive is true, the handle is not shared, and attempted port sharing results in an error. An example which listens on an exclusive port is shown below.

```
socket.bind({
  address: 'localhost',
  port: 8000,
  exclusive: true
});
```

socket.close([callback])

Close the underlying socket and stop listening for data on it. If a callback is provided, it is added as a listener for the 'close' event.

socket.address()

Returns an object containing the address information for a socket. For UDP sockets, this object will contain address , family and port.

socket.setBroadcast(flag)

- flag Boolean

Sets or clears the SO_BROADCAST socket option. When this option is set, UDP packets may be sent to a local interface's broadcast address.

socket.setTTL(ttl)

- ttl Integer

Sets the IP_TTL socket option. TTL stands for "Time to Live," but in this context it specifies the number of IP hops that a packet is allowed to go through. Each router or gateway that forwards a packet decrements the

TTL. If the TTL is decremented to 0 by a router, it will not be forwarded. Changing TTL values is typically done for network probes or when multicasting.

The argument to setTTL() is a number of hops between 1 and 255. The default on most systems is 64.

socket.setMulticastTTL(ttl)

- ttl Integer

Sets the IP_MULTICAST_TTL socket option. TTL stands for "Time to Live," but in this context it specifies the number of IP hops that a packet is allowed to go through, specifically for multicast traffic. Each router or gateway that forwards a packet decrements the TTL. If the TTL is decremented to 0 by a router, it will not be forwarded.

The argument to setMulticastTTL() is a number of hops between 0 and 255. The default on most systems is 1.

socket.setMulticastLoopback(flag)

- flag Boolean

Sets or clears the IP_MULTICAST_LOOP socket option. When this option is set, multicast packets will also be received on the local interface.

socket.addMembership(multicastAddress[, multicastInterface])

- multicastAddress String
- multicastInterface String, Optional

Tells the kernel to join a multicast group with IP_ADD_MEMBERSHIP socket option.

If multicastInterface is not specified, the OS will try to add membership to all valid interfaces.

socket.dropMembership(multicastAddress[, multicastInterface])

- multicastAddress String
- multicastInterface String, Optional

Opposite of addMembership - tells the kernel to leave a multicast group with IP_DROP_MEMBERSHIP socket option. This is automatically called by the kernel when the socket is closed or process terminates, so most apps will never need to call this.

If multicastInterface is not specified, the OS will try to drop membership to all valid interfaces.

socket.unref()

Calling unref on a socket will allow the program to exit if this is the only active socket in the event system. If the socket is already unrefd calling unref again will have no effect.

Returns socket.

socket.ref()

Opposite of unref, calling ref on a previously unrefd socket will *not* let the program exit if it's the only socket left (the default behavior). If the socket is refd calling ref again will have no effect.

Returns socket.

URL

`Stability: 2 - Stable`

This module has utilities for URL resolution and parsing. Call `require('url')` to use it.

URL Parsing

Parsed URL objects have some or all of the following fields, depending on whether or not they exist in the URL string. Any parts that are not in the URL string will not be in the parsed object. Examples are shown for the URL

`'http://user:pass@host.com:8080/p/a/t/h?query=string#hash'`

- **href**: The full URL that was originally parsed. Both the protocol and host are lowercased.

  Example: `'http://user:pass@host.com:8080/p/a/t/h?query=string#hash'`

- **protocol**: The request protocol, lowercased.

  Example: `'http:'`

- **slashes**: The protocol requires slashes after the colon.

  Example: true or false

- **host**: The full lowercased host portion of the URL, including port information.

  Example: `'host.com:8080'`

- **auth**: The authentication information portion of a URL.

  Example: `'user:pass'`

- **hostname**: Just the lowercased hostname portion of the host.

  Example: `'host.com'`

- **port**: The port number portion of the host.

  Example: `'8080'`

- **pathname**: The path section of the URL, that comes after the host and before the query, including the initial slash if present. No decoding is performed.

  Example: `'/p/a/t/h'`

- **search**: The 'query string' portion of the URL, including the leading question mark.

  Example: `'?query=string'`

- **path**: Concatenation of `pathname` and `search`. No decoding is performed.

  Example: `'/p/a/t/h?query=string'`

- **query**: Either the 'params' portion of the query string, or a querystring-parsed object.

  Example: `'query=string'` or `{'query':'string'}`

- **hash**: The 'fragment' portion of the URL including the pound-sign.

  Example: `'#hash'`

Escaped Characters

Spaces (' ') and the following characters will be automatically escaped in the properties of URL objects:

```
< > " ' \r \n \t { } | \ ^ '
```

The following methods are provided by the URL module:

url.parse(urlStr[, parseQueryString][, slashesDenoteHost])

Take a URL string, and return an object.

Pass `true` as the second argument to also parse the query string using the `querystring` module. If `true` then the `query` property will always be assigned an object, and the `search` property will always be a (possibly empty) string. If `false` then the `query` property will not be parsed or decoded. Defaults to `false`.

Pass `true` as the third argument to treat `//foo/bar` as `{ host: 'foo', pathname: '/bar' }` rather than `{ pathname: '//foo/bar' }`. Defaults to `false`.

url.format(urlObj)

Take a parsed URL object, and return a formatted URL string.

Here's how the formatting process works:

- `href` will be ignored.
- `path` will be ignored.
- `protocol` is treated the same with or without the trailing : (colon).
- The protocols `http`, `https`, `ftp`, `gopher`, `file` will be postfixed with `://` (colon-slash-slash).
- All other protocols `mailto`, `xmpp`, `aim`, `sftp`, `foo`, etc will be postfixed with : (colon).
- `slashes` set to `true` if the protocol requires `://` (colon-slash-slash)
- Only needs to be set for protocols not previously listed as requiring slashes, such as `mongodb://localhost:8000/`.
- `auth` will be used if present.
- `hostname` will only be used if `host` is absent.
- `port` will only be used if `host` is absent.
- `host` will be used in place of `hostname` and `port`.
- `pathname` is treated the same with or without the leading / (slash).
- `query` (object; see `querystring`) will only be used if `search` is absent.
- `search` will be used in place of `query`.
- It is treated the same with or without the leading ? (question mark).
- `hash` is treated the same with or without the leading # (pound sign, anchor).

url.resolve(from, to)

Take a base URL, and a href URL, and resolve them as a browser would for an anchor tag. Examples:

```
url.resolve('/one/two/three', 'four')     // '/one/two/four'
url.resolve('http://example.com/', '/one')   // 'http://example.com/one'
url.resolve('http://example.com/one', '/two') // 'http://example.com/two'
```

util

These functions are in the module 'util'. Use `require('util')` to access them.

The `util` module is primarily designed to support the needs of node.js's internal APIs. Many of these utilities are useful for your own programs. If you find that these functions are lacking for your purposes, however, you are encouraged to write your own utilities. We are not interested in any future additions to the `util` module that are unnecessary for node.js's internal functionality.

util.debuglog(section)

- `section` {String} The section of the program to be debugged
- Returns: {Function} The logging function

This is used to create a function which conditionally writes to stderr based on the existence of a `NODE_DEBUG` environment variable. If the `section` name appears in that environment variable, then the returned function will be similar to `console.error()`. If not, then the returned function is a no-op.

For example:

```
var debuglog = util.debuglog('foo');

var bar = 123;
debuglog('hello from foo [%d]', bar);
```

If this program is run with `NODE_DEBUG=foo` in the environment, then it will output something like:

```
FOO 3245: hello from foo [123]
```

where `3245` is the process id. If it is not run with that environment variable set, then it will not print anything.

You may separate multiple `NODE_DEBUG` environment variables with a comma. For example, `NODE_DEBUG=fs,net,tls`.

util.format(format[, ...])

Returns a formatted string using the first argument as a `printf`-like format.

The first argument is a string that contains zero or more *placeholders*. Each placeholder is replaced with the converted value from its corresponding argument. Supported placeholders are:

- `%s` - String.
- `%d` - Number (both integer and float).
- `%j` - JSON. Replaced with the string '`[Circular]`' if the argument contains circular references.
- `%%` - single percent sign ('`%`'). This does not consume an argument.

If the placeholder does not have a corresponding argument, the placeholder is not replaced.

```
util.format('%s:%s', 'foo'); // 'foo:%s'
```

If there are more arguments than placeholders, the extra arguments are coerced to strings (for objects and symbols, `util.inspect()` is used) and then concatenated, delimited by a space.

```
util.format('%s:%s', 'foo', 'bar', 'baz'); // 'foo:bar baz'
```

If the first argument is not a format string then `util.format()` returns a string that is the concatenation of all its arguments separated by spaces. Each argument is converted to a string with `util.inspect()`.

```
util.format(1, 2, 3); // '1 2 3'
```

util.log(string)

Output with timestamp on `stdout`.

```
require('util').log('Timestamped message.');
```

util.inspect(object[, options])

Return a string representation of `object`, which is useful for debugging.

An optional *options* object may be passed that alters certain aspects of the formatted string:

- `showHidden` - if `true` then the object's non-enumerable and symbol properties will be shown too. Defaults to `false`.

- `depth` - tells `inspect` how many times to recurse while formatting the object. This is useful for inspecting large complicated objects. Defaults to 2. To make it recurse indefinitely pass `null`.

- `colors` - if `true`, then the output will be styled with ANSI color codes. Defaults to `false`. Colors are customizable, see below.

- `customInspect` - if `false`, then custom `inspect(depth, opts)` functions defined on the objects being inspected won't be called. Defaults to `true`.

Example of inspecting all properties of the `util` object:

```
var util = require('util');

console.log(util.inspect(util, { showHidden: true, depth: null }));
```

Values may supply their own custom `inspect(depth, opts)` functions, when called they receive the current depth in the recursive inspection, as well as the options object passed to `util.inspect()`.

Customizing `util.inspect` colors

Color output (if enabled) of `util.inspect` is customizable globally via `util.inspect.styles` and `util.inspect.colors` objects.

`util.inspect.styles` is a map assigning each style a color from `util.inspect.colors`. Highlighted styles and their default values are: * `number` (yellow) * `boolean` (yellow) * `string` (green) * `date` (magenta) * `regexp` (red) * `null` (bold) * `undefined` (grey) * `special` - only function at this time (cyan) * `name` (intentionally no styling)

Predefined color codes are: `white`, `grey`, `black`, `blue`, `cyan`, `green`, `magenta`, `red` and `yellow`. There are also `bold`, `italic`, `underline` and `inverse` codes.

Custom `inspect()` function on Objects

Objects also may define their own `inspect(depth)` function which `util.inspect()` will invoke and use the result of when inspecting the object:

```
var util = require('util');

var obj = { name: 'nate' };
obj.inspect = function(depth) {
  return '{' + this.name + '}';
};

util.inspect(obj);
  // "{nate}"
```

You may also return another Object entirely, and the returned String will be formatted according to the returned Object. This is similar to how `JSON.stringify()` works:

```
var obj = { foo: 'this will not show up in the inspect() output' };
obj.inspect = function(depth) {
  return { bar: 'baz' };
};

util.inspect(obj);
  // "{ bar: 'baz' }"
```

util.isArray(object)

Stability: 0 - Deprecated

Internal alias for Array.isArray.

Returns `true` if the given "object" is an `Array`. `false` otherwise.

```
var util = require('util');

util.isArray([])
  // true
util.isArray(new Array)
  // true
util.isArray({})
  // false
```

util.isRegExp(object)

Stability: 0 - Deprecated

Returns `true` if the given "object" is a `RegExp`. `false` otherwise.

```
var util = require('util');

util.isRegExp(/some regexp/)
  // true
util.isRegExp(new RegExp('another regexp'))
  // true
util.isRegExp({})
  // false
```

util.isDate(object)

Stability: 0 - Deprecated

Returns `true` if the given "object" is a `Date`. `false` otherwise.

```
var util = require('util');

util.isDate(new Date())
  // true
util.isDate(Date())
  // false (without 'new' returns a String)
```

```
util.isDate({})
  // false
```

util.isError(object)

Stability: 0 - Deprecated

Returns true if the given "object" is an Error. false otherwise.

```
var util = require('util');

util.isError(new Error())
  // true
util.isError(new TypeError())
  // true
util.isError({ name: 'Error', message: 'an error occurred' })
  // false
```

util.isBoolean(object)

Stability: 0 - Deprecated

Returns true if the given "object" is a Boolean. false otherwise.

```
var util = require('util');

util.isBoolean(1)
  // false
util.isBoolean(0)
  // false
util.isBoolean(false)
  // true
```

util.isNull(object)

Stability: 0 - Deprecated

Returns true if the given "object" is strictly null. false otherwise.

```
var util = require('util');

util.isNull(0)
  // false
util.isNull(undefined)
  // false
util.isNull(null)
  // true
```

util.isNullOrUndefined(object)

Stability: 0 - Deprecated

Returns true if the given "object" is null or undefined. false otherwise.

```
var util = require('util');

util.isNullOrUndefined(0)
  // false
util.isNullOrUndefined(undefined)
  // true
util.isNullOrUndefined(null)
  // true
```

util.isNumber(object)

Stability: 0 - Deprecated

Returns `true` if the given "object" is a Number. `false` otherwise.

```
var util = require('util');

util.isNumber(false)
  // false
util.isNumber(Infinity)
  // true
util.isNumber(0)
  // true
util.isNumber(NaN)
  // true
```

util.isString(object)

Stability: 0 - Deprecated

Returns `true` if the given "object" is a `String`. `false` otherwise.

```
var util = require('util');

util.isString('')
  // true
util.isString('foo')
  // true
util.isString(String('foo'))
  // true
util.isString(5)
  // false
```

util.isSymbol(object)

Stability: 0 - Deprecated

Returns `true` if the given "object" is a Symbol. `false` otherwise.

```
var util = require('util');

util.isSymbol(5)
  // false
util.isSymbol('foo')
```

```
  // false
util.isSymbol(Symbol('foo'))
  // true
```

util.isUndefined(object)

Stability: 0 - Deprecated

Returns `true` if the given "object" is `undefined`. `false` otherwise.

```
var util = require('util');

var foo;
util.isUndefined(5)
  // false
util.isUndefined(foo)
  // true
util.isUndefined(null)
  // false
```

util.isObject(object)

Stability: 0 - Deprecated

Returns `true` if the given "object" is strictly an `Object` **and** not a `Function`. `false` otherwise.

```
var util = require('util');

util.isObject(5)
  // false
util.isObject(null)
  // false
util.isObject({})
  // true
util.isObject(function(){})
  // false
```

util.isFunction(object)

Stability: 0 - Deprecated

Returns `true` if the given "object" is a `Function`. `false` otherwise.

```
var util = require('util');

function Foo() {}
var Bar = function() {};

util.isFunction({})
  // false
util.isFunction(Foo)
  // true
util.isFunction(Bar)
  // true
```

util.isPrimitive(object)

Stability: 0 - Deprecated

Returns `true` if the given "object" is a primitive type. `false` otherwise.

```
var util = require('util');
```

```
util.isPrimitive(5)
  // true
util.isPrimitive('foo')
  // true
util.isPrimitive(false)
  // true
util.isPrimitive(null)
  // true
util.isPrimitive(undefined)
  // true
util.isPrimitive({})
  // false
util.isPrimitive(function() {})
  // false
util.isPrimitive(/^$/)
  // false
util.isPrimitive(new Date())
  // false
```

util.isBuffer(object)

Stability: 0 - Deprecated

Returns `true` if the given "object" is a `Buffer`. `false` otherwise.

```
var util = require('util');
```

```
util.isBuffer({ length: 0 })
  // false
util.isBuffer([])
  // false
util.isBuffer(new Buffer('hello world'))
  // true
```

util.inherits(constructor, superConstructor)

Inherit the prototype methods from one constructor into another. The prototype of `constructor` will be set to a new object created from `superConstructor`.

As an additional convenience, `superConstructor` will be accessible through the `constructor.super_` property.

```
var util = require("util");
var EventEmitter = require("events");

function MyStream() {
    EventEmitter.call(this);
}
```

```
util.inherits(MyStream, EventEmitter);

MyStream.prototype.write = function(data) {
    this.emit("data", data);
}

var stream = new MyStream();

console.log(stream instanceof EventEmitter); // true
console.log(MyStream.super_ === EventEmitter); // true

stream.on("data", function(data) {
    console.log('Received data: "' + data + '"');
})
stream.write("It works!"); // Received data: "It works!"
```

util.deprecate(function, string)

Marks that a method should not be used any more.

```
var util = require('util');

exports.puts = util.deprecate(function() {
  for (var i = 0, len = arguments.length; i < len; ++i) {
    process.stdout.write(arguments[i] + '\n');
  }
}, 'util.puts: Use console.log instead');
```

It returns a modified function which warns once by default.

If `--no-deprecation` is set then this function is a NO-OP. Configurable at run-time through the `process.noDeprecation` boolean (only effective when set before a module is loaded.)

If `--trace-deprecation` is set, a warning and a stack trace are logged to the console the first time the deprecated API is used. Configurable at run-time through the `process.traceDeprecation` boolean.

If `--throw-deprecation` is set then the application throws an exception when the deprecated API is used. Configurable at run-time through the `process.throwDeprecation` boolean.

`process.throwDeprecation` takes precedence over `process.traceDeprecation`.

util.debug(string)

Stability: 0 - Deprecated: use `console.error()` instead.

Deprecated predecessor of `console.error`.

util.error([...])

Stability: 0 - Deprecated: Use `console.error()` instead.

Deprecated predecessor of `console.error`.

util.puts([. . .])

Stability: 0 - Deprecated: Use `console.log()` instead.

Deprecated predecessor of `console.log`.

util.print([. . .])

Stability: 0 - Deprecated: Use `console.log` instead.

Deprecated predecessor of `console.log`.

util.pump(readableStream, writableStream[, callback])

Stability: 0 - Deprecated: Use `readableStream.pipe(writableStream)`

Deprecated predecessor of `stream.pipe()`.

V8

```
Stability: 2 - Stable
```

This module exposes events and interfaces specific to the version of V8 built with node.js. These interfaces are subject to change by upstream and are therefore not covered under the stability index.

getHeapStatistics()

Returns an object with the following properties

```
{
  total_heap_size: 7326976,
  total_heap_size_executable: 4194304,
  total_physical_size: 7326976,
  total_available_size: 1152656,
  used_heap_size: 3476208,
  heap_size_limit: 1535115264
}
```

setFlagsFromString(string)

Set additional V8 command line flags. Use with care; changing settings after the VM has started may result in unpredictable behavior, including crashes and data loss. Or it may simply do nothing.

The V8 options available for a version of node.js may be determined by running `node --v8-options`. An unofficial, community-maintained list of options and their effects is available here.

Usage:

```
// Print GC events to stdout for one minute.
var v8 = require('v8');
v8.setFlagsFromString('--trace_gc');
setTimeout(function() { v8.setFlagsFromString('--notrace_gc'); }, 60e3);
```

Executing JavaScript

Stability: 2 - Stable

You can access this module with:

```
var vm = require('vm');
```

JavaScript code can be compiled and run immediately or compiled, saved, and run later.

vm.runInThisContext(code[, options])

`vm.runInThisContext()` compiles `code`, runs it and returns the result. Running code does not have access to local scope, but does have access to the current `global` object.

Example of using `vm.runInThisContext` and `eval` to run the same code:

```
var vm = require('vm');
var localVar = 'initial value';

var vmResult = vm.runInThisContext('localVar = "vm";');
console.log('vmResult: ', vmResult);
console.log('localVar: ', localVar);

var evalResult = eval('localVar = "eval";');
console.log('evalResult: ', evalResult);
console.log('localVar: ', localVar);

// vmResult: 'vm', localVar: 'initial value'
// evalResult: 'eval', localVar: 'eval'
```

`vm.runInThisContext` does not have access to the local scope, so `localVar` is unchanged. `eval` does have access to the local scope, so `localVar` is changed.

In this way `vm.runInThisContext` is much like an indirect `eval` call, e.g. `(0,eval)('code')`. However, it also has the following additional options:

- `filename`: allows you to control the filename that shows up in any stack traces produced.
- `displayErrors`: whether or not to print any errors to stderr, with the line of code that caused them highlighted, before throwing an exception. Will capture both syntax errors from compiling `code` and runtime errors thrown by executing the compiled code. Defaults to `true`.
- `timeout`: a number of milliseconds to execute `code` before terminating execution. If execution is terminated, an `Error` will be thrown.

vm.createContext([sandbox])

If given a `sandbox` object, will "contextify" that sandbox so that it can be used in calls to `vm.runInContext` or `script.runInContext`. Inside scripts run as such, `sandbox` will be the global object, retaining all its existing properties but also having the built-in objects and functions any standard global object has. Outside of scripts run by the vm module, `sandbox` will be unchanged.

If not given a sandbox object, returns a new, empty contextified sandbox object you can use.

This function is useful for creating a sandbox that can be used to run multiple scripts, e.g. if you were emulating a web browser it could be used to create a single sandbox representing a window's global object, then run all `<script>` tags together inside that sandbox.

vm.isContext(sandbox)

Returns whether or not a sandbox object has been contextified by calling vm.createContext on it.

vm.runInContext(code, contextifiedSandbox[, options])

vm.runInContext compiles code, then runs it in contextifiedSandbox and returns the result. Running code does not have access to local scope. The contextifiedSandbox object must have been previously contextified via vm.createContext; it will be used as the global object for code.

vm.runInContext takes the same options as vm.runInThisContext.

Example: compile and execute different scripts in a single existing context.

```
var util = require('util');
var vm = require('vm');

var sandbox = { globalVar: 1 };
vm.createContext(sandbox);

for (var i = 0; i < 10; ++i) {
    vm.runInContext('globalVar *= 2;', sandbox);
}
console.log(util.inspect(sandbox));

// { globalVar: 1024 }
```

Note that running untrusted code is a tricky business requiring great care. vm.runInContext is quite useful, but safely running untrusted code requires a separate process.

vm.runInNewContext(code[, sandbox][, options])

vm.runInNewContext compiles code, contextifies sandbox if passed or creates a new contextified sandbox if it's omitted, and then runs the code with the sandbox as the global object and returns the result.

vm.runInNewContext takes the same options as vm.runInThisContext.

Example: compile and execute code that increments a global variable and sets a new one. These globals are contained in the sandbox.

```
var util = require('util');
var vm = require('vm');

var sandbox = {
  animal: 'cat',
  count: 2
};

vm.runInNewContext('count += 1; name = "kitty"', sandbox);
console.log(util.inspect(sandbox));

// { animal: 'cat', count: 3, name: 'kitty' }
```

Note that running untrusted code is a tricky business requiring great care. vm.runInNewContext is quite useful, but safely running untrusted code requires a separate process.

vm.runInDebugContext(code)

`vm.runInDebugContext` compiles and executes `code` inside the V8 debug context. The primary use case is to get access to the V8 debug object:

```
var Debug = vm.runInDebugContext('Debug');
Debug.scripts().forEach(function(script) { console.log(script.name); });
```

Note that the debug context and object are intrinsically tied to V8's debugger implementation and may change (or even get removed) without prior warning.

The debug object can also be exposed with the `--expose_debug_as=` switch.

Class: Script

A class for holding precompiled scripts, and running them in specific sandboxes.

new vm.Script(code, options)

Creating a new `Script` compiles `code` but does not run it. Instead, the created `vm.Script` object represents this compiled code. This script can be run later many times using methods below. The returned script is not bound to any global object. It is bound before each run, just for that run.

The options when creating a script are:

- `filename`: allows you to control the filename that shows up in any stack traces produced from this script.
- `displayErrors`: whether or not to print any errors to stderr, with the line of code that caused them highlighted, before throwing an exception. Applies only to syntax errors compiling the code; errors while running the code are controlled by the options to the script's methods.

script.runInThisContext([options])

Similar to `vm.runInThisContext` but a method of a precompiled `Script` object. `script.runInThisContext` runs `script`'s compiled code and returns the result. Running code does not have access to local scope, but does have access to the current `global` object.

Example of using `script.runInThisContext` to compile code once and run it multiple times:

```
var vm = require('vm');

global.globalVar = 0;

var script = new vm.Script('globalVar += 1', { filename: 'myfile.vm' });

for (var i = 0; i < 1000; ++i) {
  script.runInThisContext();
}

console.log(globalVar);

// 1000
```

The options for running a script are:

- `displayErrors`: whether or not to print any runtime errors to stderr, with the line of code that caused them highlighted, before throwing an exception. Applies only to runtime errors executing the code; it is impossible to create a `Script` instance with syntax errors, as the constructor will throw.
- `timeout`: a number of milliseconds to execute the script before terminating execution. If execution is terminated, an `Error` will be thrown.

script.runInContext(contextifiedSandbox[, options])

Similar to `vm.runInContext` but a method of a precompiled `Script` object. `script.runInContext` runs script's compiled code in `contextifiedSandbox` and returns the result. Running code does not have access to local scope.

`script.runInContext` takes the same options as `script.runInThisContext`.

Example: compile code that increments a global variable and sets one, then execute the code multiple times. These globals are contained in the sandbox.

```javascript
var util = require('util');
var vm = require('vm');

var sandbox = {
  animal: 'cat',
  count: 2
};

var context = new vm.createContext(sandbox);
var script = new vm.Script('count += 1; name = "kitty"');

for (var i = 0; i < 10; ++i) {
  script.runInContext(context);
}

console.log(util.inspect(sandbox));

// { animal: 'cat', count: 12, name: 'kitty' }
```

Note that running untrusted code is a tricky business requiring great care. `script.runInContext` is quite useful, but safely running untrusted code requires a separate process.

script.runInNewContext([sandbox][, options])

Similar to `vm.runInNewContext` but a method of a precompiled `Script` object. `script.runInNewContext` contextifies `sandbox` if passed or creates a new contextified sandbox if it's omitted, and then runs script's compiled code with the sandbox as the global object and returns the result. Running code does not have access to local scope.

`script.runInNewContext` takes the same options as `script.runInThisContext`.

Example: compile code that sets a global variable, then execute the code multiple times in different contexts. These globals are set on and contained in the sandboxes.

```javascript
var util = require('util');
var vm = require('vm');

var sandboxes = [{}, {}, {}];

var script = new vm.Script('globalVar = "set"');

sandboxes.forEach(function (sandbox) {
  script.runInNewContext(sandbox);
});

console.log(util.inspect(sandboxes));

// [{ globalVar: 'set' }, { globalVar: 'set' }, { globalVar: 'set' }]
```

Note that running untrusted code is a tricky business requiring great care. `script.runInNewContext` is quite useful, but safely running untrusted code requires a separate process.

Zlib

Stability: 2 - Stable

You can access this module with:

```
var zlib = require('zlib');
```

This provides bindings to Gzip/Gunzip, Deflate/Inflate, and DeflateRaw/InflateRaw classes. Each class takes the same options, and is a readable/writable Stream.

Examples

Compressing or decompressing a file can be done by piping an fs.ReadStream into a zlib stream, then into an fs.WriteStream.

```
var gzip = zlib.createGzip();
var fs = require('fs');
var inp = fs.createReadStream('input.txt');
var out = fs.createWriteStream('input.txt.gz');

inp.pipe(gzip).pipe(out);
```

Compressing or decompressing data in one step can be done by using the convenience methods.

```
var input = '.....................................';
zlib.deflate(input, function(err, buffer) {
  if (!err) {
    console.log(buffer.toString('base64'));
  }
});

var buffer = new Buffer('eJzT0yMAAGTvBe8=', 'base64');
zlib.unzip(buffer, function(err, buffer) {
  if (!err) {
    console.log(buffer.toString());
  }
});
```

To use this module in an HTTP client or server, use the accept-encoding on requests, and the content-encoding header on responses.

Note: these examples are drastically simplified to show the basic concept. Zlib encoding can be expensive, and the results ought to be cached. See Memory Usage Tuning below for more information on the speed/memory/compression tradeoffs involved in zlib usage.

```
// client request example
var zlib = require('zlib');
var http = require('http');
var fs = require('fs');
var request = http.get({ host: 'izs.me',
                         path: '/',
                         port: 80,
                         headers: { 'accept-encoding': 'gzip,deflate' } });
request.on('response', function(response) {
  var output = fs.createWriteStream('izs.me_index.html');

  switch (response.headers['content-encoding']) {
```

```
    // or, just use zlib.createUnzip() to handle both cases
    case 'gzip':
      response.pipe(zlib.createGunzip()).pipe(output);
      break;
    case 'deflate':
      response.pipe(zlib.createInflate()).pipe(output);
      break;
    default:
      response.pipe(output);
      break;
  }
});

// server example
// Running a gzip operation on every request is quite expensive.
// It would be much more efficient to cache the compressed buffer.
var zlib = require('zlib');
var http = require('http');
var fs = require('fs');
http.createServer(function(request, response) {
  var raw = fs.createReadStream('index.html');
  var acceptEncoding = request.headers['accept-encoding'];
  if (!acceptEncoding) {
    acceptEncoding = '';
  }

  // Note: this is not a conformant accept-encoding parser.
  // See http://www.w3.org/Protocols/rfc2616/rfc2616-sec14.html#sec14.3
  if (acceptEncoding.match(/\bdeflate\b/)) {
    response.writeHead(200, { 'content-encoding': 'deflate' });
    raw.pipe(zlib.createDeflate()).pipe(response);
  } else if (acceptEncoding.match(/\bgzip\b/)) {
    response.writeHead(200, { 'content-encoding': 'gzip' });
    raw.pipe(zlib.createGzip()).pipe(response);
  } else {
    response.writeHead(200, {});
    raw.pipe(response);
  }
}).listen(1337);
```

zlib.createGzip([options])

Returns a new Gzip object with an options.

zlib.createGunzip([options])

Returns a new Gunzip object with an options.

zlib.createDeflate([options])

Returns a new Deflate object with an options.

zlib.createInflate([options])

Returns a new Inflate object with an options.

zlib.createDeflateRaw([options])

Returns a new DeflateRaw object with an options.

zlib.createInflateRaw([options])

Returns a new InflateRaw object with an options.

zlib.createUnzip([options])

Returns a new Unzip object with an options.

Class: zlib.Zlib

Not exported by the `zlib` module. It is documented here because it is the base class of the compressor/decompressor classes.

zlib.flush([kind], callback)

`kind` defaults to `zlib.Z_FULL_FLUSH`.

Flush pending data. Don't call this frivolously, premature flushes negatively impact the effectiveness of the compression algorithm.

zlib.params(level, strategy, callback)

Dynamically update the compression level and compression strategy. Only applicable to deflate algorithm.

zlib.reset()

Reset the compressor/decompressor to factory defaults. Only applicable to the inflate and deflate algorithms.

Class: zlib.Gzip

Compress data using gzip.

Class: zlib.Gunzip

Decompress a gzip stream.

Class: zlib.Deflate

Compress data using deflate.

Class: zlib.Inflate

Decompress a deflate stream.

Class: zlib.DeflateRaw

Compress data using deflate, and do not append a zlib header.

Class: zlib.InflateRaw

Decompress a raw deflate stream.

Class: zlib.Unzip

Decompress either a Gzip- or Deflate-compressed stream by auto-detecting the header.

Convenience Methods

All of these take a string or buffer as the first argument, an optional second argument to supply options to the zlib classes and will call the supplied callback with `callback(error, result)`.

Every method has a `*Sync` counterpart, which accept the same arguments, but without a callback.

zlib.deflate(buf[, options], callback)

zlib.deflateSync(buf[, options])

Compress a string with Deflate.

zlib.deflateRaw(buf[, options], callback)

zlib.deflateRawSync(buf[, options])

Compress a string with DeflateRaw.

zlib.gzip(buf[, options], callback)

zlib.gzipSync(buf[, options])

Compress a string with Gzip.

zlib.gunzip(buf[, options], callback)

zlib.gunzipSync(buf[, options])

Decompress a raw Buffer with Gunzip.

zlib.inflate(buf[, options], callback)

zlib.inflateSync(buf[, options])

Decompress a raw Buffer with Inflate.

zlib.inflateRaw(buf[, options], callback)

zlib.inflateRawSync(buf[, options])

Decompress a raw Buffer with InflateRaw.

zlib.unzip(buf[, options], callback)

zlib.unzipSync(buf[, options])

Decompress a raw Buffer with Unzip.

Options

Each class takes an options object. All options are optional.

Note that some options are only relevant when compressing, and are ignored by the decompression classes.

- flush (default: `zlib.Z_NO_FLUSH`)
- chunkSize (default: 16*1024)
- windowBits
- level (compression only)
- memLevel (compression only)
- strategy (compression only)
- dictionary (deflate/inflate only, empty dictionary by default)

See the description of `deflateInit2` and `inflateInit2` at `http://zlib.net/manual.html#Advanced` for more information on these.

Memory Usage Tuning

From `zlib/zconf.h`, modified to node.js's usage:

The memory requirements for deflate are (in bytes):

```
(1 << (windowBits+2)) +  (1 << (memLevel+9))
```

that is: 128K for windowBits=15 + 128K for memLevel = 8 (default values) plus a few kilobytes for small objects.

For example, if you want to reduce the default memory requirements from 256K to 128K, set the options to:

```
{ windowBits: 14, memLevel: 7 }
```

Of course this will generally degrade compression (there's no free lunch).

The memory requirements for inflate are (in bytes)

```
1 << windowBits
```

that is, 32K for windowBits=15 (default value) plus a few kilobytes for small objects.

This is in addition to a single internal output slab buffer of size `chunkSize`, which defaults to 16K.

The speed of zlib compression is affected most dramatically by the `level` setting. A higher level will result in better compression, but will take longer to complete. A lower level will result in less compression, but will be much faster.

In general, greater memory usage options will mean that node.js has to make fewer calls to zlib, since it'll be able to process more data in a single `write` operation. So, this is another factor that affects the speed, at the cost of memory usage.

Constants

All of the constants defined in zlib.h are also defined on `require('zlib')`. In the normal course of operations, you will not need to ever set any of these. They are documented here so that their presence is not surprising. This section is taken almost directly from the zlib documentation. See `http://zlib.net/manual.html#Constants` for more details.

Allowed flush values.

- `zlib.Z_NO_FLUSH`
- `zlib.Z_PARTIAL_FLUSH`
- `zlib.Z_SYNC_FLUSH`
- `zlib.Z_FULL_FLUSH`
- `zlib.Z_FINISH`
- `zlib.Z_BLOCK`
- `zlib.Z_TREES`

Return codes for the compression/decompression functions. Negative values are errors, positive values are used for special but normal events.

- `zlib.Z_OK`
- `zlib.Z_STREAM_END`
- `zlib.Z_NEED_DICT`
- `zlib.Z_ERRNO`
- `zlib.Z_STREAM_ERROR`
- `zlib.Z_DATA_ERROR`
- `zlib.Z_MEM_ERROR`
- `zlib.Z_BUF_ERROR`
- `zlib.Z_VERSION_ERROR`

Compression levels.

- `zlib.Z_NO_COMPRESSION`
- `zlib.Z_BEST_SPEED`
- `zlib.Z_BEST_COMPRESSION`
- `zlib.Z_DEFAULT_COMPRESSION`

Compression strategy.

- `zlib.Z_FILTERED`
- `zlib.Z_HUFFMAN_ONLY`
- `zlib.Z_RLE`
- `zlib.Z_FIXED`
- `zlib.Z_DEFAULT_STRATEGY`

Possible values of the data_type field.

- `zlib.Z_BINARY`

- `zlib.Z_TEXT`
- `zlib.Z_ASCII`
- `zlib.Z_UNKNOWN`

The deflate compression method (the only one supported in this version).

- `zlib.Z_DEFLATED`

For initializing zalloc, zfree, opaque.

- `zlib.Z_NULL`